OUR
VOICES
MUST
BE HEARD

WOMEN'S SUFFRAGE AND THE STRUGGLE FOR DEMOCRACY
SERIES EDITOR: VERONICA STRONG-BOAG

The story of women's struggles and victories in the pursuit of political equality is not just a matter of the past: it has the value of informing current debate about the health of democracy in our country.

This series of short, insightful books presents a history of the vote, with vivid accounts of famous and unsung suffragists and overdue explanations of why some women were banned from the ballot box until the 1940s and 1960s. More than a celebration of women's achievements in the political realm, this series provides deeper understanding of Canadian society and politics, serving as a well-timed reminder never to take political rights for granted.

Books in the series:

One Hundred Years of Struggle: The History of Women and the Vote in Canada, by Joan Sangster

Our Voices Must Be Heard: Women and the Vote in Ontario, by Tarah Brookfield

To Be Equals in Our Own Country: Women and the Vote in Quebec, by Denyse Baillargeon

Ours by Every Law of Right and Justice: Women and the Vote in the Prairie Provinces, by Sarah Carter

A Great Revolutionary Wave: Women and the Vote in British Columbia, by Lara Campbell

We Shall Persist: Women and the Vote in the Atlantic Provinces, by Heidi MacDonald

Working Tirelessly for Change: Indigenous Women and the Vote in Canada, by Lianne Leddy

TARAH BROOKFIELD

OUR
VOICES
MUST
BE HEARD

Women and
the Vote in Ontario

UBCPress

VANCOUVER & TORONTO

27 26 25 24 23 22 21 20 19 18   5 4 3 2 1

Printed in Canada on FSC-certified ancient-forest-free paper
(100% post-consumer recycled) that is processed chlorine- and acid-free.

Library and Archives Canada Cataloguing in Publication

Women's suffrage and the struggle for democracy /
series editor: Veronica Strong-Boag.

Includes bibliographical references and index.
Contents: Volume 2: Our voices must be heard : women and the vote
in Ontario / Tarah Brookfield.
Issued in print and electronic formats.

v. 2:
ISBN 978-0-7748-6019-2 (hardcover).–ISBN 978-0-7748-6021-5 (PDF).–
ISBN 978-0-7748-6022-2 (EPUB).–ISBN 978-0-7748-6023-9 (Kindle)

Set:
ISBN 978-0-7748-3873-3 (hardcover).–ISBN 978-0-7748-3875-7 (PDF).–
ISBN 978-0-7748-3876-4 (EPUB)

1. Women – Suffrage – Canada – History. 2. Suffrage – Canada – History.
3. Women – Legal status, laws, etc. – Canada – History. 4. Women – Canada –
Social conditions. 5. Suffragists – Canada – History. 6. Voting – Canada – History.
I. Strong-Boag, Veronica, editor II. Brookfield, Tarah. Our voices must be heard

JL192.W67 2018   324.6'230971   C2017-907609-4
                                               C2017-907610-8

Canadä

UBC Press gratefully acknowledges the financial support for our publishing
program of the Government of Canada (through the Canada Book Fund),
the Canada Council for the Arts, and the British Columbia Arts Council.

Printed and bound in Canada by Friesens
Set in Gill Sans and Tundra by Artegraphica Design Co. Ltd.
Copy editor: Deborah Kerr
Proofreader: Kristy Lynn Hankewitz
Indexer: Judy Dunlop
Cover and series design: Jessica Sullivan

UBC Press
The University of British Columbia
2029 West Mall
Vancouver, BC V6T 1Z2
www.ubcpress.ca

CONTENTS

ON THE HUNDREDTH ANNIVERSARY of women's suffrage in Ontario, it may be difficult to imagine a time when women could not hold public office, let alone vote. In 2013, Ontario elected its first female premier, Kathleen Wynne. Though gender parity in government is still far off, and sexist, homophobic, and misogynistic remarks plague female candidates and elected officials, Wynne is not alone. Ontario's New Democratic Party leader, Andrea Horwath; Mississauga's longest-serving mayor, Hazel McCallion; Six Nations of the Grand River's chief, G. Ava Hill; Conservative senator Salma Ataullahjan; former school board trustee, city councillor, and federal MP Olivia Chow; and Lieutenant Governor Elizabeth Dowdeswell have also made headlines, crafted policy, and served their communities in recent years. On election day, hundreds of thousands of female voters make electoral choices they hope will produce prosperous, just, healthy, and safe communities. Others, disillusioned or indifferent, avoid voting altogether. Beyond the vote, women use many tools to address and rectify inequality and injustice: art, social media, boycotts, marches, petitions, charitable or non-governmental agency work, sit-ins, strikes, research and writing, hunger strikes, and civil disobedience. All of these acts – even the choice to be apathetic – are at least the partial legacy of the Ontario suffrage movement, a five-decade-long campaign from the 1870s to 1917 in which women fought for the same political rights as men.

On 12 April 1917, Ontario became the fifth province to grant women the right to vote. Beginning in the 1870s, its suffrage movement emerged amid the vibrant international mobilization of women who sought political representation as a means to improve their rights and to assert influence in social, economic, and political reform. Although individual suffragists held a range of political beliefs, the two most dominant views emphasized women's equality with men or positioned their maternal nature as respectable justification for the vote. Ontario suffragists largely pursued change by working within the established legal and political system, and they exhibited little of the militancy found in parts of the international suffrage movement. Collaborating with their counterparts elsewhere in Canada, the United States, and Britain, they built organizations and travelled extensively to participate in provincial, national, and international meetings. Much ink was spilled on letter writing, editorials, essays, plays, and petitions to expose the necessity and advantages of women's rights. Suffrage delegations descended upon the provincial and federal parliaments in support of pro-suffrage bills and audiences with political leaders. Activism centred in urban, rural, and northern Ontario, with Toronto being the headquarters of provincial suffrage organizations. Their efforts were derided by male and female opponents, who countered that "good" women neither needed nor wanted the vote. Many adversaries considered female enfranchisement dangerous, a risk to the sanctity of the family, good government, and the future of the province. Ontario's roots as a model British colony, grounded in social conservatism and social hierarchy, with a strong aversion to revolutionary thought, made progress on the suffrage question difficult.

Faced with suffrage victories in the Canadian Prairies a year earlier, the Ontario legislature succumbed to pressure and finally voted in favour of enfranchising women in 1917. Not all female residents immediately received the provincial vote. As with men, eligibility was restricted to women who were at least twenty-one, who were born or naturalized British subjects, and who had lived in the country for twelve months. The federal Indian Act overrode provincial voting rights, which meant that First Nations women (and men) who wanted to keep their Indian status were not enfranchised. Also excluded were female prison inmates and residents of asylums and charitable institutions, none of whom, like similarly situated men, were deemed to possess the necessary independence to vote.

Canada's history of the female franchise is fraught with contradictions. For a long time, it was one of only two narratives – along with women's voluntary and paid labour in the world wars – that reliably interjected women's history into textbooks and monuments. It was among the first subjects in women's history approached by academic and popular historians alike. And yet, the suffrage story rarely emerged as a particularly memorable slice of history. The term itself is confusing, conjuring up the gloominess of suffering rather than the democratic origins of the word, from the Latin *suffragium,* which means "to vote." The surviving images of the movement are decidedly static: groups of stern-looking women gathered together, adorned in fancy hats and voluminous dresses. The most action you can imagine here is a strongly worded letter or the occasional pounding of a podium for emphasis. In today's socially conscious era, the fact that Ontario suffragists were almost uniformly white, middle class, and deliberately exclusive makes their activism appear incompatible with twenty-first-century understandings of social justice. Given that disillusionment about politics, politicians, and the value of voting is now so prevalent, it is not surprising that suffrage history does not generate much excitement or desire for knowledge. Perhaps this is why even in my history classes, students commonly associate suffrage not with the campaign for voting rights that spanned two centuries but with the more tangible and catchy epilogue to the suffrage story: the Famous Five and the 1929 Persons case, the constitutional ruling that established the right of women to be appointed to the senate.

I came to this project as someone with my own ambiguous relationship with suffrage history. I have always been interested in the ways that women have sought change through formal and grassroots politics. My early introduction to the subject was via my master's research on Dr. Grace Ritchie-England, Quebec's first woman doctor and suffrage champion, an individual whose story highlighted the differing and divisive expressions of feminism among Montreal suffragists. Yet by the time I started my PhD degree six years later, specializing in Canadian history and women's history, suffragists went unmentioned in my coursework. Instead, we concentrated on exciting new research about women whose histories had previously been ignored: workers and immigrants, girls and widows, lesbians, black women, and Indigenous women. Quite frankly, I presumed that the suffrage story had already been told, and I was not convinced that it deserved much more attention. Not until Veronica Strong-Boag asked me to join the Struggle for Democracy project did I begin to reconsider suffrage in Canadian history. Had I been too dismissive? Was there more to discover about suffragists individually and collectively? Did their flaws, whether narrow-mindedness or inconsistencies, actually make them more interesting? Why did the vote matter so much to them and to their opponents? And what did it ultimately mean for women? I was also keen to make sense of Ontario's place within the larger struggle for political equality in Canada.

As I delved into dusty scrapbooks, newspaper accounts, memoirs, voting registries, census records, parliamentary debates, and the occasional oral history interview, I discovered that Ontario suffragists were more complicated than I had originally thought. By daring to think they were as deserving as men to choose their destinies and to claim the right to participate alongside their fathers, brothers, and husbands in a civil society, they showed great courage and defied expectations of their sex. They were also more diverse than I had assumed. Many were free thinkers on a range of subjects: religion, marriage, politics, and global governance. Even the most conservative surprised me at least once, with their insight, their compassion, or simply their boldness. At the same time, they were not the heroines we sometimes yearn to discover. Ultimately, the vast majority of Ontario suffragists represent a small privileged group, who appeared to see no contradiction in demanding equal rights for women, mostly like themselves, while simultaneously being silent about or complicit in other forms of oppression. Class prejudice, racial discrimination, anti-Semitism, eugenic assumptions about supposed mental and physical defects, and imperialist sentiments, notably but not only concerning Indigenous peoples, were commonplace. Those limitations confirm the social stratifications of late-nineteenth- and early-twentieth-century Ontario. Though the women were willing to challenge the gendered imbalances of power, only a handful mounted a broader struggle for a fully democratic or egalitarian society.

This book owes much to two ground-breaking historians, Catherine Lyle Cleverdon and Carol Lee Bacchi. Published in 1950, Cleverdon's *The Woman's Suffrage Movement in Canada* provided the first thorough account of the country's suffrage struggle. Offering a largely celebratory chronology of achievements and setbacks, it discussed key legislative victories and suffragist leaders. Written in the aftermath of Charlotte Whitton's 1946 assessment that women in contemporary Canadian politics were a "flop," its presentation of suffragists' dogged determination in the face of apathetic and sexist opposition was a wake-up call about the glacial pace of progress. Whereas Cleverdon focuses on achievement, Bacchi's *Liberation Deferred? The Ideas of English-Canadian Suffragists* questions the motivations and beliefs of the suffragists and emphasizes their relatively middle-class and Anglo-Celtic backgrounds. Written in 1983, when most of the suffragists were dead (except in Quebec), it condemns their collective commitment to British liberalism and evangelically inspired social reform: the majority were interested in political power to maintain social control. Despite substantial reservations, however, Bacchi acknowledges the importance of the suffragist achievement. Read together, these books provide a rich primer to key issues in the history of our national suffrage movement.

My own work updates the story by reassessing suffrage leaders and ideas in light of new evidence and perspectives. In the thirty-five years since the publication of Bacchi's book, women's and gender history has expanded significantly. Much more is known about ideals of femininity and masculinity, as well as their disruptions, in differing time periods and contexts. The field now pays greater attention to the rich and diverse interplay of race, class, and gender. New interpretations direct our attention to both the accomplishments and the limitations of the suffragists' arguments, tactics, and perspectives, as well as the influence of the British and American campaigns, and the connection between suffrage and other social reform movements.

Ontario's suffrage story typically begins in 1877, when Dr. Emily Stowe founded the Toronto Women's Literary Club. The club constitutes the earliest documented instance of suffrage activism in Canada, and the legacy of its founder remains central. To better understand the significance of this ground-breaking educator and physician, *Our Voices Must Be Heard* begins almost a century prior to her birth. In its search for a broader outlook, it opens with women's struggle for fundamental rights during the founding of Upper Canada, later known as Canada West and then Ontario. The United Empire Loyalist diaspora from the American Revolutionary War and reasserted British traditions created a patriarchal and imperial culture of contradiction in the new colony. On the one hand, British settler women were valued for their reproductive labour and moral potential, even if custom and law placed them at a substantial disadvantage when compared with similarly situated men. Ontario's imperial/colonial regime was still more oppressive to Indigenous and enslaved women. Despite pervasive inequality and vulnerability, women from diverse backgrounds made their political opinions known and demonstrated a capacity for demanding better terms for their sex and their communities that pre-dates the suffrage movement. Ontario's history of oppressive laws and customs – and defiance of them – inspired Stowe and her fellow activists.

Though suffragists across the province rejected the status quo, Toronto was the persistent heartland of protest. As the home of the provincial legislature and the region most affected by the late-nineteenth-century triumvirate of industrialization, immigration, and urbanization, the so-called Queen City stood at the centre of a bustling reform movement. For women like Stowe, drawn to the city for its educational and professional opportunities, it represented possibility and modernity; however, as the site of male-dominated economic, intellectual, and political power, it, like the province itself, would not easily yield to the radical idea of female enfranchisement. Despite the centrality of cities to the great cause, Ontario remained predominantly rural during the period of suffrage activism. Without support from women in farming communities and small towns, the suffrage campaign would have been far weaker. The main narrative may reside in Toronto, but *Our Voices Must Be Heard* detours whenever possible to other sites of activism, such as Hamilton, which for a short period was home to the two most vocal anti-suffragists, Adelaide Hoodless and Clementina Fessenden. From time to time, the book checks in with Haudenosaunee women's leadership and resistance at the Six Nations of the Grand River Reserve. Also featured are stories from the northern resource towns of Port Arthur and Fort Williams on Lake Superior, a vibrant suffrage hub in the early twentieth century.

In addition to chronicling the course of suffrage activism, *Our Voices Must Be Heard* examines how and when remarkable, if seemingly ordinary, women used their newfound electoral rights. You will meet voters such as Hannah Williams, daughter of Laura Secord, one of seven women who cast their ballots in Canada West in 1844, a piece of feminist effrontery that was quickly punished by the legislative exclusion of all women voters. Forty years later, when widows and unmarried women property owners gained the municipal franchise, you'll glimpse female millworkers and daughters of the town elite registered to vote in Paris, a textile town noted for women's industrial employment and opportunity. The book concludes with the story of a military nurse, Edith Anderson Monture, the only First Nations woman and status Indian in Ontario permitted to vote in 1917, a right she reportedly relished but one that set her apart from others like her. Ontario's complicated history of female activism intertwines throughout this volume with parallel histories of female abolitionists, socialists, and pacifists whose ideologies and conception of human rights sometimes linked their causes to the suffrage movement. For women whose race, ethnicity, class, and religion made them largely unwelcome in the mainstream suffrage campaign, ostracism did not mean inactivity. Black, Jewish, and working-class women typically engaged politically within their own communities, often in direct opposition to the state. Though designated the "great cause" by its true believers, obtaining the vote was only one outlet for women's protest against a status quo that consigned them and many others to subordination.

Enfranchisement did not produce the social and political revolution that some suffragists foresaw. Much like men, enfranchised women participated in existing political parties or rejected formal politics altogether. Gender might have shaped political allegiance, but it did not determine it. Yet the suffrage victories were nevertheless significant. In the nineteenth century, the democratic franchise was a key symbol of citizenship, and its denial affirmed inferiority. Its achievement raised the possibility, although never the guarantee, of using state power to challenge patriarchy. The vote offered women electoral channels for advancement and resistance that made it harder to deny them access to education, to property, to elected office, and to freedom from prejudice and violence. That promise, originating as it did in a society that had consistently dismissed women as properly subordinate to men, was far from inconsequential. Ultimately, for all its limitations and the limitations of its champions, suffrage gave unprecedented legitimacy to women's voices and choices. Voting, as the anti-suffragists who massed in opposition fully understood, mattered a great deal.

OUR
VOICES
MUST
BE HEARD

Man is strong – woman is beautiful,
Man is daring and confident – women is diffident and
  unassuming,
Man is great in action – woman is suffering,
Man shine abroad – women at home,
Man talks to convince – women to persuade and please,
Man has a rugged heart – women a soft tender one,
Men prevent misery – women relieves it,
Man has science – woman taste,
Man has judgement – woman sensibility,
Man is a being of justice – woman an angel of mercy.

– "PARALLEL QUALITIES OF THE SEXES,"
CHRISTIAN GUARDIAN, 4 APRIL 1849

ONE

WOMEN'S RIGHTS IN INDIGENOUS AND COLONIAL ONTARIO

The Polling, by English satirist William Hogarth, critiques partisan abuses of the British electoral system, which would have been familiar to Canadians. The 1758 etching shows a crowd of reform voters who are having their qualifications scrutinized, while the infirm and witless are escorted to the polls by Tory supporters. The only woman in the picture represents Britannia, the female personification of Great Britain. She sits in a broken carriage, which symbolizes the corrupt state of her electoral system.

IN 1844, DEFEATED Reform candidate James Durand accused his Conservative opponent, James Webster, of rigging the election in West Halton. Among Durand's accusations was the fact that the returning officer had allowed seven women to vote. A parliamentary committee was struck to investigate his charges of electoral fraud. At the time, no law specifically excluded female voters; however, the colony's strict property qualifications and the ineligibility of most women to own property made them unlikely to meet the necessary criteria to vote. Furthermore, dominant social attitudes assumed that they were neither interested in voting nor capable of doing so intelligently. To borrow the language of an 1849 poem titled "Parallel Qualities of the Sexes," men were strong, daring, confident, and in possession of science, good judgment, and justice. Ideal women were beautiful, diffident, unassuming, soft, and tender. Men flourished outside the home, whereas women shone within it. These principles had little grounding in lived experiences, but they informed the development of colonial Ontario's property rights, electoral system, and social customs. In Upper Canada and Canada West, women were granted respect as mothers and wives but were legally dependent on male kin for economic survival and political representation. The racial and class biases of British settlers meant that the reverence for middle-class women rarely extended to those who were Indigenous, black, or poor. In the early nineteenth century, Upper Canada's Reform Party called for more responsible government but deliberately excluded women from its vision of enhanced democracy. Therefore, the seven women who voted in West Halton challenged colonial views of womanhood even as their deed aligned with the reality of long-standing female activism in public spaces and participation in political thought and action.

INDIGENOUS WOMEN'S STATUS BEFORE AND AFTER CONTACT

In the centuries before colonization, Ontario was home to diverse Indigenous peoples, including the Inuit in the Far North, a variety of Algonquian-speaking nations in the north and northwest, and the Anishinaabe, Haudenosaunee, Delaware, and Wendat Nations in the south. Population estimates for the Great Lakes region of North America in the sixteenth century range from 60,000 to 117,000. Indigenous societies recognized differences between men and women, usually without subscribing to a gender hierarchy. Rather, as Beverley Jacobs (Gowehgyuseh), a Mohawk activist, lawyer, and former president of the Native Women's Association of Canada, explains, "Women were respected for their spiritual and mental strength and men were respected for their spiritual and physical strength ... There was always a balance between men and women as each had their own responsibilities." Though specific tasks varied from nation to nation, women tended to be responsible for childrearing, food production, hunting small game, and manufacturing clothes, tools, and shelter. Men hunted big game, made weapons, and fought in wars. Monogamy and communal property were often the norm. Oral tradition and recorded observations by Europeans suggest that there was little shame or guilt attached to premarital sex or divorce. Moreover, the Cree and Ojibwa languages present more than two categories of gender identity, suggesting gender fluidity and same-sex intimacy. This is not to imply that Indigenous societies were utopic communities free of prejudice; however, there existed the possibility of power and liberty not entirely regulated by the notion that one gender was subordinate to the other. For instance, several Wendat and Haudenosaunee nations living on or near

Lake Ontario had matrilineal kinship structures, with inheritance, lineage, and residence passed through the mother's side of the family. Matrilineal organization often involved enhanced female decision-making and leadership roles, particularly in conjunction with women's responsibility for land cultivation.

Matrilineal structures are represented by Sky Woman, an important celestial being who features in many Haudenosaunee creation stories. Though aspects of this story vary among communities and nations, the recurring element is her responsibility for bestowing human and plant life on Turtle Island, otherwise known as North America. In the Oneida version, Sky Woman falls from the sky, carrying with her the "three sisters" (corn, beans, and squash), as well as tobacco and strawberry seeds, which would become critical to agriculture and medicine gardens. Birds and animals catch her and lay her down on the back of a swimming turtle. Later, Sky Woman's daughter Lynx gives birth to the first humans, twin boys. This creation story honours women's strength, mothering, and caregiving as critical to the survival of the earth.

Beginning in the seventeenth century, colonization gradually eroded the autonomy of Indigenous women. Generally, Christian missionaries and colonial officials cultivated patriarchal dominance in marriage, the family, and property – emphasizing nuclear households and men's economic roles. So too did intermarriage with settlers, though initially marriages based on military or fur trade alliances between European husbands and First Nations or Metis women were usually advantageous to both parties. Such was the case for Molly Brant (Koñwatsiãtsiaiéñni, 1736–96), the stepdaughter of an important Mohawk chief, sister of military leader Joseph Brant (Thayendanegea), and the common law wife of Sir William Johnson, a colonial official. Brant used her uniquely situated status to protect her family interests and those of the broader confederacy during a critical period of war, migration, and land negotiations. Her role as a clan mother with intimate British ties and English-language skills raised her status among the

Sky Woman, by Haudenosaunee artist and filmmaker Shelley
Niro (2001) on display at the Canadian Museum of History. Niro
is a member of the Six Nations of the Grand River Reserve, Turtle
Clan, Bay of Quinte Mohawk.

Mohawk, which gave her an advantage in diplomatic matters, such
as deciding which side to support in the American Revolutionary
War. In turn, it was through Brant that Johnson received access
and knowledge that would help the British cultivate military

*Clan mothers of the Haudenosaunee of the Six Nations con-
federacy (Five Nations before the Tuscarora joined in 1722)
exemplified matrilineal governance. These women had hereditary rights to represent various nations of the confederacy
and were tasked with using the Great Law of Peace, their constitution, to protect land and water and to responsibly appoint,
observe, or remove male chiefs and faith keepers. A written
account of the Great Law outlines the trust in and respect for
women in decision making:*

> The women of every clan of the Five Nations shall have a
> Council Fire burning in readiness for a Council of the clan.
> When in their opinion it seems necessary for the interest
> of the people they shall hold a Council and their decision
> and recommendations shall be introduced before the
> Council of Lords by the War Chief for its consideration.

*Similarly, these female elders wielded authority in war coun-
cils, holding the power to decide if war was necessary, to lead
pre-war rituals, and to determine the fate of prisoners of war.
Women could also be faith keepers, responsible for running
Longhouse religious ceremonies.*

allies. Another outcome of the Brant-Johnson relationship was
the subsequent negotiation of the Haldimand Tract, a land grant
from the British Crown in 1784 to compensate the Six Nations for
their services in the war. These imperial connections were not
without cost, as some Mohawks viewed both Brant and her brother
as motivated solely by personal interests. For all the respectability

that Brant cultivated among the British, Johnson's will recognized her only as his "housekeeper," and she and their eight surviving children received only a small portion of his estate. Among many things, Brant's experience represents her formidable strength and the delicate balancing act necessary to adapt and operate in traditional and colonial spaces.

With change, also came resistance. For example, the enduring status and respect for clan mothers persisted despite pressure from colonial officials to shift governance to elected male-only councils. In her late-nineteenth-century fieldwork with the Haudenosaunee, Alice Fletcher, a white ethnologist and American suffragist, demonstrated that as traditional caretakers of the land, clan mothers still held considerable influence throughout the nineteenth century, even overruling a chief's decision to sell territory. Despite such endurance, Fletcher noticed the overall erosion of women's political standing. "Our custom of ignoring women in public transaction," she observed, "has had its reflex influence on Indian customs." In some communities, women nevertheless maintained responsibility for community harmony and some level of matrilineal governance. On the Six Nations of the Grand River Reserve, located on the Haldimand Tract, followers of the Longhouse who abided by traditional governance structures resisted replacing their hereditary council. They managed to do so for decades, until 1924 when the hereditary council was forcibly removed by the RCMP and replaced with an all-male elected council. As shown in this volume and others in the series, the determination of Indigenous women to oppose colonial dominance and to maintain cultural traditions, openly when they could or discreetly when necessary, means that Ontario's history of women's struggle to assert their authority properly begins with them.

SETTLER WOMEN'S RIGHTS AND STATUS IN UPPER CANADA
In the eighteenth century, the land now known as Ontario transitioned from autonomous Indigenous societies with multiple

forms of governance to a British colony headed by a distant mon-
arch and administered by a rudimentary parliamentary system.
In this process, Indigenous understandings of egalitarian gender
roles were displaced by more repressive European beliefs. After
its victory in the Seven Years' War, Britain took control of New
France in 1760, including an enormous tract of land west of the
St. Lawrence River. Ceded by Indigenous peoples, it had very little
European settlement. The 1791 Constitutional Act designated this
region a separate British colony, Upper Canada, which would be
governed by English common law and a freehold land tenure. The
first lieutenant-governor, John Graves Simcoe, strove to replicate
a mini-Britain on the Canadian frontier. Already, this had been
partially achieved by the settlement of former American col-
onists who had sought refuge in British North America after the
American Revolutionary War. They would help shape the colony's
cultural and economic development and ensure freedom from
the revolutionary spirit that had produced the American and
French Revolutions. Known as United Empire Loyalists, they included British officers and their families, free white and black
American-born settlers, thousands of Haudenosaunee allies, and
approximately five hundred enslaved African Americans. Though
subsequent waves of migrants from the United States, Britain, and
Western Europe soon arrived in the colony, Loyalists dominated
its political and economic elite, and endeavoured to become the
colonial equivalent of the British aristocracy. Until the late nineteenth century, the region remained predominantly rural, with a
handful of larger settlements at Niagara, York, and Kingston.

Women settlers who migrated to colonial Ontario between the
1770s and 1840s disagreed on whether their new homeland represented improvement. Seeking peace after a decade of war, Loyalist
refugee Nancy Jean Cameron hailed Upper Canada as "a new land
of promise." For British emigrant Susanna Moodie, Upper Canada
was simply "the bush," a frightening contrast with the civilized
landscape of England. Moodie's comment was echoed by Men-

Located in downtown Hamilton, this statue by Sydney March,
erected in 1929, commemorates the "faith and fortitude" of the
United Empire Loyalists. With one arm wrapped protectively around
his wife, the husband shows his family the land assigned to them by
the government surveyor. After years of hardship, the weary family
imagines a prosperous future in British North America.

nonite widow Barbara Riff, who exchanged one frontier for another in leaving Pennsylvania for a Waterloo farm of "bush and
flies." Writing from Chatham after the 1834 abolishment of
slavery in Canada West, black abolitionist Mary Ann Shadd noted
that "a great deal of ignorance, bigotry, prejudice, and idleness"
existed in colonial Ontario, but she concluded that it was both
"free of legal discrimination" and a land of "relative prosperity"
for black settlers and fugitive slaves. Though religious and ethnic
identities, social class, proximity to kin and neighbours, and economic resources distinguished settlement experiences, all women
were subject to the expectations and restrictions of a patriarchal
society that offered women and girls limited political rights, legal
protection, or economic independence.

In Upper Canada, as throughout the British Empire, the status of wives was determined by the wealth and reputation of their husbands and by how well they matched the ideal of womanhood, embodied in fertility and dedication to childrearing and housekeeping. Marriage and motherhood were expected, and their fulfillment was seen as women's utmost contribution to the colony. Widows commonly remarried, and unwed mothers and deserted wives were accorded little sympathy. Sex outside of marriage, although common, was considered indecent, and women who were arrested for prostitution received harsh punishments.

Of course, men and women never entirely conformed to social dictates, though exceptions often reflected class and race. Expectations of separate spheres represented the ideal; however, women frequently engaged in labour outside the home. Farmwomen worked alongside male kin to clear land, build homesteads, and establish farms or artisanal trades. Women laboured in trading posts, markets, stores, mills, hotels, and taverns. Childless unmarried women received wages as schoolteachers, domestic servants, or seamstresses. Nuns, missionaries, and laywomen served as educators, midwives, nurses, and charitable workers. The Methodist Church produced a few female preachers. Although women were expected to dedicate themselves to domestic responsibilities, the exigencies of pioneer life required that they have a public presence. Like men, they travelled within and between public and private spaces, with visibility dependent on class, kinship, and their own preferences.

Often obscured in public memory of the colonial era, slavery was a reality for black and sometimes First Nations women, men, and their offspring. Racial attitudes informed the entire system of slavery, but dominant gender norms dictated the workload of enslaved women, which included producing children for their masters. A 1763 inquiry by James Murray, military governor of the District of Quebec, observed that the value of enslaved women was determined by both manual and reproductive labour. When writing about his potential purchase of two male slaves from the United States, Murray requested "for each a clean young wife who can wash and do the female offices about a farm." Discrimination and power imbalances meant that enslaved women were unlikely to find common ground with their mistresses. In a rare first-person account, Sophia Pooley, bought as a child by Mohawk War Chief Brant in the 1760s, describes how his "barbarous" wife beat and stabbed her.

Another enslaved woman's brutal treatment illustrated the moral need to restrict slavery. Even before he arrived in Canada, Simcoe had spoken against slavery in the British House of Commons. As lieutenant-governor, he fought to abolish it in Upper Canada. He used eyewitness accounts of the violent treatment of Queenston's Chloe Cooley, who had resisted her owner when he sold her to an American buyer, as evidence that slavery was despicable. The investigation into Cooley's situation revealed that she had frequently protested her bondage by running away and refusing to work. Despite significant opposition, Simcoe persisted with his abolitionist mandate and successfully forced the Upper Canada Assembly, six of whose members owned slaves, to pass an Act for the gradual prohibition of slavery in 1793, which prevented the importation of new slaves into the colony. No slaves were freed by this act, and Cooley's ultimate fate remains unknown.

Upper Canada accorded white settler men with moral and fiscal authority inside and outside the home. British common law assigned husbands the responsibility for the care and well-being of their wives and offspring. The household was a single economic and social unit led by husbands. Only they could own property, including any land or wealth brought into the marriage or subsequently inherited or earned by their wives. The legal inability of wives to own, use, or dispose of property or wages, or even write a will, made them entirely dependent. Even their clothes, jewellery, and household goods were not their own. Nor could women sue or enter into contracts. In cases of debt, abuse, or desertion, wives had no legal protection. Sir William Blackstone, an influential eighteenth-century British legal scholar, rationalized this aspect of common law by explaining that the "legal existence of a woman is suspended during marriage, or at least incorporated and conciliated into that of the husband; under whose wing, protection and cover she performs everything." Common law also governed dowries, the property that wives brought into their marriages. If not sold, it would revert back to them when their husbands died. Widows also had rights to use, but not sell, a third of all land owned by deceased husbands, allowing some means of survival. Remaining land, cash, and personal property were commonly inherited by male relatives, though this was not required under common law. Custom dictated that unmarried daughters rarely inherited land and usually received cash sums that were smaller than those given to sons.

In colonial Ontario, property provided more than survival: its possession was a condition of voting. Owning property was presumed to demonstrate a commitment to the colony, wealth, and respectability. Under the Constitutional Act of 1791, the minimum property qualification for the franchise was relatively low: the right to vote was conferred by owning a rural freehold worth at least forty shillings per year or a town property valued at five pounds per year, or by holding a tenancy that was worth at least ten pounds per year. Most Loyalist newcomers and their descendants owned substantial amounts of land. The Crown had allotted a hundred acres for male or widowed female heads of Loyalist households, plus fifty acres per family member, and British officers could receive up to a thousand acres. As a bid to attract more settlers, subsequent homestead policies gave free or cheap land to new migrants. The land may have been free, but newcomers needed significant financial resources to clear it and establish their farms. It has been said that due to its generous land distribution policies, Upper Canada had a larger electorate of farmers and artisans than any other part of British North America.

Property alone did not guarantee the franchise. Voters had to be British subjects who were at least twenty-one. They were also required to swear a loyalty oath to the British Crown, which disqualified Jewish, Quaker, and Mennonite property owners because their faith forbade oaths. Also barred were the members of religious (effectively Catholic) orders and anyone convicted of serious criminal offences or treason. Unlike in the United States, black male property owners were not legally excluded, but white residents sometimes prevented their black neighbours from exercising the franchise. Although First Nations people were not explicitly prohibited from voting, treaty land was held in common, making it impossible for individuals to meet the property qualifications. Furthermore, a person who received annuities from the Crown, such as treaty benefits, was held to be dependent, much like all women, and they too were denied the franchise. The special status of First Nations peoples was confirmed in 1857, when An Act to Encourage the Gradual Civilization of the Indian Tribes offered voting rights to any literate adult male who was free from debt and of good moral character, requirements not demanded of other British subjects. It should be noted there was never any specific law barring Metis men from voting. Meanwhile, Inuit could not vote since their territory was under the political control of the Hudson's Bay Company, which gave no voting rights to any inhabitants, settler or Indigenous.

The 1791 Constitutional Act described voters simply as "persons" and made no reference to their sex. Technically, spinsters and widows who owned property could vote, but the surviving records for Upper Canada suggest they did not, likely because of their difficulty in amassing enough property to qualify or sufficient authority to flout convention. Upper Canada stood in contrast to Lower Canada, with its multiple examples of women who voted during the early nineteenth century, a practice attributed to its more liberal property rights for married women under the French civil code.

DEMOCRATIC EVOLUTION UNDER REBELLION AND REFORM

Despite its relatively large male electorate, Upper Canada was more of an oligarchy than a democracy. Initially, its elected Legislative Assembly had sixteen seats for its scattered settlements, and it met once a year to draft bills and assess petitions. As the legislators received no salary, they were usually wealthy, often Loyalists or their descendants. Voter qualifications were sometimes manipulated to keep these elites in power. For example, in 1800, new legislation required residents of Upper Canada who had previously lived outside the British Empire to wait seven years before they could become British subjects. This stipulation targeted new American arrivals. Even so, the assembly's democratic autonomy was limited by a constitutional process in which lawmaking passed through two non-elected bodies. Essentially, the appointed Legislative Council and the appointed lieutenant-governor could defeat the assembly's bills. Furthermore, it was the council, not the assembly, that had the right to raise and collect taxes.

Initially, Upper Canada had no political parties, but this did not preclude cohorts of like-minded men from exerting power and patronage. One such example was the network of second-generation Loyalist men who were connected by marriage, business ties, and membership in the Anglican Church, the Bank of Upper Canada, or the Law Society of Upper Canada. Renowned for their conservative outlook, they were called the Family Compact by their opponents, and they dominated positions in the assembly and council. They also controlled the Executive Council, which was essentially the governor's cabinet. The Family Compact dictated political affairs until the 1820s, when newly elected assembly members and city councillors who had no Loyalist ties began to call for more responsible government. These reformers, led by William Lyon Mackenzie, envisioned a republican-style democracy in which an appointed council and governor answered to the

elected assembly. Political insiders insulted Mackenzie's supporters by referring to them as "women and children," shorthand
for reformers being uniformed and naive, "for surely no man of
sense" would support the reformers' grievances. Infuriated by the
absence of responsible government, Mackenzie led an armed uprising in York (later known as Toronto) in 1837. It was quickly sup-
pressed; however, the threat of violence, in conjunction with
Britain's own Great Reform Act (1832), convinced colonial administrators to consider greater democracy in British North America.

Though no women have been identified as taking up arms in
the Upper Canada Rebellion, English-born migrants Mary Sophia
O'Brien and Susanna Moodie were active partisans, siding against
the reformers. The journals of O'Brien, a mother of six and the
wife of a Conservative farmer, mixed local politics with housekeeping and family news. Reflecting upon the results of an 1830
election, she wrote, "Mackenzie has got in again and we have only
the satisfaction of seeing the country is pretty equally divided."
When news of the uprising reached the O'Brien homestead, her
husband travelled to Barrie to assist the "Loyal-hearted." In his
absence, she described the rebel attacks on government men and
houses, and her own anxiety at the unknown loyalties of her
neighbours. Hearing of the rebels' defeat, she expressed relief that
"every advantage on the side of the independent party" was "far
outweighed and outnumbered by the loyal party." Opposition to
the rebellion similarly infuses Moodie's poetry, written from her
Douro County homestead and published in Kingston and
Montreal newspapers in 1837–38. Whereas her husband served in
the official militia, Moodie recounted that she "did what little
[she] could to serve the good cause with [her pen]." Though
Moodie later expressed sympathy for the Reform Party, her "Address to the Freeman of Canada" condemned any rebel as "the
trampled Despot" and "baffled traitor." Her writing also charted
the costs of partisanship: when "women entered deeply into this
party hostility ... those who, from their education and mental

advantages, might have been friends and agreeable companions kept aloof." Despite what anti-suffragists would later claim, O'Brien and Moodie's keen political observations reveal that women had strong, informed opinions.

The 1837–38 rebellion was not the only cause to prompt strong feeling or action. Abolitionism remained a fervent cause for black women, who were appalled that Britain's 1834 abolishment of slavery did not prevent Americans from retrieving runaway slaves who sought freedom in Canada. In 1837, black women in Niagara-on-the-Lake blocked the recapture and extradition of a male fugitive slave from the United States. Led by Sally Carter, herself an escaped American slave, women stood in the line of fire, singing hymns in protest. British feminist travel writer Anna Brownwell Jameson, who witnessed the resistance, interviewed Carter, "asking if she was happy here in Canada." Carter "hesitated a moment, and then replied, on my repeating the question, 'Yes – that is, I was happy here – but now – I don't know – I thought we were safe here – I thought nothing could touch us here, on your British ground, but it seems I was mistaken, and if so, I won't stay here – I won't – I won't!'" Though filtered through a white sympathizer, Carter's statement demonstrates her readiness to embrace civil disobedience to improve her life and the lives of others who were similarly vulnerable.

The glacial shift to recognize rights beyond those of the elite was visible in the 1840 Act of Union, which merged Upper and Lower Canada into one British colony and made tentative steps – cemented in 1848 – toward a government that was more responsible to the people. The new Province of Canada was to be governed by an executive council, which was responsible to an expanded Legislative Assembly with representatives from Canada West (formerly Upper Canada) and Canada East (formerly Lower Canada). Like its 1791 predecessor, the Act of Union did not include sex-specific voting qualifications. Consequently, seven women defied tradition in 1844 by casting their ballots in West Halton.

In an age before secret ballots and polling booths, voting was decidedly public. Voters approached a temporary platform erected in a tavern, church, or town square, on which the returning officers would stand, confirm voting rights, hear individual votes, and enter them into a poll book. The candidates themselves often attended, addressing the boisterous crowds and providing free drinks, creating a scene in which voters commonly faced verbal and physical intimidation. Ridings usually had just one husting, though locations sometimes rotated. Voters would carry proof of residency and deeds to their property. They may have been required to swear an oath. In Lower Canada, where more women voted in the colonial era, Louis-Joseph Papineau called women's presence at the hustings – even that of his own mother, who had voted for him in 1832 – "scandalous." For the sake of "public interest, decency, [and] the modesty of the sex," he advocated that women be prohibited from voting. Similar prejudices existed in Canada West.

ONTARIO'S FIRST FEMALE VOTERS

This incident constitutes the only recorded instance of women voting in colonial Ontario. Previous studies skim over it, concluding that male kin coerced the handful of women to vote for their favoured candidate in a tight election. Though this scenario is possible, no evidence shows that the women were dragged to the hustings. What happened looks more complicated.

The West Halton election is representative of the era's aggressive party politics and frequent deadlock in the Legislative Assembly. A parliament organized along party lines became normal during the 1830s. There was a right-wing faction, led in Canada West by the Family Compact and referred to as the Conservative Party or the Tories. On the left were those who identified as Reform, a portion of whom would go on to found the Clear Grits, a precursor to the Liberal Party, in the 1850s. Back in 1844, the election results put the Conservatives ahead in Canada West; however, their majority dropped to one when the seats from Canada East were counted. Eighteen of eighty-four results were contested, including West Halton's. The vast majority of allegations came from Reformers or the Parti réformiste (Canada East's version of the Reform Party), claiming the right to Conservative seats. What sets the West Halton contest apart is that the losing Reform candidate accused the returning officer of deterring qualified voters while allowing illegal voters, including seven women, to cast their ballots for his opponent. Given that he lost by only eleven votes, the number of women voters hit hard. The incident received considerable coverage in the Reform newspaper, the *Upper Canada Herald,* which accused the Tories of disrupting democracy. In his petition, the defeated Reformer supplied the assembly with the names of six of the seven female voters, plus those of six men who lived outside of the riding. A parliamentary committee with seven Conservatives and two Reformers investigated his charges. The overwhelming Tory representation prompted the *Upper Canada Herald* to lament that "the fate of the petition is easily foreseen."

The six identified women were all widows: Sarah McWilliams of Puslinch, Mary Hinds of Waterloo, Elizabeth Wood from Nichol, and Hannah Williams, Mrs. P. Lamb, and Mrs. E. Worsley, all from Guelph. The seventh went unnamed. As the "relicts" of relatively wealthy farmers, each would have inherited at least a third of her late husband's property and claimed the right to represent it in the election. The women may have known each other, but West Halton County was large, and it appears voting stations were set up in two locations. Census and genealogical records provide more information on three of the women. Each was white and of British ancestry. Aged seventy-five, Sarah McWilliams was an Irish Protestant. The 1851 census lists her as a farmer, living with her fifty-two-year-old daughter and nineteen-year-old female servant. A Charles McWilliams, possibly her son, lived on a neighbouring property. Mary Hinds (1772–1852) would have been seventy-two during the election. A mother of five who had emigrated from Ireland in 1824, she settled in Guelph with her husband, Thomas, who died in 1842. The third confirmed voter, Hannah Williams (1817–77), was the daughter of Laura Secord, whose heroic acts in the War of 1812 were not yet well known but would become legendary by the end of the century. Secord's youngest child, Hannah was born after her mother's daring walk to the British lines. In 1833, aged sixteen, she married Hawley Williams, an English migrant. The couple lived in Guelph, where Hannah gave birth to two girls. In 1844, when she was twenty-seven, her husband died. She temporarily moved in with Laura, who was also recently widowed but without financial resources, making it unlikely that she too had the qualifications to vote. After participating in the West Halton election, Hannah remarried in 1847 and had five more children.

We can only speculate as to why these seven women voted. Were they inspired by their own political beliefs or pressured by male relatives? Did local issues, such as the promise of more canals and roads in Canada West, precipitate their boldness? Were any of them aware that women had voted in Canada East or that vocal advocates of women's right to vote existed in Britain and the United States? Was Hannah Williams motivated by her mother's agency, displayed in her infamous wartime spying or her persistent post-war negotiations with the colonial government for a pension? Did the women meet resistance or support from the crowd and election officials? What compelled the returning officer to let them vote? Was their acceptance, as the defeated Reformers charged, a corrupt act to swell the numbers of Tory voters, or was it a matter of principle? We should also ask whether 1844 was the first time that women actually voted in colonial Ontario – or was this merely the first time that evidence survived? We need also to question assumptions that the women were puppets of Tory relatives. Given that the colony's economic wealth was disproportionately aligned with the Family Compact, propertied women, like the West Halton seven, probably needed little incentive to side with the Conservatives.

The ensuing parliamentary investigation offers few answers. In fact, the Tory victor's lawyer disputed that any women voted. Rather than debate whether unmarried women of property had the right to vote, he contended that "the Committee could not take for granted that the names sought to be expunged were those of women." He then produced 693 male witnesses and 1 female, a Mrs. Kane, each of whom swore they observed fair practices. In response, the Reform loser supplied a list of 622 men to support a contrary case. The committee hired three commissioners, lawyers from Hamilton, to interview witnesses in Halton and examine certified copies of the poll books. Unfortunately, the inquiry's evidence – including the poll books – was all lost during the process, resulting in the committee condemning the commissioners for "neglect of duty."

Because no evidence had been produced to invalidate the election, the Tory kept his seat. The investigation did, however, note that "neither the Petition nor the Opposition to it appeared to be frivolous or vexatious," suggesting that the allegations were not entirely without merit. Only one of the eighteen contested elections in 1844 was overturned. The West Halton riding is the sole instance in which the presence of female voters was singled out as election fraud, suggesting that women voting was previously unknown or unusual.

Ironically, it was Reformers, members of the party seeking more democracy, who ensured that the West Halton seven were the first and last women to vote in Canada West. When the party won the 1849 election, it immediately enacted legislation with the prohibition "that no woman is or shall be entitled to vote at any such election, whether for a County or Riding, City or Town." Similar laws were passed at the same time in the colonies of New Brunswick and Prince Edward Island. Although women's ability as voters would later be subject to debate in both the press and the legislature, the 1849 amendment occurred without any public philosophizing about appropriate gender roles and behaviour. However, it was probably influenced not only by the 1844 scandal but also by Britain's 1832 Representation of the People Act (the Great Reform Act), which clarified that only "male persons" could vote. In any case, the deliberate exclusion of women demonstrates male alarm at the prospect of female voters. The 1849 "reform" put into electoral law the principle of property law – that men were uniquely privileged as heads of households, responsible for managing families and the colony. Also significant was the addition of the sex-specific restriction that coincided with the Reform government's consideration of universal male suffrage via an end to property qualifications. That result would have left only "mental capacity" as the standard for voter competency, adding insult to the injury of exclusion. In fact, however, full manhood suffrage was rejected lest it create a "tumultuous constituency," burdened by the "worthless and intemperate." More practically, from the viewpoint of the Loyalist elite, electoral recognition of women, workers, and the poor, not to mention Indigenous peoples, threatened the profitable status quo.

Despite this setback, women did win one concession: the school franchise. School trustees were responsible for managing school budgets, hiring headmasters and teachers, opening schools, developing calendars and curriculum, and overseeing the standardization and expansion of the colony's public schools. Under the 1850 Act for the better establishment and maintenance of Common Schools in Upper Canada, all "fit and proper persons, from among the resident freeholders or householders," could vote for school trustees. The lack of further restriction effectively enfranchised unmarried and widowed female property owners.

The 1850 act's gender-neutral language was not an endorsement of women's expertise in the public education of children. Contemporary observers interpreted their inclusion as a ploy to empower the more numerous Protestant property owners to vote against Catholic agitation for separate schools. Although Catholics were a minority in Canada West, they were bolstered in the new united assembly, which was packed with French Catholics from Canada East. Subsequent reforms guaranteed separate school rights for Catholics, but propertied spinsters and widows retained the franchise for the election of school trustees.

This inclusion by Canada West was women's first electoral victory in North America and Britain, a distinction celebrated by leading American abolitionist and suffragist Lucy Stone. The previous year she had visited Hamilton to give a lecture on women rights, a phenomenon described by the *Globe* as a "rather strange and modern reformation." Later, speaking at the National Women's Rights Convention in New York in 1856, Stone recounted what "a friend of mine in Canada West told me":

> that when the law was first passed giving women who owned a certain amount of property or who paid a given rental, a right to vote, he went trembling to the polls to see the result. The first woman who came was a large property holder in Toronto; with marked respect the crowd gave way as she advanced. She spoke her vote and walked away quietly, sheltered by her womanhood. It was all the protection she needed.

This passage contrasts with another early, less respectful, account. In 1853, according to the the *Globe*, female voters in the St. James' Ward of Toronto were duped by a would-be trustee who was deemed "unfit for the office" because allegedly he could "barely write his own name." The newspaper condemned him as a "prop" of the Catholic Church, set up to defeat the incumbent trustee, who opposed separate schools. The fervently Protestant *Globe* claimed that the Catholic candidate brought "a large number of women" to the poll, plus several men who tried to vote twice. Even though women had the right to vote, the paper assumed that they had been manipulated and declared the election unfair.

Being able to vote for school trustees did not usher in immediate progress. In fact, the *Globe*, commenting on the burgeoning suffrage movement in the United States, predicted that such a phenomenon would "never make headway in Canada." While the journalist's assumptions were certainly proved wrong, forty years would pass before women themselves were elected as school trustees. Municipal and provincial voting rights came similarly slowly. However, that minor franchise victory was not without consequence. Canada provided an example that emboldened the transnational suffrage community and encouraged women in the decades before and after Confederation to arise as a political force, championing a wide range of social causes and legal reforms, including the abolition of slavery, temperance and prohibition, improvements to married women's property law, and equity in education and employment. As organizations and self-consciousness grew, the first Canadian movement dedicated to achieving the female franchise emerged.

I am not the one to set a limit to the scope of women's talents. I would have her freed to choose her vocations as her brother man, tethered by no conventionalities, enslaved by no chains, either of her own or man's forging, but I believe this occupation peculiarly on a line with woman's nature, and the one in which the great majority must forever labor.

To assume that all women must fall into this line, and excel in it, is as unjust and unreasonable as to assume that all men ought to be farmers and excel at such. The same diversities of tastes and talents are found among women as among men. In reference to occupation both sexes should choose for themselves, having reference to their special tastes, which will to some extent be controlled by their environments, and having chosen, should make in their constant study and aim to ensure by persevering toil and industry to the greatest attainable excellence in the calling of their choice.

– EMILY STOWE, 1889

TWO

ORIGINS OF FEMINIST THOUGHT AND ACTION

Abolitionist and feminist Mary Ann Shadd Cary's endorsement of equal rights for black men and women was a prominent feature of her Canada West newspaper, the *Provincial Freeman*. When she was forced to downplay her role as publisher due to gender discrimination, male colleagues rose to her support, describing her as "one of the best Editors our Province ever had," even if she "did wear petticoats instead of breeches."

FEMINISM MIGHT HAVE stirred when women voted for school trustees in pre-Confederation Ontario, but it had to counter the Victorian age's investment in the "cult of true womanhood." As Peterborough settler Catharine Parr Traill suggested in 1854, "Woman, whose nature is to love home and to cling to all home ties and associations, cannot be torn from that spot that is the little centre of joy and peace and comfort to her, without many painful regrets." Her statement, part of her advice guide dedicated entirely to frontier housekeeping tips, reinforced respectable women's proper confinement to domesticity. Yet even as she wrote, the boundaries of separate spheres were publicly challenged. Mid-century Canada West produced trailblazers such as abolitionist, publisher, and suffragist Mary Ann Shadd Cary and physician and suffragist Dr. Emily Howard Stowe. In the 1870s, the newly formed Young Women's Christian Association (YWCA), the Woman's Christian Temperance Union (WCTU), and the Toronto Women's Literary Club (TWLC) had women advocate for social reform from pulpits, newspapers, and public meetings, a robust sign they envisioned expanded roles for their sex.

Women's heightened public presence in social movements and charities, and the maternal and moral authority they used to demand government intervention and legislative reform, insisted on the value of female ideas and skills beyond the home. Some advocates envisioned boundless possibilities. "It seems to me it is with woman as man – whatever she feels is her duty and place to do, let her do it with all her heart," wrote novelist Fannie Belle Irving in 1879 for the *Toronto Weekly Graphic*. "A woman performing her duty, whatever or wherever it be," she stated, "is not so much out of her place as he who steps from his own to criticize and denounce her." Such opinions ensured that gender conformity could no longer be taken for granted in the mid- to late nineteenth century. Ontario's dominant values could now be reimagined by a persistent cohort of courageous women.

WE DO NOT KNOW HER EQUAL: MARY ANN SHADD CARY

Black women initiated human rights advocacy in Canada. Historians link their nineteenth-century activism to a long history of resistance by women of African descent in colonial North America. Some were the descendants of those enslaved by the French, British, or Americans or had migrated as free blacks. After the British Empire abolished slavery in 1834, long-established African Canadians in Toronto, Niagara Falls, and St. Catharines, were joined by free black Americans and fugitive slaves, many of whom settled in the Chatham-Windsor area. The slaves may have escaped bondage, but they encountered racism in their new country, including school segregation and discrimination. In 1849, white settlers were reported as feeling uncomfortable with nearby neighbours who "belong to a different branch of the human family, and are BLACK." That prejudice dogged black women as they raised families, supported the domestic economy, helped establish churches, schools, and clubs, and assisted fugitives to escape slavery.

Like their white counterparts, Ontario's black settlements were predominantly patriarchal, with men expected to head households and communities, and women relegated to domestic matters. This ideology informed, for example, the education of boys being privileged over girls, as when the boys' school in Elgin was established five years before that of the girls, the latter of which offered a truncated curriculum focused on homemaking. Despite such favouritism, long-standing traditions of black female leadership persisted, stemming in part from the legacy of female-headed families under slavery, when husbands and fathers were often forced to live separately from wives and children. Women led the female auxiliaries of male anti-slavery organizations, vigilant committees (which watched for American slave catchers), and benevolent associations.

The remarkable Mary Bibb (1820–77) illustrates this tradition of female community building. Bibb was born free in Rhode Island into a family of Quakers, a Christian group that opposed slavery, emphasized peace, and believed in equality between the sexes. In 1850, after training as a teacher, she emigrated to Canada West, where she became an exemplary advocate of self-improvement and human rights. Establishing private schools for black students in Sandwich and Windsor, she dreamed of starting a free school "for all irrespective of colour." Bibb spent decades seeking funding from local governments, African American benevolent societies, and Horace Mann, a white American advocate for public schools. The married and childless Bibb also helped found the Windsor Anti-Slavery Society, the Refugee Home Society, and the Windsor Ladies Club. She taught Sunday School and published a newspaper, *Voice of the Fugitive,* with her first husband, Henry Bibb.

Black women's literary societies in Windsor and Chatham predated the renowned TWLC by two decades. Literary clubs thrived in the nineteenth century, with members committed to self-improvement through writing, drama, music, and cultural debate. Particularly popular in small towns, they offered rare opportunities to connect with the world of ideas through debates and reading, and to be cost effective for shared literary subscriptions. Bibb's Windsor Ladies Club (1854), like the Ladies' Literary Society in Chatham (1850s), founded by fellow teacher Amelia Freeman Shadd, were just such ambitious offerings. For women, barred from almost all forms of higher education and most other clubs with intellectual ambitions, separate groups provided an unprecedented space to nurture ideas and develop relationships. Important connections could also be made, as Amelia Shadd's club

---

It is no coincidence that suffrage pioneers Mary Ann Shadd Cary and Emily Stowe began their professional lives as teachers. Owing to the expansion of Ontario's public school system in the mid-nineteenth century, teaching became a profession dominated by women. Hiring unmarried women saved cash-starved school boards money since it was presumed they had no dependants to support and therefore could be paid significantly less than male teachers. Furthermore, the skills and values associated with instructing children, at least young children, were closely associated with mothering. Here was a respectable, if poorly paid, occupation for women.

Initially, it was common for teachers to receive no specialized training. In 1847, the colony's first teacher's college, the Provincial Normal School, opened in Toronto. The following year, it admitted female teacher candidates, making it the first coeducational institute of higher education in the colony. Stowe, a graduate of the school, credited the school's foresight "to recognize equality in the ability of the sexes to compete in the halls of learning." Owing to their education and work experiences, teachers would be well represented in Ontario's suffrage movement. Equal pay and the right for married women to hold employment as teachers were early calls to actions taken up by suffragists.

demonstrated when it raised funds for her sister-in-law's newspaper, the *Provincial Freeman*.

The editor Mary Ann Shadd (1823–93) was once described by abolitionist leader and celebrated orator Frederick Douglass as someone with "unceasing industry ... uncomfortable zeal and commendable ability." He added, "We do not know her equal among the coloured ladies of the United States." Known across North America as an ardent abolitionist and champion of equal rights, she was born free in the slave state of Delaware. As a young woman, Shadd published articles and pamphlets on racial uplift through education and economic self-sufficiency. Travelling to Toronto in 1851 to attend an anti-slavery conference, she met the Bibbs, who hired her to teach in Windsor. Impressed by opportunities in Canada West, Shadd published *A Plea for Emigration; or Notes of Canada West,* which promoted settlement in Canada, although along very different lines from those endorsed by the genteel Catharine Parr Traill.

Though positive, Shadd remained outspoken about the need for improved race relations, affordable schools, and amenities for black communities. She openly condemned Canada West's black leaders, including the Bibbs, who promoted the financing and building of segregated settlements. Shadd argued that integration, not segregation, was the best direction. Because of her attack on the Bibbs's vision, she lost her teaching position. Undeterred, in 1853 she created her own newspaper, the *Provincial Freeman,* to act as an alternative public voice for black readers. Initially published out of Toronto, it offered subscribers in Canada West and the northern United States news and opinions, primarily about local politics and the abolition movement, but also on temperance, voting rights for black men, and women's suffrage. The *Freeman* expected the "female portion of our patrons" to be both readers and fundraisers. In return, it represented them as both active and feminine. Reporting, for example, on a meeting of Chatham voters, the *Freeman* hailed the women attendees as a "new feature in political gatherings," adding that "much of the asperity of such assemblies will be softened by their presence."

Shadd emerged as a controversial figure, a woman whose frankness, intelligence, ambition, and initially unmarried status challenged gendered expectations. Later celebrated as the first female publisher in North America, she faced abuse as "only a busy body in men's matters." Fearing that conservative attitudes would harm the *Provincial Freeman,* Shadd hired a male editor and male journalists, whereas she worked behind the scenes, publishing under her initials. As she fundraised around North America, her reputation for astute observations grew, even as she encountered outrage when she revealed herself as the paper's publisher. In 1855, Shadd temporarily removed her name from the masthead but not before directing "a word" to black women: "We have 'broken the Editorial ice,' whether willingly or not, for your class in America; so go to Editing, as many of you are willing, and able and as soon as you may if you think you are ready." Shadd soon moved the *Provincial Freeman* to the more supportive community of Chatham, where she returned to publishing the paper under her name.

Shadd continued the enterprise through the late 1850s, surviving libel charges, financial difficulties, and marriage in 1856 to a widower with three children. Apparently, she kept news of her marriage and subsequent motherhood quiet, fearful of her reception as a working mother. The *Provincial Freeman* folded in 1860, a casualty of Shadd's attention to the American Civil War and the death of her husband. Widowed and pregnant, she resumed teaching to support her family. In a testament to the prevalence of border crossing among many activists, Shadd returned to the United States. After the war, at age forty-nine, she again defied expectations to be the first female graduate to earn a law degree at Howard University in Washington, though her graduation was delayed nine years due to the university's fear of backlash. In the 1880s, much of Shadd's energy turned toward the American suffrage movement. She founded the Coloured Women's Progressive Franchise Association, which also helped its members become economically self-sufficient, and joined the predominately white National Women's Suffrage Association, where she advocated for African Americans.

Black women's lives in Canada West reveal the complexity of what it meant to negotiate personal and societal expectations about both race and gender, not to mention class, while building safe, equitable, and prosperous communities. Their activism furnished Ontario's first feminist wave, pre-dating the suffrage crusade by several decades. Nevertheless, the prevailing racism of most white women meant that when it came time to confront their own oppression, they neither sought the expertise of black women, nor drew any parallels between bigotry and sexism. As a result, the suffrage movement remained largely white. Consequently, although they encountered almost identical inspirations and challenges – both were Quakers and schoolteachers who forsook traditional paths to seek professional careers in addition to marriage and motherhood, while advocating for equality – no evidence exists that Dr. Emily Stowe ever crossed paths with her contemporary, Shadd.

BEARING THE HEAT AND BURDEN OF THE DAY:
DR. EMILY STOWE

Emily Howard Jennings Stowe (1831–1903) was the eldest daughter of Quakers in Norwich Township, Upper Canada. The family's religion and support for Reform politics placed it on the margins of the Family Compact–dominated society. As a young woman, Stowe was encouraged to question the status quo and to demonstrate intellectual equality in higher education and in medicine during the 1850s and 1860s. As Ontario's most significant nineteenth-century suffragist, she frequently bore "the heat and burden of the day" on behalf of other women. Although the term "New Woman" was not coined until 1894, her autonomy, defiance of social expectations, and willingness to break barriers made her an innovator.

Stowe's entry into an active life began with teaching. After seven years toiling in one-room schoolhouses, Stowe sought higher education, but no Ontario universities admitted female students. The only option was teacher's college, and she graduated from Toronto's Normal School in 1854. Her first-class honours and previous teaching experience won her an appointment in Brantford as the first female principal in Canada West. Two years later, she resigned, as was required, when she married Methodist carriage maker John Stowe and then bore three children. A decade later, when he contracted pulmonary tuberculosis, the mother and wife returned to teaching. Although she taught at a country grammar school, an institution markedly above local primary schools, she was inspired by her mother's work as a skilled herbalist to become a doctor.

She made this decision just as the medical profession reinforced separate spheres by insisting that the physical and intellectual strain of higher education threatened the health, femininity, and reproductive capacity of women. Unlike the majority of professional discourse, the *Canadian Lancet,* a medical journal, did not propose an outright ban on female physicians, stating in 1871 that

> as wives, mothers, sisters and dainty housekeepers we have the utmost love and respect for them; but we do not think the profession of medicine, as a rule, is a fit place for them. But if they choose to enter upon the study of medicine or any other profession which they may admire, we see no good reason why they should be denied any of the rights and privileges accorded to those of the sterner sex.

That proclamation did not stop Canadian medical schools from remaining closed to women until 1883. Stowe had to seek her training in the United States.

Stowe's daring was extraordinary. Not only were her means modest, but she dealt with the crisis of her husband's illness and

Suffragist Dr. Emily Stowe, after 1880. Her early life and career
were dedicated to improving women's access to education, health
care, and political rights. "My career has been one of much
struggle," she stated, "characterized by the usual persecution
which attends everyone who pioneers a new movement or
steps out of line with established customs."

the widespread unfriendliness toward female medical students
and women doctors. Making this bold project work was a family
enterprise. A married sister cared for her children, and everyone
recalibrated expectations of Stowe as a wife and mother. A further mark of kin support was the subsequent training of two
sisters and a daughter as physicians. Moreover, when her husband
recovered in the early 1870s, he retrained as a dentist, and the
couple set up a joint medical-dental practice.

Stowe graduated from the New York Medical College for
Women in 1867 and returned to a reimagined homeland.

MOTHERS OF CONFEDERATION

In 1867, the united Province of Canada became Ontario and Quebec, joining Confederation with Nova Scotia and New Brunswick. Nothing about the British North America Act singled out women's status or changed their rights. The only woman with an official role in the process was Queen Victoria. Reportedly, she took a keen interest in the development of Canada and met with delegates in London to discuss the terms. Private correspondence reveals the wives of the men who later become known as the Fathers of Confederation were also politically engaged. During the 1864 Confederation debates about the division of federal and provincial government, Toronto Reform politician George Brown wrote daily to his wife, Anne Nelson Brown. Though details are scant, he acknowledged her influence: "How I do wish you were here to advise me ... But never mind, I will try to do my duty to the country in such a manner as you my dearest Anne, will not be ashamed of." To mark Confederation and her new status as the wife of Canada's first prime minister, the Kingston-based Agnes Macdonald bought a lock for her diary, noting, "My Diaries as Miss Bernard did not need such precautions but then I was an insignificant young Spinster & what I might write did not matter. Now I am a Great Premier's wife & Lady Macdonald & 'Cabinet secrets and mysteries' might drop or slip off unwittingly from the nib of my pen." Such women clearly anticipated sharing ideas and even influence with the male leaders of the new dominion.

Opportunities for Canada's only female physician seemed most likely in Toronto, where Stowe started her medical practice in 1868–69. It was Ontario's largest city, with approximately fifty-six thousand residents. Though agriculture remained central, the province's economic development depended increasingly on mining and manufacturing. Immigration and industrialization nearly overwhelmed cities and transformed the family economy. Individual craftsmen and apprentices were increasingly replaced by a wage-based factory system built on less-skilled workers. Unstable wages left many in poverty and required children to supplement the family income. Although married women rarely worked outside the home for wages, they took in boarders, did laundry or sewing, gardened and raised poultry and livestock, or bartered goods. Unmarried women, widows, and adolescent daughters took on precarious and poorly paid employment as domestic servants or in factories, sweatshops, retail spaces, schools, and offices. With the exception of an 1882 strike led by female shoe- and bootmakers and a few women allowed in the Knights of Labor union, Toronto's burgeoning labour movement, like that elsewhere, had almost exclusively male members, reflecting the presumed temporary nature of women's work and the prioritization of men as family breadwinners.

As Canada's first female doctor, Stowe hoped to find patients among the working-class and poor residents of Toronto. Dedicated to the diseases of women and children, her practice reflected her conviction that her sex deserved its own physicians. Men, whether due to modesty or prejudice, would have been unlikely to seek her services. Any patient with means would have wanted a licenced physician, which Stowe was not. The 1869 Ontario Medical Act insisted that all US-trained physicians must attend at least one course in an Ontario medical school, an option unavailable to women. In 1870, Stowe and Jennie Kidd-Trout, another Canadian who was determined to become a doctor, were granted permission by the Toronto School of Medicine to take one course to meet this requirement. Their treatment by male students and faculty was nevertheless so offensive that Stowe reportedly refused to sit the exams set by the Council of the College of Physicians and Surgeons of Ontario. Instead, she risked fines to practise illegally for another ten years, an act of civil disobedience, until the college finally recognized her credentials. Kidd-Trout, in contrast, seized the opportunity and was licensed before Stowe.

Stowe made daily house calls to her patients, seeing the damage caused by poor wages and long working hours. In dirty, untidy, and unkempt homes, she saw tragedy. As a physician and a Quaker, she was especially troubled by both sexes' consumption of alcohol, and she recommended abstention. The scope of deprivation she encountered increased the appeal of social reform and suffrage activism.

WOMEN'S RISING ADVOCACY

The era's rapid changes produced radical proposals. Marxists critiqued the growing inequity produced by industrialization and capitalism. They turned to labour unions and communist and socialist political parties. Meanwhile, Protestant churches, already reeling from the secular and scientific revolution glimpsed in Herbert Spencer's "Progress: Its Law and Cause" (1857) and Charles Darwin's *Origin of Species* (1859), sought to demonstrate the relevancy of Christianity by launching the social gospel movement, which pushed for Christian-minded reform. Both movements advocated government intervention to improve community life. Not all demands were progressive. By the end of the nineteenth century, the influx of non-British immigrants had triggered reactionary demands to protect the dominance of the Anglo-Saxon race. Some would-be reformers sought solutions in romanticized visions of a homogeneous and deferential past, whereas others hoped to craft a more democratic and modern society.

Although men and women collaborated in advocacy, a significant women-only reform movement emerged in Ontario during the late 1860s and the 1870s. Most of its members were not uniquely positioned individuals, like Shadd and Stowe. Nor were they the poor or working-class women who were most dramatically injured by industrialization and urbanization. Predominantly white, Protestant, and middle class, they founded associations that were dedicated to moral uplift, education, and skills building, and they justified their involvement as relevant extensions of domestic caretaking. Lottie McAlister's 1899 novel *Clipped Wings* explained that reform channeled a maternal energy that "proposed not only to rock the cradle for the world, but to rock the world for the cradle." The participation of middle-class women was made possible by technological improvements, new consumer practices, increased availability of domestic servants, and a declining birth rate, as well as aspirations fostered variously by religious faith, political ideologies, educational advances, and professional ambitions.

Urban and rural women had taken up faith-based charitable efforts since the early eighteenth century. They had supported the so-called deserving poor and foreign and domestic mission work. Beginning in 1868, the Hebrew Ladies' Sick and Benevolent Society, managed out of the oldest synagogue in Toronto, was one of the largest female-based charities in the province. It aided orphans and the homeless, and it provided free loans to those who were seen as deserving. The biggest changes to women's reform efforts in the 1870s were the evolution from charity only to political action and the increasing numbers of women active without the supervision of male clergy. Shadd summed up the revolutionary implications of this shift: "We cannot successfully evade duty because the suffering fellow woman is only a woman. She too is a neighbour. The spirit of true philanthropy knows no sex!"

However, most ambitions remained modest. Founded to keep "our girls good," the Young Women's Christian Association (YWCA) arrived in Ontario from England in 1873. It ran boarding homes, night classes, and employment services for young urban women, many of whom had left rural toil and unequal opportunities or foreign homelands to find paid work. Though YWCA programs emphasized moral regulation and spiritual guidance, they also raised awareness about low wages and poor working conditions. By the 1890s, YWCA branches had been established in Hamilton, Peterborough, Kingston, London, Belleville, and Ottawa, with a national office located in Toronto. In settlement houses such as Toronto's Evangelia House, many activists gravitated to suffrage.

The Y's efforts were often associated with campaigns against alcohol, commonly linked with both men's abuse of women and children and a lack of industry and application among the poor. Diverse temperance societies had been advocating for abstinence and prohibition since the late 1820s. Early male-dominated organizations rarely allowed women to play significant roles. The creation of the Woman's Christian Temperance Union (WCTU) in the United States and Canada in 1874 was their first opportunity for leadership in a cause that was increasingly framed as a woman's rights issue. Temperance intended to free women and children from male aggression and the fiscal irresponsibility of intoxicated husbands and fathers, thus saving women from rape, seduction, and prostitution. Though this belief was rooted in highly classist attitudes and ignored other structural causes of domestic violence or poverty, calling for the prohibition of alcohol sales or consumption of liquor was a feminist act. Taking on temperance meant attacking three realms of male power: the liquor trade, the government, and the drinking culture of men, from gentlemen's clubs to saloons. If the hustings were considered no place for a respectable woman, neither by far was the tavern, and both spaces were targeted by the temperance

THE WAR ON WOMEN AND CHILDREN.

Liquor Traffic.—With these weapons I'm as deadly as ever, and I'll show you no mercy!

"The War on Women and Children," *Toronto Grip,* 6 June 1885. In this sympathetic look at women's temperance work, a battered but resolute mother faces off against liquor traffic, embodied as a devilish pig walking over the Scott Act, one of the first prohibition laws. In the background lurk a corrupt politician and a drunken father.

movement as symbolic and actual sites of female vulnerability. Just as abolitionism instigated black women's activism in Ontario, temperance supplied the first step toward wider protest for many white women.

The first Canadian WCTU branch was established in the hard-drinking port of Owen Sound. The second branch was founded in Picton, originally a Loyalist town, by Letitia Creighton Youmans (1827–96), who is credited with building the WCTU across Ontario. A former schoolteacher and stepmother of eight, Youmans explained in her memoir, *Campaign Echoes,* that "tales of sorrow" of the domestic violence experienced by her Sunday School pupils

led her to the cause. Her first WCTU campaign launched a petition that asked town council to stop issuing licences for the sale
of liquor. Local women collected the signatures of three hundred property holders. Years later, Youmans recalled the fear and
intimidation that WCTU members felt as they prepared their
presentation to council: "It will seem so bold. Oh! It will be so unwomanly." This anxiety was refuted when one woman asked
what could be more womanly than a mother and wife attempting
to safeguard the family.

The WCTU presented its demand in a two-day affair that
Youmans described as "a battle of words." One council member
proposed that if the radical petition were accepted, the WCTU
would need to compensate shop owners for any unsold alcohol
in stock. In response, the women asserted that compensation
should flow in the opposite direction: for example, it was owed
to a widow whose husband lay in a drunkard's grave and to another wife who was suffering "untold agonies" inflicted by a
drunken husband. Ultimately, the council refused to budge, a decision that only furthered WCTU resolve.

The WCTU was never a one-cause wonder: Canadians obeyed
the instruction of its charismatic American founder, Frances
Willard: "do everything." Campaigns focused on reforms at the city,
county, and provincial levels through support for temperance candidates, recruitment of adults and youth to take temperance
pledges, public education, protests outside of taverns, and the wearing of white ribbons. By 1891, Ontario had 175 WCTU branches, with
over 4,300 members. At its height in 1914, there were 8,000 members. Although it was not an immediate ally of female enfranchisement, the WCTU would soon champion suffrage.

The WCTU also made a conscious effort to support temperance in black and Indigenous communities. Informed by imperial
values, WCTUers believed that non-whites were particularly sus-
ceptible to alcohol. In the 1890s, following the example of its
American counterpart, the WCTU opened a department of work

among coloured people, and segregated branches led by black women aimed at serving black communities. These efforts produced little fruit, as most residents preferred to join the all-male or mixed-sex temperance groups organized by black churches.

To reach Indigenous people, the WCTU sponsored the temperance work of white missionaries stationed on reserves. That outreach, like the establishment of churches, day schools, and residential schools, was part of officially sanctioned efforts at cultural genocide. Indigenous people developed their own response to the tragedy of alcohol abuse. Among the Haudenosaunee of the Six Nations of the Grand River Reserve, several all-male or mixed-sex Christian temperance societies were founded, whereas some practitioners of the traditional Longhouse religion followed temperance as part of a cultural revival. An address by one Indigenous temperance leader, Dr. Peter Martin (Oronhyatekha), pointed to seventeenth-century roots of restraint: early clan mothers had petitioned the Council of Chiefs to "enact a prohibitory law forbidding the introduction of intoxicants among the people." His Christian female contemporaries at Grand River also led temperance efforts through the Indian Moral Association, which was co-founded by two Mohawk women, Evelyn Johnson and Mary Smith Styres. Johnson, the sister of the famous poet, drew on her earlier experience with the American YWCA in creating the reserve initiative. The extent of both Christian and Longhouse support demonstrates the agency of Indigenous people and the frequent leadership of women beyond the intervention of settler organizations.

In considering the activism of First Nations women, some historians conclude that they affirmed their traditional community power in this era through participation in colonially approved spaces, including schools, churches, and voluntary organizations. Overall, however, the 1876 federal Indian Act and its subsequent amendments reinforced efforts at assimilation. The act, not the Indigenous communities themselves, defined who was Indian

and who was not. It also regulated the reserve system and restricted traditional forms of governance, education, language,
travel, and religious ceremonies. Voting rights applied solely to
First Nations men, but only if they renounced their Indian status
and achieved sufficient property qualifications. Attaining a university degree or professional designation as a doctor, clergyman,
or lawyer meant automatic loss of Indian status. The Indian Act
further legislated that all chiefs and band councillors must be
"male members of the band of the full age of twenty-one years."

The act excluded First Nations women from participating in
the band council. Even more of a burden, if they married white
men or First Nations men who lacked Indian status, they would
lose their own status and treaty rights, as would all children produced by that union. This abuse was far more important than
being unable to vote in colonial elections. Not surprisingly,
Indigenous women resisted it, both individually and communally.
Take, for example, Catherine Sutton (Nahnebahwequay, 1824–
65), a Christian Ojibwe woman who challenged the colonial government's sale of treaty lands around Georgian Bay. In 1859,
Sutton petitioned the Canadian Parliament on behalf of family
and neighbours who had lost treaty land and highlighted the injustice of denying treaty rights to women who, like herself, had
married white men. Refused compensation by Ottawa, Sutton
then appealed to Queen Victoria, whose only redress was to allow
her to buy back her own land. Reflecting on her meeting with
the Ojibwe petitioner, the queen wrote, "She speaks English quite
well, and is come on behalf of her Tribe to petition against some
grievance as regards their land." Upon returning to Canada,
Sutton resisted until her death against the "wholesale robbery
and treachery" visited upon Indigenous peoples. Despite Sutton's
activism and the resistance of other First Nations women, the
Indian Act would discriminate against generations, denying their
identities and rights to land. Later, the establishment of manda-
tory residential schools and the out-migration of children for

education further destabilized Indigenous women's identities and status as mothers. None of these cruelties drew the attention of white women reformers. Even suffragists, who were so attuned to discrimination on the basis of sex, were generally insensitive to or ignorant of issues of racial prejudice.

CLANDESTINE SUFFRAGE ACTIVITY

The irreverent Emily Stowe lectured on "woman's sphere" across southern Ontario, openly condemning the "conventionalities of society," which prevented a woman from exploring "whatever fields of nature her God-given faculties qualify her for." The *Toronto Star* summed up the public response to Stowe as "the fiercest dislike, opposition and even persecution." Most white women remained blind to their own oppression; however, Stowe gathered a small but well-positioned following that was interested in exploring women's political inequities in patriarchal culture. The first women's suffrage organization in Canada began quietly, as the Toronto Women's Literary Club (TWLC). Anxious about reception, Stowe likely chose the name to disguise the fact that the TWLC was a political body keen to advance women's rights, most significantly the franchise. Inspired by attendance at meetings of the American Association for the Advancement of Women, Stowe founded the intellectually driven club and became its first president in 1877. She hoped that Canadian clubs would encourage "widespread intelligence among the women." Pointing out that "gentlemen have long felt the need and have acknowledged the advantages of such unions," she intended to awaken Canadian women to "the social and economic injustices" they suffered.

Predictably, given its overwhelmingly white, middle-class membership, the early suffrage movement targeted access to higher education and professional careers. The earliest TWLC recruits were connected to Stowe through her Quaker, professional, and reform channels. Early stalwarts were author and playwright Sarah Curzon; school reformer Jessie Turnbull McEwen; WCTU leaders Annie Parker, Mary McDonnell, and Margaret McDonnell; Jennie Gray, a later graduate of Toronto's Trinity Medical School; and Eliza Noble Rogers, a Quaker and wife of a coal baron. Most lived in Toronto and were married with children. Gathering in private homes, meetings covered multiple subjects and lessons, ranging from Stowe's dissection of a sheep's eyeball to flower arranging and a dramatic reading of *Taming of the Shrew,* all linked by participants' commitment to think critically. Women's rights inevitably came up, and discussions centred on placing woman in political equality with man, with the "general opinion being in favour of the subject." Subcommittees reviewed charitable institutions, foreign missionary work, and conditions of working women. On at least one occasion, the TWLC investigated the working conditions for female shop clerks and factory workers, and its activists pressed employers for more humane hours, breaks, and separate toilets. The club also endorsed Stowe's dream of opening the University of Toronto to women.

By 1884, Ontario suffragists had won small victories, such as amendments to married women's property laws and municipal voting rights for unmarried women and widows. Despite such gains, opponents insisted that wider suffrage measures would only threaten the well-being of families and society. The patriarchal prejudices, rooted in the province's early conservatism, kept the TWLC and its sympathizers on the sidelines of political life.

We ask to have the franchise extended to our property qualified women, because it is just. Justice is the heart-principle of every true Canadian; and every form of injustice removed from us as a nation, is a good gained for all our people. We ask this privilege, not as a selfish benefit, but so whatever good is in us may have an ever increasing influence on the upward and onward development of the people.

– JENNIE FOULDS, SECRETARY OF THE CANADIAN
WOMEN SUFFRAGE ASSOCIATION, 1883

THREE

EARLY LEGISLATIVE VICTORIES AND DEFEATS

Unlike her mother, Dr. Augusta Stowe-Gullen completed her medical training in Ontario. Dressed here in her convocation robes, in 1883, she became the first female physician to graduate from the Faculty of Medicine at Victoria University. As a suffragist, she condemned men's narrow-minded approach to politics: "In man's legislation his ideals in nearly every instance relate to property and as a class, men are not concerned with human rights, especially of women, children and the home."

THE STRENGTH OF PERSISTING resistance to a fair deal for women was summed up in 1879 by Francis Parkman, an American who researched Canadian history: "Let us pray for deliverance from female suffrage." Though conceding that some "savage tribes of this continent listened, in solemn assembly, to the counsels of its matrons," he insisted that women's many defects of character and lack of experience in self-government, particularly among those in the lower classes, prevented them from being effective political actors. Furthermore, though women could own property, they could not serve as soldiers and thus could never be full citizens. He used the frequently repeated refrain that good women simply did not want the vote and that they would find it "a cruel and intolerable burden." Like many other scholars, he used his professional authority to reinforce old prejudices and, not so incidentally, to undermine possible academic rivals. Such warnings did not deter the brave. Global protest gradually mounted against conventions that consigned much of the population to second-class status. The mid-nineteenth-century Chartist reformers in Britain and abolitionists in the United States disrupted class and racial privilege. Women's rights, however, were generally not at the top of reform agendas. Although white settler women gained the vote in the Wyoming and Utah territories (in 1869 and 1870 respectively), early British and American suffrage bills could not surmount fears about supposed threats to marriage, democracy, and civilization. Suffragists fiercely rejected such slurs.

Invoking a host of precedents from the mythical Amazons to Elizabeth I and Joan of Arc, not to mention the Virgin Mary, suffragists in Western nations insisted that they were on the right side of history. American Lucy Stone pointed to heroic women: nursing pioneer Florence Nightingale and educational reformer Mary Carpenter were recent examples of great women who under current law were categorized with "idiots and felons." Another leader of the suffrage crusade in the United States, Elizabeth Cady Stanton, cited Ontario's thirty-year history of women's school suffrage as proof that female voters could be trusted. By 1883, growing self-confidence had encouraged the Toronto Women's Literary Club (TWLC) to change its name to the Canadian Women's Suffrage Association (CWSA). Over the next year, Emily Stowe rallied male and female suffragists, with varying degrees of success, on three campaigns: coeducation at the University of Toronto, property rights for married women, and municipal franchise rights for all female property holders.

PUBLIC OUTRAGE AND MOCKERY

Opponents dismissed every claim to equal rights at the ballot box. Anti-suffragists mobilized across the country and globe, but Ontario reactionaries found their own leader. This was Goldwin Smith, a former professor of modern history at Oxford and Cornell Universities, who was married to a wealthy Toronto widow. He condemned "votes for women" alongside a litany of evils: imperialism, temperance, and socialism, all of which he routinely criticized in essays published in British and North American periodicals, including the three he founded. Recanting his previous enthusiasm for British equal rights philosopher John Stuart Mill's petition for the female franchise, Smith insisted that women's subordination in public life was a historical artifact, necessary to the establishment of higher civilization: "Without it," he claimed, "the germs of nations and of humanity would have perished." This system worked well because relationships between men and women were supported by sexual affection and a division of labour that was based on men's superior strength for labour and soldiering. The victory of women's rights would bring unconsecrated cohabitation and would promote the sexual exploitation of women, who would no longer be protected by men. Prior to the founding of the TWLC, Smith celebrated Canada as free of feminist demands, with the exception of calls for coeducation. Although ignoring the details of subsequent Canadian suffrage activism, Smith remained as a well-known pontificator. The British satirical magazine *Punch* singled him out in 1889 for resembling the "shrews" he condemned:

> So Goody – I mean Goldwin – Please
> To moderate your ecstasies
> Of anger, lest the feebler sex,
> Whose aims your manly soul so vex,
> Should think you share – wildest notions!
> Their "irresponsible emotions."

That anonymous verse reminded suffragists that they had both supporters and opponents all around the globe, some of whom could be found in the Toronto press.

The *Globe,* a newspaper with Reform Party origins, published monthly summaries of TWLC meetings. This recurring feature did not suggest that the paper formally endorsed the suffrage cause, but it did give the club a public forum to share its ideas and possibly attract new members. The *Globe* often published letters to the editor highlighting multiple perspectives on women's enhanced public presence. Notably, in 1877, its coverage of a Woman's Christian Temperance Union (WCTU) meeting prompted a month's worth of letters on the topic of women as effective public speakers. This extended into a discussion about the relative merits of "strong-minded" women.

Illustration from "O.P. Dildock Visits the Woman's Club: Make
Way for Liberty. Great Cackalations," *Toronto Graphic*, c. 1870s.
Having shaved off his whiskers in hopes of looking more
feminine, the reporter lurks in the shadows, observing the
proceedings before heckling the members. Note the deliberate
misspelling of "rights" as "wright" and "writes."

The *Toronto Graphic*, a weekly paper that favoured jokes and
gossip, delighted in mocking suffragists. One of its regular col-
umnists, whose pen name was O.P. Dildock, reported on his infil-
tration of a local woman's literary club soon after the TWLC was
founded. Disguised as a woman, he ridiculed everything from
the ages and looks of members to the rights they demanded. The
piece concluded with Dildock run out of the "hen convention." For
all the mockery and contempt, the choice of pseudonym suggests
that the author himself was not too bright (O.P. rhymes with
"dopey") and therefore not reliable. Stowe pasted the Dildock article in her scrapbook next to another satirical piece entitled
"Women's Rights," which included the line, "When each strong
minded matron changes places with her mate," she will "rock
the state." Clearly, mayhem was the inevitable consequence of
equality.

More provocative press coverage of the TWLC arose when Stowe was charged with attempting to procure a miscarriage in 1879. In May of that year, a pregnant nineteen-year-old domestic servant named Sarah Ann Lovell had consulted Stowe, asking for an abortifacient. Stowe gave her a prescription for the appropriate drugs, but later claimed she deliberately made the dosage too weak to bring on a miscarriage. Three months later, still pregnant, the young woman died of unknown causes, and the subsequent inquest uncovered Stowe's involvement. Ultimately, Stowe was acquitted due to lack of evidence. Though her stance on abortion remains ambiguous, the trial and media accounts reveal public and professional hostility toward female physicians. Throughout the trial, the TWLC stood by its president, filling the courtroom with twenty-five to thirty "lady spectators" described by the conservative Toronto newspaper the *Mail* as Stowe's "woman's rights army." Literary subterfuge or not, the TWLC was apparently known for being more than a book club by 1879.

A WOMEN'S RIGHTS ARMY

Stowe did not retreat. From the beginning, she had made it clear that the TWLC was interested in "all questions of a social or moral nature affecting our sex at the present time, as well as everything pertaining to women's welfare or work ... We have no sympathy with the idle butterflies of our sex." Given her own experience of institutional and public hostility, she took for granted that winning the franchise would be an uphill battle. This is why the TWLC devoted five years to mobilizing support before it flaunted its suffrage ambitions in public.

To formally mark its politicization, the TWLC disbanded in 1883 to reconstitute as the Canadian Women's Suffrage Association (CWSA). Though the moniker suggested claims to the national stage, the organization was Toronto-centric. The new association was officially fledged at an invitation-only meeting for men and women who had shown an interest in suffrage. Toronto City Council lent its chambers for this meeting, an early sign of the city government's consistent open-mindedness about suffrage. A few women from Quebec attended too. At the meeting, Mayor Arthur Radcliffe Boswell said, "I do not feel called upon to commit myself in my official capacity, yet I do not know any good reason why ladies should not have a voice in municipal and parliamentary affairs. Their intelligence on many of the problems presented to public men is equal, and in some respects superior, to that of the male sex." When asked the rationale for pursuing female enfranchisement, CWSA members explained that their first goal was to address the lack of democracy that came from taxation without representation. Next, they would focus on "several questions that cannot be satisfactorily settled without the presence of women among the legislators." They listed temperance, educational matters, fairer remuneration for female workers, and "all moral questions." Extending the franchise would not only be good for society, but it would also allow women to have "perfect freedom to express ourselves in all directions." Furthermore, CWSA members "also anticipate an enlarged sphere of usefulness."

At the meeting, a mixed audience of 130 voted unanimously in favour of granting the franchise to women on the same basis as men. Contextualizing the CWSA cause within the theories of iconoclast British thinkers John Stuart Mill and Herbert Spencer, the CWSA constitution laid down its objective: "To obtain for women the Municipal and Parliamentary Franchise, on the same conditions as those on which these are, or may be, granted to men." TWLC founding member Jessie Turnbull McEwen (1845–1920) was elected president. A mother of four, McEwen remained CWSA president for only one year before her family moved west to Manitoba, where she remained active in a variety of women's clubs and causes. Subsequently, Stowe took over leadership of the CWSA. Unlike in the TWLC, men could become CWSA members and could sit on the executive, an acknowledgment that political revolution required a joint effort. William Fenton McMaster (1822–1907), an Irish-born merchant and captain of the Naval Brigade, was the first man elected to one of four vice-president positions. Although suffrage was often a family affair, particularly for men, McMaster's wife, Jane Sumner, and his two daughters are not listed on the existing membership rolls, leaving his particular inspiration unknown. Five other men sat on the twelve-person executive committee. Some suffragists would later lament the loss of female autonomy that occurred in a mixed-sex group, but that was not a current concern. The new organization quickly had cause to celebrate women's admittance into the University of Toronto, reforms to married women's property law, and the municipal enfranchisement of single women.

1884: A TRIO OF VICTORIES

Since their establishment during the 1840s, Ontario's three universities – King's College (Toronto), College of Bytown (Ottawa), and Queen's University (Kingston) – had been closed to women. Those who wished to pursue higher education could undertake teacher training at the Provincial Normal School or, after the 1870s, could attend church-sponsored ladies' colleges in towns across southwestern Ontario; however, these offered diplomas, not degrees, and their curriculum did not stray far from art, music, and the liberal arts. In 1877, the University of Toronto permitted women to take its admission exam, but even if they passed, female students were forbidden to attend lectures, lest their presence be a distraction to male students. They could, however, sit their course exams. In 1881, female students were allowed to compete for the university's scholarships, but since they still could not attend lectures, they had to spend their awards on private tutors. By 1882, fifty-four women had passed the entrance exam, but only

THE SWEET GIRL GRADUATE

In 1882, J.W. Bengough, the editor and chief cartoonist of the Grip, a Toronto-based satirical reform magazine, solicited a play to mock the discriminatory state of affairs in higher education. Authored by Sarah Curzon, a TWLC member and writer who had immigrated to Toronto from England during the 1860s, The Sweet Girl Graduate tells the story of Kate Bloggs, an honour student who is denied admission to the University of Toronto lest "the young men would be demoralized by [her] presence." Undaunted, Kate cuts her hair, dresses as a man, and enters the university as Tom Christopher. She wins academic honours, illustrating Curzon's insistence that gender was a social construct and that sex roles could evolve.

Near the end of the play, Curzon places the case for co-education in an imperial context by reminding the audience that Canada was lagging behind New Zealand. Bloggs states, "Now let the New Zealanders boast, and the Cambridge girls bite their tongues, Canada has caught them up! ... But never mind! I've proved that Canadian girls are equal in mental power with Canadian boys." Singling out New Zealand would prove prophetic. Ten years after Curzon wrote the play, it became the first country to issue voting rights to women. Suffragists consistently held up the Dominion of New Zealand as an example of enlightenment in the face of Canadian backwardness. Curzon would later gain fame for her play Laura Secord, the Heroine of 1812, credited for rescuing Secord's role in history from obscurity.

five had successfully written their first-year examination and three their second-year. Clearly, progress was difficult without access to the faculty and classes.

In 1883, the TWLC organized a petition in which the "unlawful and unjust" exclusion of women from the University of Toronto was called "an insult to the sex and a wrong to the individual and society." It noted that the integration of female students had gone well at Queen's University and other educational institutions, including the Provincial Normal School, "where both sexes mingle on an equal footing." Sixteen hundred men signed the petition, including alumni, professors, businessmen, and clergymen. John Morrison Gibson, the Liberal member of Provincial Parliament (MPP) for Hamilton West, who was also a Toronto alumnus, presented it to university president Daniel Wilson and the Legislative Assembly.

Wilson refused to change university policy unless ordered to do so by the government. Instead, in the interests of decorum, he championed a separate university for female students. The student newspaper, the *Varsity*, fell in line with Wilson, expressing fears that coeducation would feminize men and masculinize women. Despite this resistance, the fall of 1884 produced an Order-in-Council that forced the admission of women to lectures. Wilson insisted that the new situation could give rise to sexual impropriety. To protect the modesty of female students, he appointed a female superintendent to act as a chaperone. Regardless, women flocked to the campus to take up degrees in the arts and sciences.

Among the university's first female graduates was Curzon's daughter, Edith, who took a natural sciences degree in 1889. Other early alumnae included future judge Helen Gregory (BA 1889), Canada's first female lawyer, Clara Brett Martin (BA 1890), and poet Jennie Stork Hill (BA 1890). The victory came too late for Stowe's daughter, Augusta Stowe-Gullen (1857–1943), who had graduated in 1883 with a degree in medicine from the Toronto School of Medicine, then operating at the Faculty of Medicine at Victoria University. She was its sole female student, and accounts differ regarding how well she was accepted by faculty and class-mates. One report states that her brother had to accompany her to class each day to protect her from jeers and to remove morgue specimens that had been left on her desk. When she graduated, the dean's convocation speech suggested that things had gone well for the college's first female student: "Although she had received her instruction in a mixed class of both sexes, there had never existed the slightest difficulty in the class owing to her presence there." After graduation, Augusta married John B. Gullen, a classmate, and the two pursued postgraduate studies in New York. Returning to Toronto, she opened a practice and joined the newly established Ontario Medical College for Women as a demonstrator of anatomy. Her husband went on to found the Western Hospital, where Stowe-Gullen also worked from time to time and where she or-ganized a women's board.

The CWSA's second legislative triumph was municipal voting rights for unmarried female property owners. Even though the numbers involved were few, the group believed that such gains helped enlarge support. In 1881 and 1883, it organized delega-tions to Liberal premier Oliver Mowat in support of the munici-pal franchise for widows and unmarried women. Mowat had a good reputation for electoral reform, which must have given the suffragists hope. Recently, he had significantly reduced the prop-erty qualifications for voting and had replaced the tradition of public verbal declarations of votes with the secret ballot. His democratic sympathies, however, did not extend to women. CWSA persistence nevertheless produced an 1883 revision of the stat-utes of Ontario to enfranchise "every unmarried woman and every widow who possesses the property qualification and other qualification which would, if she were a male ratepayer, entitle her to vote on bylaws requiring the assent of electors."

The CWSA continued its pressure and appreciated the support from Liberal MPPs William Douglas Balfour (Essex South) and John Waters (Middlesex North). Both were defenders of temperance and had legislative histories of championing equal rights for women and minorities. In 1884, Balfour moved a bill to permit propertied widows and spinsters to vote in municipal elections. In the same year, he introduced legislation that allowed Delos Rogest Davis of Essex County to receive accreditation and become Canada's second black lawyer. Later, he supported women in the practice of law and was essential to the passage of the 1892 legislation that admitted Clara Brett Martin to the Law Society of Upper Canada. A loyal suffrage supporter, Waters would introduce nine bills between 1885 and 1893, all arguing for women's voting rights. Initially, he focused on extending the municipal franchise to unmarried female property owners. To justify this step, he compared voting to teaching, suggesting that if the state trusted women with the "great public duty" of teaching, surely it should allow them to vote because "it did not require so much talent to exercise the franchise at municipal elections as it did to teach a school successfully." The opposition preferred to prattle about uncharted consequences and possible unfairness. Liberal MPP Christopher Finlay Fraser (Brockville) argued that disenfranchised men (such as those who did not meet the property requirements) should be the next to receive the vote. Fraser also feared that suffrage rights would produce female candidates. Much to the assembly's surprise, Balfour's 1884 bill narrowly passed. Afterward, Liberal James Marshall Ferris (Northumberland East) radically proposed that the words "unmarried" and "widow" be struck out, giving the municipal vote to all women, but that amendment was thoroughly defeated by ninety-one to three.

Forty years after the seven women voted in the 1844 West Halton riding, propertied single women in Ontario had gained the franchise at the municipal level.

Many anti-feminists insisted that enfranchised women would not bother to vote. Documented turnout of Ontario male voters in the latter half of the nineteenth century ranged from a low of 66 percent to a high of 82 percent. Surviving voter registration lists, news stories, and individual voter testimony suggest that newly enfranchised women cast their ballots in large numbers. Letitia Youmans noted that her recent widowhood was "a dear price to pay for a vote." Grief aside, she rose to the occasion to organize all eligible WCTU members in Picton. They travelled together to the polling station, heavy with smoke and full of men who were shocked by the intruders. Youmans set them straight: "You will remember, gentlemen, that I am a citizen this morning." She further highlighted the historic moment by adding, "While alone marking that paper, a deep sense of personal responsibility rested down upon me. None but the eye of God was cognizant of the act, and I would not have dared to be influenced by mere party principles, or other unworthy motive." She also showed an understandable flash of temper in observing that "if only widows and spinsters are allowed to vote, then surely bachelors and widowers should be the only men eligible to the same privilege."

Inaccurate property assessment lists and intimidation could nevertheless deter some women from voting, as was the case in Toronto's 1886 municipal election. This featured a heated race between incumbent mayor Alexander Manning, who co-owned a brewery, and William Holmes Howland, an evangelical Christian member of the Temperance Electoral Union. Howland deliberately courted new women voters with the slogan "Toronto the Good." Despite bad weather on election day, the *Globe* reported that "women were to be seen hustling to the polls," only to discover that many could not vote due to discrepancies in the voter lists. The newspaper described one woman who "besieged" a city clerk when she was denied her rights. "I have been paying taxes for years, and it's a funny thing if I haven't got a vote," she complained. Because her property assessment failed to identify her as a "Miss" or a "Mrs.," she could not be proven eligible. Angrily, she stated, "I think it is a mean, dirty shame that I haven't a vote after all the bother I have been put to." She added, "I wanted to vote for Mayor Howland because I would just love to see him elected."

In other Toronto wards, women reported being intimidated by Manning's scrutineers and representatives of the liquor trade. In one case, sixteen of thirty women supposedly left without exercising their franchise because they felt uncomfortable swearing an oath, which was required when a would-be voter was suspected of being unqualified. In contrast, a neighbouring polling station reported that ten women had voted without difficulty. In another ward, a hotelkeeper insulted two women at the poll housed in his establishment, perhaps because he feared that a Howland victory would result in prohibition. In spite of irregularities, Howland won a "huge" majority and expressed his "warm thanks" to the ladies, adding that he had "never been so angry in his life as he was today at seeing the way the women voters were treated in some of the polling places." A female voter whom the *Globe* interviewed focused on celebrating her recognition as a citizen: "I am 80 years old; I have been steeped up to my neck in taxes for a long time, but I thank God I have lived to get a vote." In the aftermath, Toronto City Council considered installing separate voting booths for women, allegedly to protect their modesty rather than to stop male misbehaviour. Stowe vigorously protested this unnecessary expense. Men and women shared public space all the time, and segregation allowed voters to be identified by sex, potentially leading to fraud: "Men who have only recently learned to regard women's opinion as worthy of record," she warned, "would have no scruple in tampering with our votes." No such booths were ever created.

Though most qualifying municipal voters appear to have been upper and middle class, less economically privileged property owners appeared too. In Paris, a manufacturing town centred on the production of knit goods, the 1895 voter registry records 1,027 total voters. Of these, 163, or 15 percent, were women, two-thirds of them widows; 127 owned a residence or business, and the remaining 36 were tenants who paid the property equivalency in rent. Census records, city directories, and death records reveal that these voters were overwhelmingly British or Ontario-born, with ages ranging from twenty-one to seventy-five, though most were in their forties. The vast majority had deceased husbands or fathers who had been small-business owners, professionals, or skilled workers. A few were farmers, and the census described a handful as gentlemen. This cohort of women had no listed occupation, and most apparently lived off the income from their properties. Such was the case for Jane Capron and Cornelia Capron Stuart-Jones, the daughters of Hiram Capron, the founder and first reeve of Paris. His daughter Jane, who never married, qualified to vote in 1895 due to her ownership of four properties. Her sister Cornelia, a widow with four young children who had returned to Paris from New York in 1890, owned two properties in Paris. Given their family history and investments, the sisters probably had opinions on local politics and future development, which encouraged their political engagement.

Other Paris voters had humbler origins. Upon his death in 1882, Lucy Chapple's husband was a labourer and handyman. The 1891 census lists Lucy as forty-seven years old and gives her occupation as a nurse. Five of her six children lived with her, including daughters who were employed, one as a mill knitter and one a cuff machine operator. One son worked as an errand boy, and another was an apprentice. Only the youngest son was not in waged

Making winter underwear in Penman's Sewing Department, Paris, c. 1910. Paris was widely hailed as a woman's town because of the close association between textile work and female labour. At Penman's, the largest mill in Paris, the majority of workers were unmarried women, many of whom were teenagers, young adults, and widows of all ages. Among the widows, several were registered to vote in the 1895 election.

employment. In 1895, Lucy Chapple appeared on the voter registry as owning a residence. Elizabeth Pierce was also a nurse, whose husband had been the night watchman at a mill. At least six other registered voters were widows whose children were also mill employees. Another three, two of whom were widows, worked before or after 1895 as wool spinners. Six others laboured for wages around the time of their voter registration: five as dressmakers or tailors and another as a cigar manufacturer. Another four ran boarding houses, sometimes in addition to other labour. Though the 163 registered female voters of Paris differed in economic and marital circumstances, all shared the experience of living independently without men, something to prompt their interest in political decisions and candidates.

These electoral advances coincided with a third major legal victory, the 1884 Married Woman's Property Act. Since the 1850s, letters to editors and government petitions had sought property law reform. One 1857 petition bore the names of 1,300 married women. Between 1859 and 1873, this agitation produced legislative changes that allowed married women to technically retain the property they had brought into the marriage but made their husbands trustees who could sell or use the land without consulting them. These reforms also included limited rights for abandoned or abused women to collect alimony and not be burdened with the debts of their husbands. Conspicuous by its absence was any concept of autonomous property rights for married women. A series of open letters to *Toronto World,* written in 1883–84 by an anonymous woman, maybe Stowe or one of her followers, blamed the short-sightedness of all-male parliaments. Some people, the writer stated, were "shocked at the idea of women having to think about politics and say we pay our male relations a poor compliment when we cannot trust them to vote for us." She added that "if men were so anxious to do perfectly right by women we should have equal pay for equal labour and have no need for the married women's property acts and other protections that come between us and the other sex."

In 1884, keen to appear up-to-date with recent married women's property reform in England, Mowat ushered in revisions that gave wives the right to own and manage property separately from their husbands. This landmark legislation recognized marital partners as separate legal entities and provided more economic security for women. Though progressive in some ways, the act had significant limitations. Since most married women did not work for wages, and single women rarely earned enough to purchase property before marriage, the reform predominantly empowered wealthy women with inheritances. Still, historians cite the large quantity of investments and mortgages held by Hamilton women between 1860 and 1930 as proof that the act bestowed considerable financial agency, even upon middle-class women. Significantly, no reforms allowed wives to claim rights to family property that had been acquired through the labour of both spouses during their marriage.

FEDERAL PARALLELS

While Ontario women were receiving new rights, Parliament held its first official debate on suffrage. Triggered by the female enfranchisement portion of Conservative Prime Minister John A. Macdonald's controversial 1885 electoral reform bill, members of Parliament expressed a range of opinions, mostly in the negative, about the consequences of unmarried women property owners receiving federal voting rights. Many mimicked the anti-feminist rhetoric of Francis Parkman and Goldwin Smith. Either women were simply uninterested in or unsuited for politics or the process would de-sex them. Others, such as Liberal James Edgar (Ontario West), worried about how to balance chivalry and politics in an integrated House of Commons. In contrast, a few, such as Conservative MP and lumber baron Alonzo Wright (Ottawa County), cited the unfairness of denying voting privileges to half the human race. Meanwhile, Liberal John Charlton (North Norfolk), who was known for his religious devotion and social reform interests, stated that female enfranchisement would be inherently good for Canada because "it would create a large vote which would be on the side of moral, social and religious reform." Charlton was not the first or the last male ally to suggest that women were more morally upright than men, an easier pill to swallow than conceding that they were equal.

JOHN A. MACDONALD: A SUFFRAGIST?

In 1885, Prime Minister John A. Macdonald attempted wide-reaching electoral reform that, among other things, proposed the federal enfranchisement of unmarried female property owners. Macdonald's bill produced a contentious seven-day debate, resulting in the women's franchise clause being deemed outrageous by the majority of parliamentarians. Macdonald himself said little but expressed the hope that "Canada would have had the great honour of leading in the cause of securing the complete emancipation of women, of completely establishing her equality as a human being and a member of society with man." Scholars have questioned his sincerity. When he was the MP for Kingston, Macdonald absented himself or abstained from voting on the 1849 Reform Party bill that formally excluded women from the electorate. Drafts of his franchise reforms from the 1860s and 1870s defined a voter as a "male person." Even without the women's suffrage portions, Macdonald's 1885 bill was controversial enough. Given the unpopularity of female suffrage, some historians have concluded that he would not have burdened his bill with it unless he were a true believer. Indeed, only eight Liberals and four Conservatives supported him, which left the vast majority of MPs in opposition. Alternatively, it is possible that Macdonald always intended the women's suffrage portion of his bill to be a sacrificial clause, that once excised, would make rest of the bill look more reasonable. Either way, Macdonald's subsequent silence on suffrage post-1885 suggests it was not a cause close to his heart.

Rather than debate the worthiness of the female sex, the leader of the Opposition and former premier of Ontario, Edward Blake, focused his critique on Macdonald's exclusion of wives. What purpose would be served by enfranchising unmarried women property owners who, he estimated, represented only one-fifth of all women? In doing so, "you are driven to treat marriage as a disability," Blake claimed. Several MPs agreed, while expressing anxiety about the unnaturalness of single women. In an awkward attempt at humour, Liberal James McMullen (Wellington North) fretted about "old maids" who might trade their votes for a marriage proposal, thus increasing the popularity of bachelor candidates. Displaying racial and gender prejudice, Liberal George Landerkin (South Grey) asked how Macdonald could give "the franchise to an unmarried female, who may be Chinese, or a squaw, or any other person naturalized, and deny it to the mothers of this country." This debate linked the privilege of voting not with property but with the respectability conferred by marriage and motherhood, and of course, whiteness. Ultimately, the bill denied the vote to most Indigenous people, as defined by the Indian Act, and to residents of Chinese origin. Furthermore, the exaltation of married women did not result in the Liberals' endorsement of their suffrage. Instead, Blake's rant about their exclusion was intended to show that Macdonald's entire bill was ill conceived. Blake went on to say that there was "no more dangerous element in the voting community of a country than the mass which does not take a keen and active interest in public affairs." Most particularly, however, the Liberals opposed the legislation because it removed the determination of the franchise from the provinces, where their party tended to do better at the polls.

The 1885 Electoral Franchise Act, which Macdonald called the "greatest triumph of his life," passed after the women's suffrage part was dropped. For thirteen years, it standardized voter qualifications across the country and put Ottawa in control of voter lists. After the Liberals came to power in 1898, Prime Minister Wilfrid Laurier returned the franchise determination to the provinces. Their capitals, not Ottawa, then became the target of suffragists.

I am delighted to have met all of you gentlemen here today, and I am quite sure my colleagues share in the delight I feel. I have, and I am sure they have, listened with the greatest possible interest to your address. Your arguments on behalf of your claim have been forcible, eloquent, logical, and clear. If any person can answer the reasons you have advanced in favour of manhood suffrage, I am sure that I cannot.

– EMILY STOWE,
IN THE ROLE OF ATTORNEY GENERAL, ADDRESSING
A DEPUTATION FROM THE MEN'S ENFRANCHISEMENT
ASSOCIATION, *A MOCK PARLIAMENT*, 1896

FOUR

WAKING UP
TO THE POWER

- - - Plan of Members' Seats - - -

			SPEAKER, Hon. A. O. Rutherford			
Noxon, A. / Brant	Abercrombie, W. / Welland				Forster, M. C. / Perth	Allen, B. / Lanark
Savigny, A. G. / Victoria, W.	Burwash, M. / Ottawa	Stowe, Hon. Dr. R. H. / Oxford	Clark, H. Johnson	McDonnell, M. / Toronto, N.	Riches, S. / Lennox	Harrington, I.C. / Stormont
Redmond, M. A. / Peterboro	Stevens, Hon. H. / Kingston	Gullen, Hon. Dr. A. S. / Brant		Hunter, G. / Dundas	Rose, C. M. / Grenville	Brown, A. / Muskoka
Vance, A. / Nipissing	Ford, Hon. E. A. / Monck	Hughes, Hon. A. M. / Middlesex, W.		Parker A. / Halton	Jackson, M. M. / Addington	Henderson, O. / Victoria, E.
Lelean, E. / Waterloo	Teskey, S. Ray. / Northumberland	Sims, Hon. A. / Hamilton		Biggs, S.E. / Norfolk	Smith, M., B.E. / Lincoln	Hilborn, S. / Parry Sound
Summerfeldt, J. / Simcoe	Campbell, F. R. / Huron	Wiggins, Hon. I. E. / Ontario		Spence, S F. / Prince Edward	Walker, H. / Cardwell	Bowbeer, C. / Carleton
Duff, A. J. / Peel	Yeigh, K. / Algoma	Doane, S. A. / N. York		Brown, M. A. / Frontenac	Youmans, I. / Lambton	Wrigley, G. / Dufferin
Cook, C. / Wellington	Forest, L. / Glengarry	Laing, M. R. / N. Middlesex		Sanderson, A. / Bruce, N.	Chamberlain, A. J. / Elgin	Faircloth, I. S. / Bruce S.
Cowan, A. M. / Kent	Ward, F. C. / S. York	Rose, J. M. / Essex		Orr, W. H. / Stormont	Coad, E. / Wentworth	Mason, W. / Leeds

Asst. Clerk, M. J. Lake

J. Semple, Sergt-at-Arms

The inside of a Mock Parliament program,
distributed to theatregoers on 18 February 1896,
features the names of all the performers and acts as a handy
visual aid to imagine an all-female legislature.

ONE FEBRUARY EVENING in Toronto 1896, Dr. Emily Stowe received a delegation of men, who summoned their courage to beseech her "on behalf of our downtrodden sex that men, fully half of the population, so long denied a role in the political decision-making of this country, be granted that first right of a citizen, the ballot." Stowe expressed sympathy: "The most precious of all human rights is the right to think – to form opinions – and the expression of such opinions into words or languages is what characterizes us as humans." Although Stowe praised the men for their good use of the school and municipal ballots, she ultimately concluded that they had little hope of getting full suffrage this year or next. After this gloomy prediction, the men withdrew and a session of parliament began. All the MPs were women. Dr. Augusta Stowe-Gullen, the representative from Brant, and Letitia Youmans, representative from Lambton, were among the fifty MPs who read bills intended to "keep men out of the medical profession! Give men one third of women's pay for equal work! Censor men's dress! Enforce a curfew for unchaperoned men!" Citing Scripture, the minister of education gave a speech proclaiming the superiority of matriarchal governance. The minister for Crown lands warned that allowing men to vote would lead to polygamy, broken homes, and societal distress. Parliament closed with the defeat of the male suffrage bill, a sign that women would retain their position as stewards of Ontario.

This fantasy was an inspired theatrical performance at Toronto's Allen Gardens. As a piece of feminist propaganda, the play showcased the suffragists' flair for spectacle, as well as their claims on parliamentary democracy. Described by the *Toronto Star* as "heaps of fun" and "amusing," as well as the work of "strongminded women," the event used role reversal to showcase the absurdity of denying the vote to women. The play embodied the enhanced public presence of the suffrage cause and its expansion to include the right to stand for public office, no longer matters to be discussed behind closed doors. The idea that women could hold office upset at least one anonymous Torontonian, who urged city council to cancel the Mock Parliament as "a deep-laid scheme for the new women to show that they are capable of filling legislative positions." He complained, "It would simply be dreadful if the Board of Control should ever come under the management of women."

The Toronto play was just one of at least seven versions performed in late-nineteenth- and early-twentieth-century Ontario, including Grey County, Wentworth, Cornwall, and Galt, in collaboration with local chapters of the Woman's Christian Temperance Union (WCTU). At the Allen Gardens production, Stowe cast herself as the provincial premier, and her dialogue echoed fifteen years of Oliver Mowat's polite condescension to suffrage delegations. The performance was Stowe's last major suffrage effort before her death. In fact, the entire production represented the culmination of her decades of activism, including attempts to work with American suffragists, the start of a new suffrage organization, an alliance with the WCTU, and the expansion of suffrage clubs outside of Toronto. Furthermore, the presentation of Stowe and her fellow performers as female politicians paralleled women candidates' actual election to the Toronto Public School Board and the candidacy of socialist Margaret Haile, the first woman to stand for a seat in the Legislative Assembly.

TRANSNATIONAL COLLABORATION AND LOCAL ALLIES

The Mock Parliament hoopla arose after suffrage activism went through a dormant period. The seeming break from 1885 to 1889 owes something to a sense of accomplishment that stemmed from the 1884 legislative victories, combined with the fatigue of almost a decade's worth of activism. Furthermore, the passage of John A. Macdonald's 1885 Electoral Franchise Act made voting rights a federal matter, which directed reform efforts to Ottawa, beyond the Toronto stronghold of the Canadian Women's Suffrage Association (CWSA). Another factor may have been the "demoralizing" move from the all-female Toronto Women's Literary Club (TWLC) to the mixed-gender CWSA. In hindsight, Stowe argued that male members had reinforced "the old idea of female dependence," where "the ladies began to rely on the gentlemen rather than their own efforts." That downturn did not last. Soon, women's transnational collaboration renewed the Ontario movement.

Ontario suffragists had always been inspired by their American and British counterparts. They exchanged correspondence and shared news of accomplishments and setbacks. In return, Canada's suffrage progress, often singularly represented by efforts in Toronto, was noted in each edition of the *History of Woman Suffrage,* a multivolume series tracking suffrage achievements published by Susan B. Anthony and Elizabeth Cady Stanton, whom Stowe had probably met during her medical training in the United States. More significant transnational collaboration waited until 1888, spawned by the first meeting of the International Council of Women (ICW) in Washington, DC. Founded by Anthony, the ICW assembled fifty-three women from nine countries to jointly advocate for women's rights. Stowe represented Canada, along with WCTU leader and suffragist Mary McDonnell and four other Canadians. In Washington, Stowe reconnected with Anthony and met Reverend Dr. Anna Howard Shaw, a Methodist minister and physician who was an active player in the American WCTU and the National American Women's Suffrage Association. At Stowe's invitation, Shaw and Anthony travelled to Toronto twice in 1889 to lecture on the American suffrage struggle. The lack of inter-change between Canadian and British suffragists during this period speaks not so much to disinterest, but rather to the expense and lengthy nature of crossing the Atlantic.

Between Shaw and Anthony's visits, Stowe revived the Toronto movement by shuttering the CWSA and creating a new club called the Dominion Women's Enfranchisement Association (DWEA). She served as its president until her death in 1903. Stowe intended to turn the DWEA into a national network that extended beyond Toronto. Previously, the only other vibrant centre of activism in Ontario had been the St. Catharines and Niagara Falls area. There, under the leadership of two WCTUers – Sarah Curzon's literary friend Emma A. Currie and a Miss M. Phelps – suffrage work had persisted since the early 1880s, around the time when Currie began corresponding with Anthony. In hopes of recruiting new followers, the DWEA paid New York suffragist Mary S. Howell to undertake a lecture tour of Ontario towns to find existing suffrage clubs and start new ones. Within a year of its formation, DWEA branches were formed in the farming communities of Ingersoll, Aurora, Midland, and Woodstock. As the home riding of Premier Mowat, Woodstock was a particularly symbolic area for suffrage activity. Led by John W. Garvin, principal of the Model and Public Schools and a YMCA member, the Woodstock DWEA branch recorded sixty-five members in 1890. Advocating for the female franchise, Garvin stated in the *Woodstock Sentinel-Review* that "woman is man's equal intellectually, morally, spiritually." Activity in small towns such as Woodstock showed that suffrage was more than an urban phenomenon.

One of the DWEA's most notable accomplishments was organizing a two-day Toronto convention in 1890. The event was attended by over two hundred women, whom the *Globe* described as "drawn from the ranks of the well-to-do" in Ontario and the United States. Yellow banners reading "Women Are One-half the People," "Women Man's Equal," and "Canada's Daughters Shall Be Free" framed the speakers' platform, over which hung a portrait of Anthony. Stowe chaired the convention, which featured speeches and papers on all aspects of women's rights, as well as an address by Shaw.

Notably absent from Stowe's convention were women from Quebec or Western and Atlantic Canada. This signalled that Canada would rely on regional movements rather than one national umbrella organization centred in Toronto. Indeed, Manitoba, Nova Scotia, and New Brunswick had already founded their own suffrage clubs by the 1880s. The influence of Ontario can nevertheless be measured in other ways. A number of women who would lead the suffrage cause on the Prairies and in British Columbia were born and educated in Ontario, including Emily Spencer (born in Toronto in 1860), Ella Cora Hind (born in Toronto in 1861), Helen Emma Gregory MacGill (born in Hamilton in 1864), Emily Murphy (born in Cookstown in 1868), Louise McKinney (born in Frankville in 1868), Nellie McClung (born in Chatsworth in 1873), Laura Marshall Jamieson (born in Park Head in 1882), and Francis Marion Beynon (born in Streetsville in 1884). Whereas women's organizations in Quebec would not focus on suffrage for another decade, their anglophone and francophone members had a long tradition of visiting Toronto to meet suffragists and exchange ideas and frustration.

Honoured at the 1890 DWEA convention was John Waters, the Liberal MPP who had helped usher in municipal voting rights. Described by the *Globe* as "the best type of public man," the Scottish-born Waters had supported women's suffrage and temperance during the fifteen years that he was in office. Citing the British and American suffrage movements as proof of international sympathy, he referred to Ontario women's work as church volunteers and paid teachers as further evidence of female merits. Waters tried to convince his constituents and fellow parliamentarians that suffrage was part of a natural evolution in political life. In contrast, his opponents asserted that it threatened domestic life. "Someone must mind the baby," insisted Henry Edward Clarke, Conservative MPP for Toronto. Nor could fellow Liberals be counted on for support. The MPP for Brant South, Arthur Sturgis Hardy, who would succeed Mowat as premier, dismissed suffrage victories in Utah and Wyoming because they occurred in "cowboy territory, where women were few in number, and where the woman with a shotgun was the hero of the hour." Rather, the lack of female enfranchisement in the great European civilizations was a better standard for a proper British dominion.

A particularly outspoken Liberal opponent was MPP John Dryden (Ontario South), a farmer and businessman who served as minister of agriculture in 1893. Quoting Scripture as evidence that God had ordained different paths for women and men, Dryden joined Francis Parkman and Goldwin Smith in insisting that most women did not want "to be dragged into party politics against their will and consent." They preferred to "shine in their own sphere, and in their own homes." Dryden also anticipated that discord would arise if "men and women voted differently, the mother against the son, the husband against the wife, and so on." Alternatively, if women voted as their husbands did, nothing would be gained by their enfranchisement. The strength of such sentiments was demonstrated by the sneers and criticism from within and outside Waters's own party, which greeted his repeated efforts.

Although parliamentary allies were essential, so too was an active alliance between the DWEA and the WCTU. There had always been an overlap in membership, but the provincial WCTU did not at first openly champion suffrage, though individual branches and members had voiced support since the late 1870s. For example, a Toronto WCTU periodical, *Canada Citizen and Temperance Herald,* devoted a weekly column to TWLC efforts, written by Sarah Curzon. Still, many WCTU members believed that a woman's influence was better exercised at home, not the polling station. Others worried about linking temperance with another controversial cause. Soon, however, the lack of legislative progress on temperance forced the WCTU to reconsider its stance.

By the 1880s, more WCTUers had moved publicly into the suffrage camp. The partnership gave the DWEA access to a larger membership base, with substantial connections in rural parts of the province. In return, the WCTU benefitted from suffragist expertise in political lobbying. "If women were allowed to vote," one pro-temperance bulletin announced, "progress would be made in dealing legislatively with the evils arising from the traffic in intoxicating drinks." To put it more bluntly, the dominion WCTU declared, "We can fight Christ's battles armed with ballots." In 1887, the Ontario provincial WCTU opened a Department on Legislation, Franchise and Petitions, and in the following year, they passed a resolution in favour of women's suffrage. Cementing the new open alliance, Youmans invited Stowe to give a suffrage address at the 1889 WCTU convention. To mark this new partnership, subsequent suffrage delegations to the Legislative Assembly would always include prominent WCTU members in the platform. Some local WCTU branches, including those of Dunnville and Ottawa, nevertheless resisted the call to support enfranchisement until the early twentieth century.

Following its suffrage awakening, the white-dominated WCTU attempted to renew relations with black women, hoping that they would encourage support from their enfranchised male kin. In extending its appeal, the WCTU tried to make amends for past prejudice. It founded a section titled "Work Among Colored People" (renamed the African department in 1898), whose new

THE ONLY REASON.

P. C. HARDY—"Tut, tut, lady; I can't let you open that door New Year's Day, because I'd then have to shut this door, and me friends in the trade wouldn't like it."

This *Toronto Evening Telegram* cartoon of 13 January 1898 demonstrates that temperance was the presumed outcome of women's suffrage. The fear that one would automatically follow the other kept Premier Hardy, here dressed as a police constable, from extending the municipal franchise beyond single women.

superintendent confessed, "the whites had no compassion on the Black man, but now we come to them for help, for assistance. We need them." The superintendent added, "Our common enemy," meaning alcohol, "has united us ... as I looked the race line seemed to vanish entirely ... It is one of the greatest triumphs of Christianity that the barriers between nations and races are being lowered every year." Under this new attitude, black communities emerged as partners, not problems. Despite this effort, the absence of black women as visible WCTU spokespeople for temperance or suffrage speaks to the deep gulf that remained.

The temperance and suffrage alliance may have curtailed feminist ambitions. Temperance supporters seemed less likely to invest in other women's rights issues, such as access to education or equal pay. Given that the main message of the WCTU focused on alcohol's danger to the home and family, it naturally emphasized women's domestic lives and their identities as wives and daughters. Furthermore, the WCTU's preoccupation with women as the victims of male alcohol abuse often sprang from a middle-class myopia in which condemning working-class masculinity had more to do with assumptions about class and ethnicity than with a critique of patriarchy. Despite such limitations, the WCTU put violence against women and children high on the suffrage agenda. After most women were enfranchised in 1917, that issue would not regain its place of prominence until the end of the twentieth century.

Since the beginning of the movement, suffragists offered both maternal and egalitarian rationales for women's involvement in politics. The first claimed that women deserved voting rights because their superior morals and maternal nature would enhance political life. The egalitarian viewpoint emphasized human rights. The two perspectives were not oppositional. Depending on the preference of advocates or audiences, they could be linked or distinguished. When one reads suffragist manifestos, it is easy to conclude that the choice of maternal or equal rights arguments was as much about expediency as principle.

Around the time of the Ontario WCTU endorsement, Stowe began to downplay the language of egalitarian feminism in public appeals, while highlighting the less threatening maternal feminist message. Her 1889 essay "Housewifery" typified this new orientation: "I believe homemaking, of all the occupations that fall to woman's lot is the one most important and far reaching in its effects on humanity." Though Stowe approved of giving women the freedom to choose their own path, her praise for wives and mothers ultimately concluded that "no trade, profession or calling demands more versatility than [homemaking]." On the other hand, she also extended the metaphor to insist that "governing a state is merely keeping house of a large scale": women's maternal nature would make them effective legislators. So as not to reinforce women's natural affinity for housewifery, nor to dismiss it as inherently simple, Stowe insisted that women should receive professional training in home economics during public school. Stowe's ode to housewifery reflected the practical centrality of women's domestic role in the society and the economy of Canada. Furthermore, she never suggested that women should surrender their traditional roles and did not do so herself in her own pursuit of higher education, a career, and suffrage. The housewifery essay may have been aimed at maintaining new WCTU allies. It is also possible that after twenty years of framing suffrage as an equal rights cause, Stowe was trying to broaden its appeal. In any case, the language of equal rights never disappeared from DWEA arguments.

The suffragist experimentation with tactics is visible in presentations made by the joint DWEA-WCTU delegations to Premier Mowat between 1889 and 1894. In the first delegation, suffragists combined maternal and egalitarian rationales with Christian ideals and democratic principles. Stowe began by characterizing women as "educated citizens" who were "moral and loving" and who "desire to be placed in a position to impress directly our thought upon our nation and times." Her statement reassured legislators that training and natural abilities would make women responsible and trustworthy voters. In an attempt to shame governments, she reminded them that denying women the vote placed them in the same category as "imbeciles and the insane." To make the bitter suffrage pill easier to swallow, she claimed that "we are not office seekers," contradicting her own earlier TWLC commitment to women in legislative roles and her 1893 support for campaigns by her daughter and others to be school trustees. Such caution seemed designed to reassure timorous male legislators.

Stowe's WCTU colleague McDonnell spoke next, appealing to morality and justice: enfranchisement was surely ordained by God, who saw men and women as different but equal. Framing

SUFFRAGE: A FAMILY AFFAIR

Though often politically conservative, progressive school reformer and Toronto public school inspector James Hughes (1846–1935) was a vocal suffrage champion. Hughes served on the first mixed-sex CWSA executive. When he was president of the Toronto Woman's Equal Franchise Association, he authored Equal Suffrage, *a fifty-eight-page pamphlet that combined Christian dogma and Liberal principles to explain why it was rational for women to vote:*

Equal suffrage is a fixed element in human development. Women have shown themselves capable of taking an intelligent part in public affairs; they have to submit to laws on the same condition of men; they pay taxes; they are producers of wealth; they are deeply interested in moral and philanthropic work; they naturally represent the home, and they are responsible human beings.

human rights as Christian justice, McDonnell made a similar argument in 1893: "We often hear it is asserted that the voice of the people is the voice of God. If that be true the voice of God has never yet been heard in human governments for half the race is silent." She added, "The great questions of the future will be economic and social ones. Moral questions are also involved, and deeply involved, in politics."

Similar themes were evoked by the 1894 DWEA-WCTU delegation, but this time none of the speakers was female, perhaps in hopes that the male legislators would listen more carefully to members of their own sex. Thus, two men, temperance leader

Hughes' interest in women's rights pre-dates his 1885 marriage to an American-born feminist and kindergarten teacher, Adaline Marean (1848–1929). The couple met in 1878 when Hughes recruited Marean, a graduate of the New York Normal School, to open Toronto's first kindergarten, an accomplishment that led to her becoming locally and internationally renowned in early childhood education circles. Marean, too, was an active suffragist; for example, she took a role in the 1896 Mock Parliament. Yet, it was her husband's suffrage efforts that received greater publicity and notoriety. As a well-respected public figure, Hughes was invaluable in lending prestige to the movement and was often called upon to lead suffrage delegations. At times, his persona as a male suffragist made him the subject of public ridicule (see the illustration on p. 131).

James and Adaline had one daughter, Laura (1886–1966), who followed in her parents' reform-minded shoes, engaging in suffrage, labour, and peace activism.

F.S. Spence and school inspector James L. Hughes, led the delegation of 150 women. Whereas Spence and Hughes told Mowat that full suffrage was desired, they proposed taking small steps in the form of the municipal enfranchisement for married women. Hughes also polished the apple, noting that "the government granting such legislation deserved to stay in power for twenty years." Apparently, Augusta Stowe-Gullen had prepared a speech, but whether due to time constraints or deliberate exclusion, she did not deliver it and could only leave a copy for the government.

Whatever the tactic, the slippery Mowat always exuded paternalistic sympathy. He consistently offered a variation of polite disinterest to the annual delegations: "I do not say you will get what you want this year, or next year, but this I do say, that I hope I shall remain long enough in power to be the humble instrument of carrying your wishes into effect." As the *Toronto Star* reported, "he had no doubt that many who were present in this deputation would live to see woman suffrage, but whether or not it would be in his own time he could not say."

During his twenty years in office, Mowat refused to budge on suffrage. Besides having few supporters of the cause in his own party, he felt personally confident most women were disinterested in voting rights. To test this theory, during the 1894 municipal elections, widows and spinsters were given a blue ballot to distinguish their votes from men, who used a yellow ballot. This was done to measure female voter turnout and allegiance in an election that included a province-wide plebiscite asking: "Are you in favour of the immediate prohibition by law of the importation, manufacture and sale of intoxicating liquors as a beverage?" Given women's interest in temperance, observers predicted a high turnout of women voters. Across the province, 14,628 women and 288,581 men participated in the plebiscite; an overwhelming majority (63.5%) voted in favour of prohibition. Proportionately, the disparity between men and women voters made sense given that only a minority of adult women qualified to vote; however, female voter turnout in rural and urban regions was significantly lower than male voter turnout. To naysayers, this was proof that women had no interest in voting. Meanwhile defenders of suffrage claimed the low turnout had many factors, the main one being that the majority of women interested in temperance – married women – were excluded from the process. "How many men would be out if the manhood franchise was restricted to widowers and bachelors and men with property who have been taught to believe that such a proceeding was unmanly," asked suffragist Dr. Margaret Gordon.

SAMPLE OF VOTER TURNOUT ACROSS ONTARIO,
1894 PROHIBITION PLEBISCITE

Electoral district	Male voter turnout	Female voter turnout
Algoma East	44%	29%
Brant South	61%	45%
Hamilton	61%	39%
Halton	54%	29%
Muskoka	45%	26%
Ottawa	48%	31%
Toronto	47%	25%
Stormont	57%	33%
Welland	62%	34%
York East	46%	20%

AWAKENING SLEEPING SISTERS

Even as the provincial campaign seemed stuck in aspic, advocates turned to Toronto school boards. Ontario women had been electing school trustees since 1850. It was, however, unclear whether they were entitled to run for the position. The wording of the law was ambiguous. There was no explicit exclusion. Anyone who paid

property taxes could stand for office, with the only added requirement being that they were "fit and proper." Presumably, who was
"fit and proper" would be left up to voters to determine. There is
no evidence that women stood for or were elected to public or
separate school boards between 1850 and 1892.

Debates on women's potential as candidates for school trustee
surfaced in the Toronto press during the late 1870s, just as the
suffrage movement was born. Advocates argued that if women
could be teachers and could vote for trustees, was it any less
womanly for them to be on a school board? An anonymous letter
to the *Globe* in 1877 noted that England had recently changed its
laws to allow women to run as school trustees. It mentioned the
success of a female candidate in London. The author called upon
the Ontario legislature to enact a similar law, because "with all
our boasted liberality we have not, in this respect at least advanced as rapidly as Conservative England has done." An 1885
letter to the editor repeated the point and drew attention to the
vagueness of the law: "If women are forbidden by law to be trustees let the law be altered. If as the law is at present they can stand
as candidates and be chosen, provided they get enough votes, by
all means let some brave one put the matter to the test." By the
1880s, revisions to Statutes of the Province of Ontario provided
some clarity when the phrase "fit and proper" was replaced with
the less value-laden term "persons," defined as "resident rate-
payers within the school section, and of the full age of twenty-one
years." The new language did not result in immediate female
candidates, suggesting that nebulous vocabulary had not been the
only roadblock.

According to Phelps and Curzon's update on Canada's progress for the 1887 edition of the *History of Woman Suffrage,* Ontario
women were always eligible for school offices but had "been slow
to avail themselves of this privilege, owing to their ignorance of
the laws and their lack of interest in regard to all public measures.

When they awake to their political rights they will feel a deeper responsibility in the discharge of their public duties." Even the politically inclined were cautious. In 1883, the CWSA had proposed presenting a female candidate, noting that some two thousand women were eligible to vote in Toronto and that they could determine the outcome. Nothing happened, however.

Progress first appeared in appointments to the high school board. In January 1888, Mary McDonnell, president of the Toronto WCTU, petitioned city council to appoint two female trustees. This founding member of the TWLC and the DWEA probably saw an opportunity to ensure that the board (and by proxy high school students) was influenced by social-reform-minded women and that women could demonstrate their public capabilities. With the exception of one alderman, Toronto City Council agreed and appointed two women who were immersed in mission work and local voluntary associations. One was Catherine Seaton Skirving Ewart, a mother of three. She was also the widow of Thomas Ewart, who had been a legal partner and brother-in-law of Mowat. The epitome of maternal morality, Ewart was president of the Women's Foreign Missionary Society of the Presbyterian Church in Canada, which supported female missionaries in India and missionaries of both sexes in northwest Canada. Citing pre-existing volunteer commitments, Ewart declined the appointment. She was replaced by Mary Carty, an unmarried woman who regularly appeared on the society pages. Like Ewart, she was involved in reform and educational clubs, including the Ramambai Mission to India, the National Council of Women of Canada, the Women's Art Association, and the city's Canadian Women's Historical Society. Two other women who were active in foreign mission work later joined Carty on the board. Such women often saw overseas and local outreach as related expressions of Christian duty, as well as opportunities for leadership. In response to these appointments, the *Toronto Grip,* already an advocate for the female franchise, suggested that the board would benefit from "women's gentle influence." Borrowing from the broader suffrage argument that women's presence made politics more dignified, it speculated that female trustees would inject a measure of "common justice and wise expediency" into board meetings, which sometimes resembled "beer garden scenes."

In 1892, the public school trustees in Toronto oversaw thirty thousand students. They were expected to meet bi-monthly to determine finance, staffing, curriculum, and management. Key issues included expanding the budget required for free texts – a matter put to a referendum – and board-funded teachers' pensions. Unlike their appointed high school counterparts, public school trustees were elected during municipal elections. The top four vote-getters in each ward drew lots to determine whether they would serve a one- or two-year term. In preparation for the election, the DWEA fielded a female candidate in five of the six wards. The DWEA candidates were Mrs. Vance (Ward 1), Mrs. J.A. Harrison (Ward 2), Mrs. Humphrey (Ward 3), Augusta Stowe-Gullen (Ward 4), and Mary McDonnell (Ward 6). The latter two received the bulk of the pre-election-day publicity, probably because they were already well known and had been nominated by male members of Toronto's political, business, and social reform elite.

During the brief campaign, the *Globe* stated that McDonnell had made "a favorable impression by the clear and forcible way she treated" her support for free school texts and her opposition to board-paid teacher pensions. At her nomination meeting, Stowe-Gullen spoke of the need for female trustees and expressed her opposition to school military drills because they fostered militarism. McDonnell received the most votes of the eleven candidates in her ward, and Stowe-Gullen squeezed in as the fourth in a field of six. The *Globe* initially reported that Harrison came in fourth, but her absence from school board records suggests that she never took up her position, whether due to ballot recounts or her own resignation. She ran unsuccessfully in 1893. Having drawn a one-term marker, McDonnell ran again in 1893 and secured a two-year term. Stowe-Gullen was re-elected in 1894 and would serve four years on the board.

Female trustees did not generate much opposition – quite the contrary. An 1892 letter writer who called herself "A Woman Voter" saw the awakening of "my sleeping sisters to the power that lies in the ballot." The election roused "an army of women to see that they have possibilities, responsibilities, and duties outside the four walls that environ them." Speaking directly of female trustees, she wrote, "anyone who thinks at all must recognize the school as woman's legitimate place. Men by their own confession often aspire to the trusteeship because of some other axe to grind or self good to gain. The women teachers and our children need the sister and mother influence on the board."

Once installed in office, McDonnell and Stowe-Gullen put their feminist principles into action. They endorsed equal pay and defeated a motion barring women from principal positions in schoolhouses with eight classrooms or more. When one male trustee put forth a motion banning female teachers from wearing bloomers because he equated the style of dress with prostitution, Stowe-Gullen launched into a defence of the bloomer costume, calling it a modest style of dress akin to long trousers with a skirt to the knee that she herself had worn.

Throughout 1893 and 1894, the board wrestled with whether to employ married female teachers. Some male trustees argued that the practice threatened single women, who needed the income. Another male trustee asserted that married women should be re-engaged only if their husbands were ill, unemployed, or underemployed, as had been the case for Stowe-Gullen's own mother. Even this recommended limitation was problematic for some male trustees, who worried that the offspring of female teachers would be neglected if their mothers returned to work. Others disliked the idea of a wage-earning married woman simply because "it lowered the queenly name of woman to have her, after her marriage, go into the world to make her living." In contrast, a few board members believed that their job was to "engage the best talent" and that the previous teaching experience of married women, in addition to the possibly of their own child-rearing expertise, made them superior to other candidates. McDonnell reminded the board that she represented married women and that she had no problem with women of any marital status teaching. Furthermore, she pointed out that "no complaints were recorded against the married women who were teachers in Toronto, and the small number of married women who were teachers showed that no woman left her home except under peculiar circumstances." When the vote was finally called, the resolution to bar married women teachers was defeated nineteen to six.

Other cases were less successful. For example, in 1893, Stowe-Gullen discovered that the board had no legal authority to appoint public school supervisors. As a matter of fiscal responsibility, she suggested that the position of supervisor be eliminated, thus saving $6,000 annually. According to the sympathetic *Toronto Grip,* the board ignored her recommendations, and the illegal appointments were subsequently maintained, although unreported by the mainstream press. In the end, Stowe-Gullen declined to seek re-election, explaining that what she could accomplish, along with "five or six well-disposed men," was not able to compete with the lack of progressive thought in regard to the board as a whole.

The battle for inclusion on school boards was significant. Although giving female property owners the school vote in 1850 had largely been designed to favour Protestants, it proved useful over the years in demonstrating that Ontario women made trustworthy voters. McDonnell and Stowe-Gullen represented a new, if limited, confidence that women could play a more expansive role in public affairs.

FRONTIER SUFFRAGE VICTORIES

Developments elsewhere in the British Empire and the United States suggested that further change was possible. In 1893, New Zealand passed a landmark act that gave women the parliamentary vote, regardless of their marital status and ethnicity. This victory, the product of a coalition between suffragists and WCTU members, had been prompted in part by a petition that contained more than sixty-one thousand signatures. Ten weeks after the legislative change, both white and Māori women headed to the polls, though none could stand as candidates until 1919. Nine years later, Australia became the second nation-state to enfranchise women.

Given the similar origins and governance structures of British settler colonies, why did Ontario suffragists face much more resistance? Scholars generally argue that the vote was pioneered in regions of lesser economic importance. On the fringes of the British Empire, New Zealand and Australia were freer than Canada to experiment with democracy. In comparison, Canada's democratic evolution was constrained by its greater proximity, cultural intimacy, and trade relationships with Britain. This explanation also accounts for the regional differences in the enfranchisement of Canadian women. Although the suffrage battle started in Ontario, the fundamentally conservative values instilled by the Loyalists were largely unchanged by the later entry of Reform dissidents, at least in terms of gender and race. In the nineteenth century, Ontario remained socially conservative, even though it elected so-called Liberal governments. Atlantic Canada and Quebec provided other examples of deep-rooted conservatism. In contrast, the fight in Western Canada, though difficult, was more quickly resolved, a reflection of the more diverse European immigration to the region, fears about significant Indigenous and Asian populations, and less entrenched governance structures.

This theory resonates with developments in the western United States. In 1893 and 1896, Colorado and Idaho joined Wyoming and Utah in enfranchising white American women. The more egalitarian frontier spirit and fewer constitutional obstacles have been cited as a reason for the speedier resolution of suffrage in the West. Boosters even commented that enfranchisement would attract female settlers to balance the population and tame the region's rough bachelor culture. In Utah, scholars speculate that the anti-polygamy lobby wanted women voters to oppose Mormon polygamy. Unaware that their own battle was far from over, Ontario suffragists took hope from news of such victories elsewhere.

Distinctions of geography made no difference to Mrs. J.H. Brown, an Ottawa suffragist who organized a letter-writing campaign to all the wives of Ontario legislators. Her campaign highlighted the absurdity that Canada had fallen below the standards of other British dominions. Enlisting "sympathy and active cooperation" on the matter on suffrage, Brown called upon this cohort of uniquely positioned women, whom she described as "loyal daughters of the largest, and we had ever felt, the most progressive, of British colonies," to express their distaste that "our sisters in New Zealand and Australia welcome to the full rights of citizenship, while we remain outcasts, classed with 'undesirables' and 'deficients.'" Brown went on to equate the lack of suffrage with the lack of respect shown to the women, particularly regarding their contributions to the development of Canada. "Have our sisters, over the seas, excelled us?" she asked. "Have we not willingly risked our lives to give our country its sons and daughters? Have we not cared for and instructed these future citizens, safeguarding them in every way possible in our disabled position?" Brown's potent combination of imperial, colonial, and maternal visions of citizenship appealed to the first ladies of Ontario. According to her, except for six recipients, all promised to influence their husbands' support of suffrage in the legislature.

WOMEN'S PLACE IN SOCIALISM

The dawn of the twentieth century injected socialists into the Ontario suffrage campaign. In what had been predominantly a middle-class and elite women's movement, socialists put the spotlight on class as well as gender inequity. In 1899, the Canadian Socialist League was established in Toronto, expanding so quickly that it founded sixty locals across the country within three years. In 1902, it added a provincial headquarters, the Ontario Socialist League (OSL). Two years later, another national organization, the Socialist Party of Canada (SPC) had a presence in Ontario. This momentum reflected working-class demands for a fair redistribution of wealth and power. Amid socialist battle cries for equality, women found a mixed reception. Though their support and labour for the movement were welcomed, few socialist policies prioritized the conditions and wages of working women. In fact, the principle of female economic independence contradicted a key socialist demand that employers pay male breadwinners a family wage, thus eliminating the need for women and children to work. Turn-of-the-century radical rhetoric included little support for independent female wage earners. In fact, the socialist preoccupation with wives and mothers, safely installed in the home, did not stray far from the traditional ideology entrenched in the mainstream middle-class concept of separate spheres. A few socialist women active in Ontario – Edith Wrigley, Mary Darwin, and Margaret Haile – nevertheless determinedly argued in favour of female wage earners and supported universal suffrage.

As the wife of socialist George Wrigley, Toronto's Edith Wrigley recruited women into radical politics, while simultaneously trying to provide a more welcoming forum for female members. Although most socialist women were wary of bourgeois women's organizations, Wrigley backed the ideology and gumption of the WCTU, approving its frequent condemnation of the industrial system, even if it identified different roots for its evils. Wrigley's linking of socialist and evangelical Christian demands for social justice had precedents. The socialist sympathies of American WCTU icon Frances Willard produced a temperance department that was dedicated to working people and an 1886 alliance with the Knights of Labor union. As the Ontario WCTU superintendent for temperance in Sunday Schools, Wrigley encouraged members to see socialism not as a radical departure from their values, but as a kindred spirit in solving social problems. In her column for *Citizen and Country,* her husband's socialist paper, Wrigley wrote about social reform and domestic issues, often focusing on women's primary purpose as wives and mothers. Despite her maternal feminism, she offered space to critique the indifference of socialist men. She believed that until women had the vote, male socialists would ignore their voices. Later, as one of three female delegates to the Ontario Socialist Convention, Wrigley favoured a motion in support of female lecturers and literature addressing women's issues. She also advocated the elimination of all property and gendered barriers to voting. Although the motion passed, the party refused a specific endorsement of female suffrage as part of its broader universal suffrage aims.

Many male socialists remained ambivalent regarding female enfranchisement. In part, this arose from their hostility to the suffrage organizations of middle-class women, which, aside from dabbling in the rights of working women, generally ignored labour movements, particularly in Ontario. More influential was the assumption that gender-based rights distracted from the party's class interests and the destruction of capitalism. As an editorial in the *Western Clarion* insisted, suffrage loyalties could subordinate "the struggle between the classes" to "the struggle between the sexes." Others theorized that capitalism encouraged conservatism in women, who could not be trusted to vote social-ist. One exception to such conclusions was the OSL. Much as the WCTU came to terms with suffrage, the OSL decided that female voters would improve its electoral chances. In 1902, it put uni-versal suffrage on its platform and supported female candidates in Toronto North, first Mary "May" Darwin (1859–1924) and then Margaret Haile, for the provincial legislature.

Most socialist women worked behind the scenes, but Darwin and Haile were exceptional. Darwin came from an English family with five brothers who were labour activists, including Robert Glockling, a bookbinder and prominent Toronto unionist. At the time of the 1902 election, Darwin, a married mother of five, had become Toronto socialism's de facto spokeswoman on the ef-fects of capitalism on women and children, and the need for equal pay. In 1902, she was nominated as one of seven Socialist Party candidates running in the provincial election. Darwin's OSL nom-inators hoped that a female candidate would raise awareness of their universal suffrage platform. Almost immediately, however, Darwin stepped aside to let Haile, the more experienced socialist organizer, take her place. Darwin would go on to make an un-successful run for school board the following year. Later, she led union label committees.

Before her candidacy in Toronto North, the Canadian-born Haile had been active in the American socialist movement. Listed in 1900 as one of the "One Hundred Well-known Social Dem-ocrats" in the United States, she had served as secretary for the Massachusetts Social Democratic Party and was one of a handful of female delegates who founded the American Socialist Party in 1901. She was also a speaker for the Boston Labour Church, which preached Christian socialism. Like Wrigley, Haile admired the WCTU, which she saw as a cross-class sisterhood opposing the destructive impact of alcohol. She shared these views in the British periodical *Justice,* the first English-language socialist paper to print a woman's column. Haile insisted that women needed a space in which to discuss "things and explain them in our own way, and see how they affect us and what we are going to do about it." She drew parallels between the socialist awakenings of male wage earners and the consciousness raising of feminists: "The new woman believes in being herself right down to the end of life, living out her own personal life."

Haile's personal life provides a rare glimpse of politicized women who also had to combine parenting with employment. Working at various times as a teacher, stenographer, and journalist, she experienced economic hardship. In 1900, an acquaintance commented on the shabbiness of her clothes and connected it with poverty:

> I understand that she has *lost* the good place she has had, or that she has given it up, in order to be able to give more time to the movement, and that she is working as a typewriter in a lawyer's office. The pay there cannot be very much, I suppose, and she has to support herself and child.

The press identified Haile as both a "Miss" and a "Mrs.," so her marital status is unknown, though she seems to have supported herself and at least one child. As the similar histories of Mary Ann Shadd Cary and Emily Stowe demonstrate, low and discriminatory pay made self-support difficult.

When Haile returned to Toronto in 1901, her radical politics undoubtedly hindered her acceptance by leading female activists, at least until her MPP candidacy singled her out. Desiring to attract more women to the Socialist Party, she hosted a lecture on socialism at the Toronto WCTU headquarters. Despite Wrigley's linkage of the socialist and temperance communities, the *Toronto*

Margaret Haile, the first woman to run in an Ontario
provincial election, is featured in this 1902 leaflet
advertising Toronto's Socialist candidates and their
worker-centric platform.

Star described WCTU women as apprehensive about socialists oc-
cupying their hall. Whatever the hesitation, Haile became Canada's, and likely the British Empire's, first female candidate for any
legislative office. Almost overnight, she gained support from long-
time suffragists. Stowe-Gullen publicly endorsed her at a socialist
candidates' meeting two weeks before the election. And she was
joined by physician Margaret Gordon, artist Jean Grant, and Clara

Brett Martin, Canada's first female lawyer, who had recently been elected to the Toronto School Board – the first female trustee since Stowe-Gullen and McDonnell. Haile's candidacy tested the legitimacy of especially progressive female political contenders.

Fears were well-founded. As the sympathetic *Globe* reported, "Doubt has been expressed as to a woman's right to offer herself as a candidate." Asked to comment, the deputy attorney general of Ontario could not immediately "express definite opinion" on Haile's legitimacy, though he did not prevent her from running. As a socialist and a woman, her odds of winning were low; it is possible that the state did not take her candidacy seriously enough to investigate the legality of a woman being elected.

Outside of socialist and suffragist circles, Haile found little support. The Conservative-leaning *Toronto Mail and Empire* reported that her opponents left an all-candidates meeting before Haile's address. Disgusted by the lack of respect, George Wrigley berated the crowd as it left and subsequently collected an impromptu audience so that Haile could at least outline the socialist platform. During the campaign, Haile was especially daring in raising the issue of prostitution, which she described not as a moral flaw, but a consequence stemming from the lack of well-paid employment for women, a conclusion that resonated with social reform, suffragist, and socialist supporters alike. Ultimately, however, Haile received only eighty-one votes, the poorest showing among the seven Socialist Party candidates. She did, however, triumph over one socialist-labour candidate in her riding, who placed below her with only twenty-three votes.

Not much is known about Haile after the election. A year later, she was publishing in a Canadian socialist magazine and contributed to a special edition of a Wisconsin paper titled the *Vanguard,* written by socialist women. She then disappears from the historic record. Nevertheless, the 1902 Ontario election was interpreted as a victory for socialists internationally because it placed Canada

as "another red spot on the socialist map." Although no other female political candidate of any stripe would appear until after
women were enfranchised in 1917, Haile's candidacy prompted
Toronto suffragists to work more closely with labour unions.
This prospect would have varying degrees of success.

In 1903, Dr. Emily Stowe died of kidney failure. Accolades
flowed in. Writing to Augusta Stowe-Gullen, the American leader
Susan B. Anthony hailed "your mother" as "a pioneer in every
sense of the word." Over a lifetime, the remarkable physician and
suffragist had witnessed a transformation in women's opportunities and had done much to clear educational, professional, legal,
and economic roadblocks for future generations. She had aided
the creation of a suffrage movement that was skilled in political
rhetoric and receptive to alliances and evolution, a legacy that
helped her successors weather challenges as they navigated inter-
nal discord, continued opposition from government, and the first
anti-suffragist organization.

Our whole social structure has been founded on a basis of inequality and injustice and while this continues we cannot possibly attain a satisfactory grade of social development. Can anyone doubt for a moment the vital and beneficent part played by our women who are devoting their time, ability and energy to better social conditions ... More women are giving of their time to help run this city [Toronto] then there are men elected to official positions to run it. Then why should women's work be handicapped by being unofficial?

– FLORA MACDONALD DENISON,
"THE MENTAL ATMOSPHERE," C. 1911

FIVE

RESISTING
A REVOLUTION

Portrait of dressmaker and Canadian Suffrage Association president
Flora MacDonald Denison, c. 1911–14. Her embrace of militant
British suffragettes disturbed conservative suffragists. Denison also
encouraged collaboration with American suffragists, noting, "It is
impossible to separate the work of American and Canadian women
in their fight for the ballot. We are just as interested in their
progress as we are in our own for in the great Conventions, we have
learned that this is an international movement and a gain in one
country means a gain in every country."

FOLLOWING THE DEATH of Dr. Emily Stowe, the trajectory of the Ontario suffrage movement must have provoked a sense of déjà vu. Once more, the movement was under the leadership of a female physician named Stowe, this time Dr. Augusta Stowe-Gullen. Like her mother three times before, Stowe-Gullen started anew by closing one club, the Dominion Women's Enfranchisement Association (DWEA), and founding the Canadian Suffrage Association (CSA) in 1906. As in the past, CSA membership was drawn from the ranks of educated, white professional women and middle-class social reformers who had varying commitments to maternal and egalitarian feminism. Members identified themselves with sunflower badges of yellow and brown "symbolizing light and wisdom." With the Woman's Christian Temperance Union (WCTU) as a firm ally, the CSA sought the support of another significant women's organization that was initially resistant to suffrage, the National Council of Women of Canada (NCWC). There may have been a new premier in office in 1905, but Conservative James Whitney proved just as reluctant a suffragist as his Liberal predecessor. Yet again, however, the CSA found a handful of allies in the legislature, but huge majorities defeated their suffrage bills. Despite almost thirty years of activism, opposition remained substantial.

New directions and fresh challenges also abounded. In northern Ontario, the new suffrage hub of Port Arthur-Fort William saw clubwomen and Finnish socialist women unite behind the enfranchisement cause. A coalition of sorts emerged with the Toronto District Labour Council, but this was weakened by suffragists' general disinterest in trade unionism and the rights of working women. Overseas, the tactics of British suffragettes and American militants produced a transnational debate and division regarding appropriate resistance. Partly in reaction to British militancy, a significant anti-suffragist opposition arose, inspired by the ideology of domestic science guru Adelaide Hoodless and championed by vocal anti-suffragist Clementina Fessenden and the Association Opposed to Woman Suffrage in Canada (AOWSC). It marked unprecedented public conflict. Suffrage iconoclast Flora MacDonald Denison stood at the centre of this storm. Eager to revolutionize the Ontario suffrage movement, she marshalled aggressive activism, even as the suffragist majority adhered to less radical methods and visions of social change.

A NEW GENERATION OF SUFFRAGISTS

As president of the DWEA and CSA between 1903 and 1911, Augusta Stowe-Gullen led a new generation, most born around the time of Confederation. Growing up amid the province's industrial development, booms in urbanization and immigration, and powerful evangelical and secular efforts at reform, suffrage newcomers came of age when spaces for women who defied convention did exist – at least in most cities. They were the beneficiaries of suffrage clubs, coeducational universities, and the leisure and consumption habits associated with the turn-of-the-century cultural phenomenon of the New Woman, especially dress reform, bicycles, and exposure to bohemian art and literature. As a result, the numbers of professional women had increased dramatically, with many suffragists employed in medicine, journalism, or teaching – often before and in conjunction with marriage and a family. Like her mother, Stowe-Gullen defended possibilities for women in the workforce and the home. She advised parents that

all girls should be taught one vocation in life, whether it be as housewives, doctors, lawyers, ministers, artists, farmers

or dressmakers ... Do not educate your daughters to think
marriage is the Alpha and Omega of their earthly career, but
rather a happy incident in their life's work, and then women
will only marry from the highest and purest motives.

Altogether, the suffragists remained relatively privileged women
who explored more options and autonomy than their mothers
and grandmothers. In their hands, suffrage activism became – if
not mainstream – slightly less of a fringe endeavour. As American
May Wright Sewell expressed during an 1898 visit to Toronto, a suffragist was no longer regarded as a "creature with horns."

Among the most important of the new suffragists was Flora
MacDonald Merrill Denison (1867–1921), a dressmaker and
writer from the small Ontario town of Bridgewater. She grew up
in a middle-class family that was impoverished by her father's
failed prospecting schemes. Her schoolteacher mother supported
the family while her father practised spiritualism, the communication with spirits in the afterlife. After a stint as a teacher, which
she found unsatisfactory, Flora moved to Detroit, where she
started a relationship with a salesman, Howard Denison. By 1898,
she was in Toronto, where she designed clothes and managed the
custom-dress department of Simpson's department store. In
1905, she started her own business, Denison Costumer, and continued to work after the birth of her son, Merrill. On the side, she
wrote fiction and articles for local periodicals. Providing high
fashion to Toronto's social elite gave Denison insight into class
inequities and the exploitation of women garment workers – a
subject she tackled in an 1898 article for *Saturday Night*. Her expansive spirit was also evident in the exploration of an eclectic
array of reforms, including suffrage, temperance, single tax, free
thought, free love, state welfare reform, equal pay, dress reform,
and wilderness conservation.

As an equal rights feminist, Denison greatly admired Stowe,
whom she met shortly before her death, and likewise championed

equal rights and freethinking. "Nature did not divide men and women," Denison wrote. "Human institutions and systems" were responsible for that, and "a sorry story is the tale they have told." Jumping headlong into the suffrage movement, she joined the executive of the DWEA and the CSA, as well as the Progressive Ideas Club. She represented Canada at the 1906 International Suffrage Convention in Copenhagen. Suffrage and women's rights dominated the weekly column that she published in the *Toronto World* between 1909 and 1913. First titled "Under the Pines: What Women Are Doing for the Advancement of Civilization" and later "The Open Road towards Democracy," Denison's column, for which she received no salary, combined personal thoughts on suffrage agitation and justice for women with news of the local, national, and international movements. One early column reached out to women who considered themselves "indifferent to the vote" and attempted to raise their consciousness about suffrage as a doorway to all other rights. She argued that all Ontario women "owe their gratitude to the women suffrage pioneers," such as Stowe, for higher education and property reforms. In a list of remaining injustices, she prioritized the lack of custodial rights for mothers and the scourge of child labour.

Though many suffragists shared Denison's reform interests, her politics and personal life were highly unconventional. An agnostic and committed spiritualist, Denison's devotion to a belief system that emphasized the survival of the soul after death and communication with the dead set her apart from the majority of suffragists aligned strictly with Protestant churches. One exception was Stowe, who had transitioned from the strict Christian tenants of Quakerism to Methodism, Christian Science, Unitarianism, and the even more peripheral theosophy, a set of principles that joined together religion, philosophy, and science. Around the time of her death, Stowe admitted to something close to atheism. Moreover, Denison's vocal support for free love, the belief in sexual freedom outside of marriage, as well as birth control and divorce, bordered on the scandalous. So did her relationship with her husband. He already had a wife when they first met, and Denison's marriage to him may have been only common law. Her refusal to be silent about her lack of convention readily made her a lightning rod. In one speech about marital oppression, Denison invoked *Lysistrata,* the Aristophanes play in which the women of Athens refuse to sleep with their husbands until they abandon a senseless war. Denison irreverently suggested that the quickest route to suffrage would be a walkout of all wives. At another point, in reference to widows being able to vote municipally, she quipped, "I have no particular desire to see my husband dead, but I do want the vote." Despite her avant-garde beliefs and lifestyle, Denison initially found acceptance in the Toronto suffragist community, succeeding Stowe-Gullen as CSA president in 1911.

Also on the Toronto scene was Constance Hamilton (1862–1945), an English immigrant and a transplant from Winnipeg. A trained musician married to a civil engineer, Hamilton was active in the Big Sisters, YWCA, and the Bach Society. She also used the settlement movement to help immigrants adapt and sought to improve the working conditions of servants and farmwomen. Friendships bound such activists. Hamilton was close to Charlotte Constance Rudyard Boulton (1865–1940), a journalist and cycling enthusiast who was known for her strong commitment to imperialism. A poet, graduate student, and protégé of Denison, Laura Elizabeth McCully (1886–1924) was recruited to the movement in 1908, the same year she gave an outdoor address on suffrage to a crowd of seven hundred in Orillia. Stowe-Gullen had four medical colleagues to draw on for support – Dr. Margaret Blair Young Gordon (1861–1928), Dr. Margaret Macallum Johnston, Dr. Isabella Smith Wood, and Dr. Margaret McAlpine. Aside from Stowe-Gullen, Gordon was the most prolific of the twentieth-century doctor-suffragists. Born in London, England, she was schooled in Toronto. In 1885, she married the sales manager of a roofing company, with whom she had one child in 1887. She entered medical school after marriage and motherhood, and completed her medical degree at the University of Toronto in 1898. A member of several progressive and women's clubs, Gordon would lead the Toronto branch of the CSA.

With the Toronto movement growing, meeting space became an issue. Since the days of the Toronto Women's Literary Club (TWLC), suffrage meetings had commonly been held in members' homes. For larger gatherings, rooms or lecture halls were rented or borrowed from the WCTU or YWCA. Therefore, it was a cause for celebration when in 1910 the CSA opened its first public headquarters on Yonge Street. Such an effort gave suffragists a downtown storefront in which to publicize their cause and recruit members. To help finance it, the CSA operated a vegetarian restaurant on the premises. It was a short-term venture, closing after only one year due to the financial burden.

By the early twentieth century, Ottawa had also established a burgeoning suffrage community under the motto "For the taxes we pay, And the laws we obey, We want something to say." The Ottawa Equal Franchise Association was led by Mrs. J.H. Brown and Miss Belfrage Gilbertson, the latter of whom was the private secretary to Earl Grey, the governor general. Despite the elite connections of its members, the association encountered obstacles in its development, one being the loss of its right to meet at the public library because the library council felt that it did not fit the criteria for an educational association. Brown perceived the ejection as "criticism of an unjust kind" and argued that no other organization had done more in the last six months to educate the public mind. Specifically, she called attention to the fact that Queen's University had asked the suffrage association to supply material for a debate on women's rights. Unyielding, Brown persisted and, several months later, regained the right to use the library. The city's proximity to Montreal meant that Quebec's leading Anglo suffragists were sometimes hosted in Ottawa, including Professor Carrie Derick and Caroline Kenney.

Another energetic addition to the Ontario movement emerged in Port Arthur-Fort William (later Thunder Bay), a twin city on Lake Superior. Originally a fur trade post and mining town, it had become a key stop on multiple railway lines, resulting in rapid development and modernization. Between 1901 and 1911, the combined population jumped from 7,211 to 27,719, making it Ontario's fifth largest city. As early as 1899, the *Weekly Herald and Algoma Miner* noted local interest in suffrage and described the cause as a matter of human rights. Led by Dr. Clara Todson, Mary J.L. Black (1879–1939), and Anne J. Barrie, reform and suffrage agitation was a robust force in the twin city. Todson, one of the region's first female physicians, was a recent arrival, having moved from the United States, where she had been active with the Illinois Civic Equality League. Jumping into local activism, she became president of the newly formed West Algoma Equal Suffrage Association. Though she lived in the city for only three years before her mother's illness forced her to return to the United States, Todson quickly gained a reputation as a celebrated reformer whose frequent letter writing called upon local and provincial politicians to improve civic life through support of temperance and suffrage. Mary J.L. Black, a librarian, was renowned for transforming the local library from a neglected facility to a celebrated hub of culture and education in the predominantly working-class community and for being the first female president of the Ontario Library Association. Anne J. Barrie, a musician noted for having written the song "Lil Suffragette," made up the trio, leaving behind a scrapbook that chronicled the West Algoma campaign. Their endeavours included collaboration with the CSA on municipal voting rights for married women, rallying around female school trustees, channelling energy toward the provincial franchise campaign, and fighting anti-suffrage efforts at home. The *Fort William Daily Times-Journal* devoted a regular column to the association's affairs.

Todson, Black, and Barrie were single and childless – it is thought that Todson and Black never married and that Barrie was widowed. Consequently, they probably enjoyed more liberty than the average wife or mother, but it also became a conspicuous identity to defend against opponents who equated suffrage with the end of marriage. Tackling this prejudice, Todson argued the opposite: poverty and social evils were what drove women to seek alternatives to marriage. If female voters forced the legislature to make economic and social improvements (such as the reduction of poverty, alcoholism, and prostitution), Todson predicted that marriage rates would soar and result in more stable families. In the meantime, being unmarried brought Todson, Black, and Barrie themselves a step closer to accessing municipal voting rights, but it is unknown whether they met the property qualifications. What information has survived about their residences and livelihoods suggests that in the early twentieth century, Todson shared a home with a male relative, Black's wages were precarious, and Barrie boarded in the household of the local jailer. Even among these leading women, economic security could remain elusive.

Port Arthur-Fort William's suffrage cause was aided by sizable support from members of the Finnish community, many of whom were also embedded in the local labour movement and socialist politics. In Finland, women had been enfranchised in 1906, a product of their political organizing since the late nineteenth century and the success of legislative reforms sought by socialists and anti-czarists alike, who pushed for universal suffrage in the early twentieth century. Finnish women were the first to be enfranchised in Europe and the first anywhere in the world to hold elected office. Drawn to cheap land and industrial employment, many Finns immigrated to Canada between 1900 and 1914. For women, migration meant relinquishing hard-fought voting rights and returning to suffrage activism in their new homeland, primarily through socialist organizations. Such was the case of Sanna

Kannasto (1878–1968), a recruiter for the Socialist Party who, after a brief sojourn in the United States, moved to Port Arthur with her common law husband. Much like her Anglo counterparts in Toronto, Kannasto pushed the Socialist Party to focus on issues related to gender as well as class. In addressing women workers, she spoke of the need for suffrage, birth control, and equality within marriage. Kannasto concentrated on the Port Arthur-Fort William region, enlisting workers in mining and lumber camps, but she participated in at least five national recruitment tours. Her travels gained the attention of the RCMP, who labelled her a "dangerous radical" and threatened deportation. Even among the less radical Finns, suffrage was widely supported. "Equal rights for everyone regardless of sex" became a rallying cry of the *Canadan Uutiset,* a right-wing Finnish newspaper published in Port Arthur that came out in favour of women's suffrage in 1915.

It is unknown whether the "radical" Kannasto or other Finnish suffragists interacted with the "respectable" ladies of the West Algoma Equal Suffrage Association or if language barriers and political difference kept the two communities apart. One clue to possible overlap appears in the suffrage column and women's page of the *Daily Times-Journal,* which sometimes voiced support for putting the ballot in the hands of working women. The efforts of dedicated, hard-working women such as Kannasto, Todson, Black, and Barrie in Port Arthur-Fort William demonstrate that the suffrage cause was alive and well outside of Toronto. They did not work in isolation. Railways connected northern suffrage enthusiasts to national and transnational networks of speakers and resources.

Back in Toronto, the CSA continued to lobby for the municipal enfranchisement of married women and for the provincial vote for all women. Between 1905 and 1906 alone, new MPP defenders of women's suffrage presented seventy-two petitions on municipal voting to Premier James Whitney, who rejected them all. Thus, the 1906 endorsement of Toronto mayor Emerson Coatsworth

Socialist parade on Bay Street in Port Arthur, 1913. Carrying a
"Women Should Vote" banner, the suffrage contingent is positioned
behind the banner calling for the abolition of child labour.

was welcomed when he chaired a public meeting. "I wish you all
had votes," Coatsworth thundered to the audience of seventy-
five women and a few men. Speaking at the same event was
Dr. Willoughby Ayson, a female physician from New Zealand who
argued that her dominion's enfranchisement of Māori and white
women thirteen years earlier had elevated the colony, not doomed
it: "Men there prefer their wives and mothers and sisters shall be
their equals, and not their subjects." Moreover, she added, the failure to revoke the measure demonstrated widespread public satisfaction with it.

No argument seemed to shake the prejudices at Queen's Park,
however. Even a March 1909 petition with nearly 100,000 signatures, delivered to Whitney by a five-hundred-person delegation
led by Stowe-Gullen, produced no action. Denison, Johnston, and
Gordon, plus representatives from the WCTU, Women's University Clubs, the Women's Teachers' Association, and the Medical

Alumnae of the University of Toronto, had joined male allies School Inspector James L. Hughes, Unitarian reverend R.J. Hutcheon, and Council Controller Horatio Clarence Hocken to head the delegation. For the first time, there was also significant representation from the Toronto District Labour Council (TDLC), the Socialist Party, and the International Brotherhood of Electrical Workers. To Stowe-Gullen, the event disproved the government's

THE CHURCH AS AN ALLY

Whereas the social gospel movement had launched much of women's social reform efforts, enfranchisement strayed too far from women's traditional roles for churches to quickly endorse suffrage. In the early twentieth century, Dr. Margaret Gordon, who was an active Congregationalist, organized a Church Work Committee to survey suffrage support in local churches. As with other male allies, clergymen brought respectability, as well as a regular pulpit, to the suffrage cause. Moreover, being able to present suffrage as approved by God could win over conservative naysayers. One outcome of Gordon's research was the publication of favourable statements by fourteen Toronto ministers from mainstream Protestant and other liberal churches. Half were Methodists, reflecting that denomination's relatively progressive views of women's role inside and outside the church. Much like the suffragists themselves, the clergymen supported enfranchisement for diverse reasons. Positioning women's rights as human rights, the minister of the Christie Street Baptist Church insisted, "Women have proved themselves the equal of men in practically every department of life." Though they paid taxes and contributed to the economy and tired refrain that suffrage was of interest only to "a few faddist women." To ignore the demands of thousands was "tyranny," she declared. "Would they stand for this injustice for themselves?" Stowe-Gullen asked. "Should they stand for it for their mothers, wives and daughters? No race or class or sex can have its interests properly safeguarded in the Legislature of any country unless represented by direct suffrage."

government in other ways, "we give them no voice in electing the men who shall make the laws the State forces them to obey." A minister at the Queen Street Methodist Church argued, "objections to woman's suffrage are founded on prejudice only. Christ teaches equality, and nowhere did Christ teach the subjection of women." Invoking maternalism, he cited Queen Victoria as proof that "a woman may be an exemplary wife and mother, devoted to the interests of a home, and yet spare some time to help advance the welfare of her country." No minister acknowledged the subordinate role that women played in their churches. By 1916, only the Baptist and Congregationalist Churches gave women full voting rights on church affairs. With the exception of the limited role of deaconesses in the Methodist Church, women could not hold the role of church clerk or elder positions, let alone stand at the pulpit. By the time suffrage was made legal in Ontario, the Methodist Conference and the Presbyterian and Anglican synods had already come out in favour. Viewed as a threat to family sanctity, the Roman Catholic Church remained firmly staunchly anti-suffrage throughout the campaign.

Addressing the suffragists, Whitney replied that although he could not "deny the depth of woman's influence in whatever direction it was exercised," his "government would have to examine the moral and social aspect of the question." Like Mowat before him, he invited the petitioners to "call again, and we will try to give you better accommodation." Supremely cautious, Whitney would have known that the largest women's organization in Canada, the NCWC, was not yet onside and that a few of its prominent members were strongly opposed to suffrage.

THE (UN)POPULAR THING TO DO

The heightened anti-suffrage agitation before the First World War can be partially explained as outrage over the escalating radicalism within the British suffrage movement. It also reflected some lingering resistance among some of Ontario's leading women reformers. Notably, the NCWC, the product of Canadian women's participation in the International Council of Women, had become something of a public force while declining to take an explicit stance on enfranchisement. Committed to non-partisanship as a means of uniting the diverse and often divided regions, religions, and politics of Canada, it promised to facilitate women's "greater unity of thought, sympathy and purpose" and to "conserve the highest good of the family and the state." An 1893 mass meeting in Toronto, attended by over 1,500 women, marked its official founding under the presidency of Lady Ishbel Aberdeen, an English aristocrat, wife of the governor general of Canada, and long-standing British reformer.

The NCWC met annually, whereas the sixteen local Ontario councils established between 1893 and 1914 held monthly meetings attended by representatives of various women's organizations to share news and collaborate on mutual interests. The local councils put forward motions to the NCWC executive on subjects that deserved national attention. Most causes demonstrated maternal feminist concerns that centred on improving the well-being of children and families. At the local level, they focused on municipal services, such as clean water, public health, or playgrounds. The Ontario Council typically lobbied for province-wide reforms such as the creation of children's aid societies. Suffrage and temperance were regularly sidestepped as too divisive for the varied membership. A suffragist herself, Aberdeen acknowledged that many founding members of the NCWC saw politics as unwomanly. This timidity frustrated Denison, and in 1909 she openly chastised the NCWC's preference to "endorse measures only after it is quite sure it is the popular thing to do."

One of the highest-profile NCWC anti-suffragists was Adelaide Sophia Hunter Hoodless (1858–1910). Born on a small family farm in Brant County, Hoodless moved to Hamilton, Ontario's second largest city, after she married a furniture manufacturer. As president of the Hamilton YWCA, she met young rural and urban women whose entry into the paid workforce disturbed her. She believed that wage earning led to inadequately trained wives and mothers, unhappy homes, and by proxy, crime, delinquency, immorality, and divorce. She condemned Ontario's education system as designed to serve male students who were destined for careers, leaving female students unprepared for homemaking. Hoodless never, however, saw women as unequal; she wanted their domestic labour to be accorded professional respect. Women did not need to be emancipated from domestic duties but to undertake them using efficient modern techniques and ideas.

Therefore, she embraced a new American-created course of study called domestic science, the academic study of sanitation, nutrition, and childrearing. Initially, it was taught in private institutes but was later amended for use in elementary and high schools and universities. As Canada's leading advocate of domestic science, Hoodless promoted it across North America and created the Women's Institutes (WI) in 1897, which enabled rural women to update their domestic skills after marriage and motherhood. In a sign of the close links between personal experience and politics of every sort, Hoodless's determination was probably spurred by the death of her toddler son due to drinking contaminated milk.

Hoodless abhorred suffrage as the antithesis of domestic life. Anyone, she predicted, "who has been brought face to face with the great truths presented through a properly graded course in domestic science or Home Economics in its wider interpretation, will never be found in the ranks of the suffragettes." Women exercised enough influence in their familial roles. "A woman who has not succeeded in training her sons to vote so they guard their mother's best interest and the best interests of the nation," Hoodless declared in 1904, "is not herself worthy of the vote." Furthermore, she did not accept that suffrage was the antidote to the shortcomings of male politicians: "Good men have never denied the women of this country anything they have gone about getting the right way."

Given their geographic proximity, Hoodless probably knew the influential anti-suffragist Clementina Trenholme Fessenden (1843–1918), who was also an NCWC member. Born in Canada East to an English family with Loyalist roots, Fessenden married a minister and relocated to Canada West. Remembered primarily for her imperialist zeal, Fessenden created Empire Day, a holiday for schoolchildren to celebrate the British identity. She admired Queen Victoria and, like her idol, dressed in mourning clothes long after her husband's death. She joined the WI, the Wentworth Historical Society, and the Imperial Order Daughters of the Empire, a nationwide women's organization dedicated to celebrating imperialism – a trio of causes that linked their members to frequently romanticized interpretations of Canadian history.

Whereas Hoodless was a long-time anti-suffragist, Fessenden espoused the cause in 1909, the year of heightened militancy in the British movement. Between 1909 and 1913, she wrote numerous anti-suffragist letters to Hamilton and Toronto newspapers. The *Hamilton Herald* sometimes titled her column "Anti-suffrage

Notes." Like Goldwin Smith, Fessenden believed that God had ordained a special role for women, which was centred on motherhood. Suffrage, she foretold, would threaten births and marriages. Neglected children, with their "baby hands stretch[ed] out to a paid nurse or the forgotten father," would be its true victims. Nor did she accept that women would make good political candidates. Spinsters, in her opinion, were abnormal, wives had more important duties, and poor women were too ignorant – "So let us continue to hope that the high treble of the suffragist may never impair the sweet melody of Home, Home, Sweet, Sweet Home." Unlike Smith, however, Fessenden did see a role for female leaders in charity and education – hence her own significant participation in women's organizations.

Both Hoodless and Fessenden found comfort in their identities as wives and mothers. Yet, much like their suffragist foes, both spent their adult lives immersed in public affairs: holding meetings, giving speeches, writing letters and newspaper columns, appealing to governments for endorsement and financial support – activism that in Hoodless's case occurred when her children were still small. Despite their critique of the public engagement of suffragists, neither Hoodless nor Fessenden addressed this contradiction. Nor did they accept that suffragists too believed they were building a better world for children. For such antis, female enfranchisement remained a selfish indulgence with great risks.

Their views did not prevail. Mounting international support kept pressure on the NCWC. In 1904, the International Council of Women, backed by national councils in Italy, New Zealand, Argentina, France, Austria, Switzerland, Norway, and Greece, came out in favour of suffrage. Closer to home, Stowe-Gullen's 1906 motion to establish an NCWC standing committee on "political equality" was approved by a wide margin. Even after it passed, Hoodless objected, and she was called out of order. Two years later, the Victoria, British Columbia, chapter of the NCWC sanctioned suffrage, the first Canadian branch to do so. In 1909, Toronto hosted the International Council meeting, where Aberdeen endorsed a motion that "women ought to possess the vote in all countries where representative government existed." After a lengthy debate the following year, the NCWC became suffrage-friendly in a vote of seventy-one to fifty-one, a margin that revealed continuing opposition. Still, the backing of the NCWC and the fact that it represented ten thousand members were immensely useful. It helped to redirect attention to the national campaign, and its endorsement of the female franchise answered the old objection that women did not want the vote. The NCWC, in its endorsement of suffrage, framed voting rights as pragmatic, a way to accomplish social reform, rather than as a human rights issue.

Despite the NCWC ratification, some member groups remained opposed to suffrage. The Hamilton Local Council of Women was recalcitrant, perhaps due to the influence of Hamiltonians Hoodless and Fessenden. Moreover, Hoodless directed the WI, considered the most widespread and influential organization for rural Ontario women, not to take up suffrage activism. Indeed, the WI had a legitimate fear of risking its funding from the provincial Department of Agriculture. Despite the official rejection, not all WI members or branches kept to the sidelines. Particularly in isolated northern Ontario, where defiance may have been easier and the WI the only woman's organization in a community, branches used funds to host suffrage speakers. "We have got the suffrage microbe in our District and we are hopelessly infected," reported a member of the WI for Lee Valley, a tiny town near Sudbury, in 1917. "Headquarters may give all the orders they like," she stated, "but when women get interested in anything, it is going to come out in the Institute, and indirectly our Institute, although officially opposed to suffrage, has been the best medium we have had to spread the suffrage doctrine."

THE ASSOCIATION OPPOSED
TO WOMAN SUFFRAGE IN CANADA

Founded in 1913, the Association Opposed to Woman Suffrage in Canada (AOWSC) marked the first known effort among women to organize against suffrage in Ontario. Perhaps due to its size or subsequent embarrassment, this group left few records. A wealthy Toronto widow, Sarah Warren, who was active in the Girl Guides, the Spadina Lodge for Working Girls, and the Royal Ontario Museum, was its leader. Other members included the female kin of politicians and industrialists. More so than suffragists, the vast majority of AOWCA members were married and did not work outside the home. One member, Mary Plummer, daughter of the president of Dominion Steel, described AOWSC's goals as being, "to give those who are opposed to the [suffrage] movement ... an opportunity to express their conviction that such a measure would be against the best interests of the State." She insisted, "questions of civic, social and moral reform ... can best be advanced without the extension of the parliamentary franchise to women." Premier Mowat's nephew, Herbert Mowat, a lawyer and justice on the Ontario Supreme Court, once addressed the club on the inadvisability of suffrage. According to the Toronto Star, *suffragists infiltrated and attempted to address AOWSC meetings. Any momentum built by AOWSC dissipated with the First World War. Its visibility dropped precipitously as members turned to war work, and its arguments seemed all the more out of date.*

SEEKING SUPPORT FROM LABOUR

From the beginning, working-class women were largely missing from the Ontario suffrage crusade, and for good reason – they were not sought after as allies, and their needs were not prioritized. Suffrage grounded in this spirit probably had little appeal to them. Just as they tended to ignore non-white or non-British immigrant women, suffragists rarely spoke or acted in a way that suggested they felt solidarity with working women. Yet it is not as if the average suffragist were completely disconnected from the lives of the less well-to-do. Indeed, poor and working-class families made up the bulk of female physicians' patients in Toronto, supplied pupils for the suffragist schoolteachers, and were targets of their frequent social reform interventions and journalistic investigations. These relationships involved significant power imbalances and the potential for moral judgments that made friendships or loyalty difficult. For example, Emily Stowe evidently felt some sympathy for Sarah Ann Lovell, the domestic servant who asked her for an abortifacient, yet she revealed Lovell's pregnancy to her employer, thus costing the young woman her job.

Most suffragists might well have employed domestic servants of their own to balance the demands of careers and households. In an article for *Everywoman's World,* four professional women were interviewed about managing their responsibilities inside and outside the home. Augusta Stowe-Gullen acknowledged, "it is often difficult to keep the domestic machinery moving smoothly." Only by "securing efficient domestic help" could she "practice her profession and still find home a haven of rest instead of a nest of worries." Yet even when their labour was recognized as valuable, servants themselves rarely were. The article's author, Elizabeth Becker, suggested that the "average maid" was unschooled, dim-witted, and unreliable, often merely adding to the burdens of busy career women. "Those that have brain enough to respond to the test of greater responsibility, usually enter some other occupation," she remarked, an observation that typically linked social stratification with ability and opportunities. Nowhere did Becker or the four women whom she profiled consider the difficulties of servants and other working women in juggling paid employment with home duties.

Nor did suffragists often discuss or attempt to improve the working conditions of working-class women, at least not with the same focus and energy they directed to gaining access to universities and the professions. Whereas Denison lamented the lack of female workers, issues affecting the vast majority of them – namely, unsafe working conditions, lack of job security, and low pay – had little initial purchase. Commitment, such as the early TWLC foray into factory inspection reports, went little beyond making recommendations. In 1889, the same year the DWEA joined forces with the WCTU, Stowe and Mary McDonnell had been speakers for the Silver Fleece Labor Assembly, a Knights of Labor local for 409 female tailors in Toronto, but the alliance was short-lived. The next significant suffrage-labour link did not occur until 1902, when Margaret Haile ran for the Ontario legislature and there was a brief flurry of support for the socialists' universal suffrage platform.

Indifference was often mutual. Female socialists and labour advocates complained that unions frequently showed little interest in addressing women's labour issues. Employment for women was contentious not only because men of all classes preferred them at home but also because many unionists saw women's labour as a threat to fair pay and job security for men. Rather than embrace equal pay to nullify the problem of cheaper female rivals, organized labour chose to demand a breadwinner wage for all men. Wives and daughters could remain properly dependent. In 1910, an organizer for the Garment Workers insisted that there would be no need for the "advocacy of equal rights or suffrage for women were they permitted to remain in their natural sphere, the home." It was "greed for wealth by corporate and other employing interests [that] had driven the women and the girls into

commercial and industrial fields." The idea that paid work generated fulfillment, independence, and equality, so vital to many suffragists, was noticeably absent.

In short, little evidence suggests that Ontario suffragists
thought highly enough of their working-class sisters to seek their
council, recruit them, or make them feel welcome. Indeed, in their
quest to prove that women deserved the vote, they often highlighted the maternal morality or equal intellect demonstrated by
respectable mothers, university students, and professionals. The
hardships or exploitation of working women were rarely part of
this calculation. The lack of outreach, combined with decades-
long characterization of working and poor women as downtrodden or immoral and in need of middle-class guidance and uplift,
helps explain why the relations between working-class and suffragist women were negative or non-existent. Ontario's deep-seated
conservatism made co-operation among the classes less inviting
than it sometimes seemed in more recently settled regions.

Therefore, the attempts of Ontario suffragists to befriend the
labour movement in the years leading up to the First World
War should be viewed less as a recognition of shared sisterhood
and more as a calculated effort to gain influence over union men,
who could throw their weight (and votes) behind candidates
who favoured suffrage. In 1909, the CSA approached the Toronto District Labour Council (TDLC), a central labour body with
representation from the city's various unions, asking for its support. The union men voted thirty-four to three to support a CSA
motion asking for union endorsement. Nevertheless, fears about
backing a bourgeois cause brought an almost immediate retrac-
tion. Despite this complicated scenario, the TDLC sent a representative to stand alongside Stowe-Gullen when she submitted
the 1909 petition to Queen's Park. Thus began a tradition of
labour representatives in such delegations and campaigns. For instance, Mrs. Duncan McDougall, a member of the Labour Union
of Women, was part of the 1911 provincial delegation, and R.J.

Stevenson represented unions in the 1913 effort to gain municipal voting rights for married female property owners. Stevenson's involvement triggered familiar concerns from a labour newspaper, the *Industrial Banner,* which reported that the TDLC debated whether the CSA's focus on female property owners was a slight to the wives of the working men. The vote to appoint Stevenson nevertheless passed unanimously, as it was concluded that the partial franchise was only one step toward the CSA goal of full enfranchisement.

Denison was a force behind the outreach to labour. As a dressmaker, she had close ties to the garment industry, and unlike more highly educated and wealthier suffragists, she understood dependence on uncertain wages. Her poem "Woman with the Needle," published in *Saturday Night* during the 1890s, suggests a compassionate perspective on the disparities between those who sewed gowns and those who wore them:

> *Pale blue lips – a ghastly sight,*
> *Stitching she to dress a world,*
> *That, perchance, does not dress her,*
> *No indeed but barely feeds her,*
> *Hardly gives her bread enough,*
> *To keep her soul and flesh together.*
> *This "The Woman with the needle."*

Whatever her sympathies may have been, Denison did not pay her own employees more than standard wages. In 1913, the seamstresses she hired earned just five to ten dollars a week, although more skilled cutters got eighteen to twenty. Denison justified her pay scale as necessary to support her family, sustain her small business, and generate some profits to fund reform causes.

Nonetheless, Denison addressed the sixty female strikers from the T.E. Braime Clothing Company in 1910. These garment workers, most of whom were Russian and Jewish, walked out in protest when the cost of thread they used to sew shirts and overalls was deducted from their wages. The strikers marched, picketed the factory, and tried to discourage other women from applying for work there. The CSA invited the strikers to visit its headquarters one night, but no other signs of support have survived.

To be sure, Denison was not entirely alone in her sympathies. Alice Amelia Chown (1866–1949), Laura Hughes, and Harriet Dunlop Prenter were other middle-class women with an interest in labour activism and labour party politics. Among the three, Chown's activism was most significant during the pre-war years. An economics and political science graduate from Queen's University, Chown had been raised in a strict Methodist household in Kingston. As the caretaker of her ailing mother, she remained at home until the age of forty. Her mother's death freed her for travel and a career in welfare work, reform, and journalism. Writing for the *Christian Guardian* in 1911, Chown gained notoriety for her scathing critique of the poor pay and conditions endured by the deaconesses (essentially social workers and ministerial aides) of the Methodist Church. Though Chown favoured home economics, she did not see it as women's only respectable option for higher education. Still more radically, Chown shared Denison's sympathies for free love, dress reform, and Freudian psychoanalysis. Chown's niece recalled that her aunt was the family black sheep because of her eccentricities, forthright feminism, and commitment to social justice.

Chown's vocal support for the 1912 Eaton's strike also distinguished her from other labour-friendly suffragists, including Denison. Fed up with deplorable working conditions, job losses, and low wages, over eight hundred male and female garment workers employed by the popular department store and catalogue company went on strike for sixteen weeks. A third of the strikers were non-unionized female cloak makers. Their complaints included sexual harassment by foremen. When the TDLC asked women's groups to support the strikers, Chown was reportedly the only suffragist to respond. Her highly fictionalized 1921 memoir, *The Stairway*, describes how the picketers were subject to heckling and rough treatment from pedestrians and police. When she joined them, she too was rounded up by police officers as they attempted to disperse the strikers. Although Chown tried to use her press connections to get Toronto papers to cover the strike, none dared to take on Eaton's, a major source of advertising revenue. She also recruited a female strike organizer from New York to raise public consciousness. According to Chown, her sister suffragists expressed disgust at sexual harassment but little more: "The common, everyday longings for better conditions, for a life that would provide more than food, clothes and shelter, were not recognized in justifying the strike." Even the most zealous ignored Chown's fundraising, and her plans to boycott Eaton's were rejected, lest their own "pet causes would be hurt through being linked with an unpopular one." Although the Eaton's strike ultimately failed, its length and the possibility of wider progressive alliances were historically significant. Stifled by Ontario conservatism, Chown eventually moved to New York, where she continued labour activism and attended lectures by feminist activist and anarchist Emma Goldman.

Given that most of the Eaton's strikers were Jewish and born outside of Canada, anti-Semitism and xenophobia probably played a role in the indifference of suffragists. Over 3 million immigrants came to Canada between 1897 and 1914, a third from Continental Europe. Most headed for the prairie wheat boom, but approximately 30 percent settled in Ontario, primarily in Toronto, to work in factories. Their arrival deepened xenophobia. Even liberal suffragists such as Denison employed anti-immigrant rhetoric in juxtaposing enfranchised foreign-born men with voteless female British subjects. Denison dismissed "most" immigrants as "ignorant, illiterate and often the scum of the earth," warning that "in a few years they will be empowered to vote and make laws for the women of our land." With rare exceptions, suffragists regarded foreign immigrants as a threat to British values. Unlike respectable women, they would not usher in a better nation.

Though the wider public and possibly even her suffragist friends were unaware of it, one CSA member had Russian Jewish origins. Sonia Marie Natanson Leathes (1871–1964) was a Jewish concert pianist who fled Russia at the end of the nineteenth century. While working in Switzerland as a language tutor, she met and later married an English physician and lecturer. The couple moved to Canada in 1909 when her husband became professor of chemical pathology at the University of Toronto. Leathes joined the University College Women's Literary Society and the CSA, and became the vice-president of the Toronto Local Council of Women. Her status as the spouse of a British scholar gave her access to the elite social circles of Toronto, even as Jews were openly barred from certain neighbourhoods, workplaces, schools, and clubs. There is no evidence that Leathes joined the National Council of Jewish Women, which was established in Toronto in 1897. Given that her daughter discovered her mother's religious heritage only after her death, it seems probable that her suffragist friends were equally ignorant. Leathes retained her Russian accent, which prompted the local press to consistently identify her as a foreigner, despite her class. Assimilation remained incomplete.

As a leading CSA member between 1909 and 1912, Leathes called for the creation of a women's court and spoke out against child labour. In linking employment and social abuses, she denied that suffragists wanted to overturn all gender conventions:

> Many people think that women want to become like men, to wear men's clothes, to smoke and grow a mustache. We do not. To men food is merely a thing to sell; to women it is a thing to eat. We want to be able to say to men, "You make money, but you shall not make it by selling dirty milk, you shall not make it by sweating women."

Her broad sympathies led her to join an international effort by women's groups seeking clemency for Angelina Napolitano, an Italian immigrant and mother of four. In 1911, while living in Sault Ste. Marie, Napolitano murdered her husband in retribution for his assaults and demands that she prostitute herself, even when pregnant. Her case became a *cause célèbre*, and she was found guilty and sentenced to death. Believing that the trial was unfair because the all-male jury ignored evidence of domestic abuse, Leathes publicized the case in the *Globe*, arguing that women should be judged by a jury of their peers. "All women know that Angelina Napolitano's act is most likely the effect of temporary insanity," Leathes asserted, "caused by the most terrible provocation on the part of a man who naturally ought to have sheltered and protected her in her present condition." Resulting public outrage prompted the government to commute Napolitano's sentence to life in prison. In the end, she served eleven years. (Ottawa suffragists rallied around a similar case of a young Polish mother, who was charged with infanticide in 1913. They set up a legal defence fund for the woman, whom they described as poor and homeless, not a murderer.)

Elsewhere, Leathes hailed the revolutionary spirit of Russian women. In a 1912 article for the *Woman's Journal*, an American suffrage periodical, she pointed to the absence of a Russian suffrage movement and suggested that Russians were slow to develop "any political solidarity as a sex." This was not entirely surprising since under the czar's rule even Russian men could not vote until 1906. Russian women nevertheless sought "political liberty" with "fearless enthusiasm" – sometimes violently – alongside men. Their "common suffering" allowed women to "ignore the circumstance of sex perhaps more readily than is the case elsewhere."

Though Ontario suffragists remained extremely limited in their sympathies, Leathes, Chown, and Denison demonstrate that the movement was not entirely predictable or homogeneously

Anglo-Celtic. Overall, however, the broader labour-suffrage partnership floundered in the years leading up to the First World War.
Suffragists wanted the backing and electoral power of working
men, without any accompanying radicalism. In turn, labouring
men and women remained suspicious of a cause that American
labour leader Margaret Drier summed up in an *Industrial Banner*
article as "controlled by privilege and reaction" and as lacking
working women among its leadership.

THE IMPACT OF SUFFRAGETTE MILITANCY

Petitions, delegations, and public meetings – the stalwart and
rarely sensational core of Ontario suffragist campaigns – were
interrupted when news of British suffragette militancy landed in
Toronto. In 1903, a section of Britain's National Union of Women's
Suffrage Societies (NUWSS) broke off to form the Women's Social
and Political Union (WSPU). Its founder was Emmeline Pankhurst
(1858–1928), a charismatic middle-class Manchester widow with
long-standing ties to radical causes. Like many Canadian reform
groups, the WSPU was a family endeavour. When Pankhurst was
driven to militancy by frustration at the slow pace of NUWSS lobbying and almost fifty years of peacefully seeking democratic
reform, her daughters Christabel and Sylvia joined her in the fore-
front of agitation.

Under the slogan "Deeds not words," the WSPU initiated public
demonstrations, often deemed unlawful assembly. Its members
smashed windows, torched mailboxes, and painted "Votes for
Women" on walls or burnt it into lawns. When police officers attempted to stop them, they pushed back, but the violence directed
at them by male spectators and the police far outweighed their
own. WSPU members were arrested multiple times. During one
bout of imprisonment in 1909, fourteen of Pankhurst's followers
launched a hunger strike and endured force feeding – the first of
many such outrages suffered by Emmeline and others. The brutal

confrontations generated unprecedented global media attention for the great cause.

WSPU members became known as suffragettes, a label distinguishing their militancy from the more conventional politicking of law-abiding moderate suffragists elsewhere, although in practice the name was often applied indiscriminately to any women's rights activist. Pankhurst became an international sensation, praised by admirers for her magnetic oratory and personal sacrifices. Her detractors labelled her morally appalling, unladylike, and counterproductive. She responded by noting that civil disobedience was a time-honoured British remedy for electoral injustice. Early Chartists had rioted, destroying property in 1832, and disenfranchised men had broken the law in 1867. Women's militancy was part of a distinguished tradition. Pankhurst blamed escalating violence not on militants but on Parliament's resistance to constitutional equality.

The WSPU vision was not limited to Britain. It was always "imperial in its scope," anticipating that "success in one part of the Empire will contribute to success in every other part." In particular, Pankhurst felt that Canada, as the only white settler dominion not to have achieved suffrage, was ripe for revolution. Militancy might not be required, she mused in a private letter, but Canadians needed leadership and inspiration. The CSA seemingly agreed, and in November 1909 it sponsored a Canadian stop at the end of Pankhurst's American tour. By the time she arrived in Toronto, she had a lengthy arrest record for obstruction, inciting a crowd, and assaulting a police officer, for which she had served two prison terms. Sympathy and curiosity attracted huge crowds to her three talks in Toronto. She was the first female speaker ever to address the men's Canadian Club, and she drew a large crowd of women at Massey Hall. Popular demand produced an additional last-minute speech at the Princess Theatre. While in Toronto, she reportedly had tea with suffrage foe Goldwin Smith.

MAYOR OLIVER – "WONDER WHO TOLD THEM WE DIDN'T ENCOURAGE THE SUFFRAGETTE MOVEMENT IN TORONTO?"

Under the spell of Pankhurst, cartoonist Newton McConnell imagines Toronto suffragists as succumbing to similar unruliness as they give chase to the mayor, c. 1910.

According to newspaper accounts, Toronto audiences were won over by Pankhurst's charming oratory and downplaying of militancy. The media proclaimed the rabble rouser to be "sweet," "attractive," "gracious," and "logical." Subsequently, the CSA hosted the visit of a more moderate British suffragist, Ethel Snowden, a NUWSS member and Christian socialist. At Massey Hall, Snowden argued that "physical violence was [not] the best method of gaining their end but it was justified in certain causes." Though she did not condone Pankhurst's militancy, she condemned the government's harsh policing and punishments as "most unjustified."

Despite reasonably favourable impressions left by Pankhurst and other suffragettes, Canadians continued to fear militancy. A *Toronto News* cartoon depicted a mob of angry, yet well dressed,

In a cartoon titled "James L. Hughes, One of Toronto's Leading Suffragettes Rehearsing for the Coming of Mrs. Pankhurst," Newton McConnell skewers male suffragist James Hughes, c. 1910.

women sprinting after Toronto mayor Joseph Oliver and an unnamed political crony. In the background, two suffragists brandish the spoils of war – the men's top hats. In the foreground, the two women at Oliver's heels raise an umbrella and a cane, threatening greater violence. Missing from the drawing is any rationale for suffrage: the women are little more than a hysterical mob. The tone invokes O.P. Dildock's similar portrayal of the women's literary club three decades earlier. Although the cartoonist made Oliver, not Mowat, the suffragist target, he had in fact chaired Pankhurst's Massey Hall talk, which suggests at least some allegiance. Readers are left to wonder whether Oliver was selected in order to emphasize the senselessness of suffragists or even to ridicule him for any sympathies he might have harboured. Another cartoon by the same artist depicts suffrage ally James Hughes in drag, complete with high heels, feathered hat, and raised umbrella, dancing a jig in excitement over Pankhurst's visit. Such cartoons obviously emasculated and thereby discredited male supporters while at the same time diminishing women as political actors. Militancy was made to look foolish rather than meaningful or strategic.

British militancy required delicate navigation by the CSA. Visiting suffragettes were given a forum to explain their divisive tactics. Yet the CSA never gave outright support of their militancy or championed use of such methods in Ontario. What did happen was that Denison and a few others began to hero-worship Pankhurst and her followers, a sentiment often paired with an expressed desire for more rapid change in Ontario. In 1906, Denison and Stowe-Gullen met Pankhurst during the International Suffrage Convention meeting in Copenhagen and bonds were clearly established. Denison hosted Pankhurst during her 1909 Toronto visit and expressed great admiration for the militant for making the suffrage cause globally known. The dressmaker also valued Pankhurst's outreach to both privileged and working women. Denison's sympathy for militants went further still. She publicly defended British Australian WSPU member Dora Montefiore, a poet who had barricaded herself inside her home and refused to pay taxes until women had political representation. "She is neither insane or a fanatic," Denison insisted, pointing to press misrepresentation. Though Denison stopped short of accepting violence, she reminded readers that the suffrage movement had long protested unjust laws. Celebrated American suffragist Susan B. Anthony was singled out as having been arrested and tried in a criminal court in 1872 for her attempt to vote. Under Denison's leadership, the CSA maintained ties with the increasingly militant WSPU.

One of Denison's youngest followers, Laura McCully, was similarly inspired by Pankhurst. Restless with the snail-like progress and polite activism, she felt it was time to "torment members of parliament, march through the streets, or raid sleepy legislatures." In one of her poetry collections, she wrote an ode to Emily Wilding Davidson, the British suffragette who sacrificed her life at the 1913 Epsom Derby to draw attention to the suffrage cause:

And thou, who bravedst the whole world's scorn
Meeting thy death in sordid wise
To keep a cause before their eyes
And flaunt a flag that fools have torn
I deem thee knight of high emprise,
Dear comrade, whom with tears we mourn.

With friend Helen Cunningham, McCully formed the "Women's Political Club, Militant Section." Though the two young women claimed to have recruited others to their cause, no apparent civil disobedience was forthcoming.

The boldest militant action in Ontario amounted to a mild commotion at Queen's Park. In 1910, English visitor Olivia Smith rose from the gallery at the legislature to protest that it had concluded business for the year "without doing justice to women." Choosing to speak just as the lieutenant-governor exited the floor and the prorogation ceremony began, Smith called out, "Women are as much entitled to votes as men. I hope that in your future deliberations you will do justice to the cause of women. This is all I have to say at present. Thank you." Noting that Smith was dressed in a brown suit, fur toque, and fur ruff, the *Lindsay Post* identified the polite instigator as a "real suffragette" and explained that her prison-bar–shaped brooch signified that she had "suffered imprisonment for her cause." Indeed, the thirty-year-old Smith, who worked as nurse, had been jailed in 1908 for chaining herself to the gates outside Prime Minister Henry Asquith's residence and shouting "Votes for Women," a diversion that allowed two other suffragettes to sneak inside. When asked to account for her much tamer Toronto-based disturbance, Smith said that she spoke "impulsively," a course of action that "might be more effective than are the present methods here." In hindsight, she presumed that Canadians might think her actions "vulgar." Certainly, Premier Whitney was annoyed at her gall. He called the sergeant-at-arms to remove her, but she left before that was necessary. Allegedly, Whitney also expressed a wish that "some-body had been there to throw a bucket of water on her." Even a long-time suffrage advocate, the labour MPP Allan Studholme, disavowed knowing Smith or approving of her methods. Speaking a few days later, Smith gave a harsh assessment of the Canadian suffrage campaign. "The movement here is dead," she declared. "You need a revival and a few martyrs." She would return to Canada in 1912 for a tour of local suffrage organizations, including a newly established club in Owen Sound.

When Pankhurst made her second tour of Canada in 1911, with Ontario stops in Toronto, Ottawa, and Port Arthur-Fort William, the earlier enthusiasm was not reproduced. No longer a novelty, Pankhurst's unrelenting militancy had grown less appealing to the mainstream. A crowd of only 1,500 attended her Massey Hall address, down from the 5,000 of two years earlier. Other activists nevertheless made similar tours. Sylvia Pankhurst arrived in 1911, and WSPU member Barbara Wylie came in 1912. Just prior to her visit, Wylie joined a five-member delegation that met with Prime Minister Robert Borden during a visit to London, England. Borden explained that he had not given much thought to suffrage and did not know enough to comment on the British movement. In response to this brush-off, the delegation threatened "agitation" across the Atlantic. Borden deflected the threat by claiming that franchise conditions were determined by the provinces, not he himself. He also sidestepped efforts at recruitment by British anti-suffragists. Denison minimized the confrontation with Borden, telling the *Globe* that the CSA had nothing to do with London events and that its "policy is to gain supporters for our cause through peaceful means. We want the press on our side, and we want the movement to spread through example and by correct instruction regarding our principles." Ontario activists seemed equally lukewarm in greeting Wylie.

Public disapproval of militancy nevertheless soared as the WSPU rolled out an arson campaign between 1912 and 1914. It

mailed letter bombs and bombed public buildings and unoccu-
pied homes belonging to the British elite. Violent acts by individual suffragettes, such as Mary Leigh's hatchet attack on Prime
Minister Asquith's carriage and Mary Richardson's slashing of a
picture in the National Gallery, saw suffragettes condemned.
Following the assault by Leigh, NUWSS leader Millicent Fawcett
called upon Pankhurst to end the violence before it harmed the
cause further. A 1913 article in *Saturday Night,* perhaps Canada's
most conservative general magazine, questioned Pankhurst's
sanity, pointing out that even if women were enfranchised, her
arrest record meant that, as with other criminals, she would be
denied the vote. This censure was echoed by Toronto legal scholar
Augustus Henry Frazer Lefroy, who observed that the actions of
the English suffragettes "are a good argument for denying the
vote to the great body of respectable, law-abiding English
women." In contrast, the "abstinence from militant methods is,
quantum valeat, an argument in favour of enfranchising Canadian
women."

Denison, nevertheless, remained steadfast. During Emmeline
Pankhurst's 1911 visit, she hailed her mentor as "beyond any
woman in the world." In England, Denison once addressed a WSPU
rally and signed her own WSPU membership card. By 1913, she
had identified herself as a suffragette, renaming her *Toronto Sunday World* column "Stray Leaves from a Suffragette's Notebook."
Denison was not the only vocally staunch supporter of Pankhurst.
After being criticized in the press for her stance, Ottawa suffragist
Lulu Abbot predicted, "Mrs. Pankhurst will go down in history as
the Joan of Arc of the twentieth century and Asquith's name will
be a blot on the page."

PERFORMING SUFFRAGE IN WASHINGTON
Britain was not the only source of inspiration. Denison also aligned
herself with American suffragists Lucy Burns and Alice Paul,
Pankhurst disciples who introduced non-violent but aggressive

suffrage tactics into the US movement. Hoping to have the Constitution amended, they staged a mass public demonstration in 1913, on the eve of President Woodrow Wilson's inauguration. Eight thousand women, dressed in costume and waving placards and banners, marched down Pennsylvania Avenue in front of the White House. Paul designed a spectacle that demanded attention while simultaneously portraying the suffrage movement as dignified, respectable, and patriotic. The parade included celebrated members of the US women's rights movement: Reverend Dr. Anna Howard Shaw and Carrie Chapman Catt, activist Helen Keller, and journalist Nellie Bly. Invoking a warrior goddess, labour lawyer Inez Milholland, garbed in a white cloak and crown, led the parade on a white horse. Floats displaying key scenes in American suffrage history followed, accompanied by delegations of suffragists from each state and collectives representing homemakers, professionals, labour, college graduates, and political parties, including socialists. Thirteen American Indigenous women led by Blackfoot Daisy Norris marched in the middle of the procession. Referring to Norris as an "Indian Maiden," newspaper accounts focused on her captivating beauty. According to one report, she was an "ardent suffragist" who "longed to be like her white sisters" and had begged her father's permission to travel from Washington state to join the parade.

The Norris contingent was small and exotic enough to fit the harmonious vision of parade organizers, but black suffragists were not. Much to the ire of African American women's rights leader and journalist Ida B. Wells-Barnett, the National Association of Coloured Women and other black women's groups were given a mixed reception. There is evidence that black women were instructed to march in the rear, behind a delegation of white male supporters, lest integration deter southern participants. Speculation arose as to whether black suffragists would boycott the parade. In Toronto, Denison was asked to comment. She stated that the CSA did not bar any women, though she did not say whether its membership included non-white women. In re-marking on the US affairs, she explained that southern suffragists "might not care to have a coloured person ruling them." In the end, approximately fifty African Americans participated.

Suffragists from Europe and across the British Empire joined the American march. Though Pankhurst was notably absent, the presence of enfranchised and non-enfranchised women from a dozen nations allowed the organizers to showcase a widespread Western phenomenon. Denison led the eighteen-person Can-adian delegation, made up entirely of Ontario suffragists, many of whom were CSA members, including Augusta Stowe-Gullen, Margaret Johnston, and Margaret Gordon. Constance Hamilton joined Harriet Prenter to represent the newly formed Ontario suffrage club, the Equal Franchise League (EFL). Also present were Miss Amereaux, president of Toronto's Junior Suffrage Club, and Jessie Campbell MacIver, editor of the NCWC magazine *Woman's Century*. Others came from London, Ottawa, and Orangeville. Long-time suffrage supporter and *Grip* editor J.W. Bengough walked with his wife. Denison was accompanied by her son, Merrill, a university student. Merrill, who would later be a re-nowned playwright, shared his mother's feminism. "I had no illu-sions about the women being a secondary, inferior sex," he explained, "because I had evidence ... around me of great femin-ine capability, as thinkers, administrators, just as capable as given the same opportunity as men. I always had taken a dim regard of the polarization of the sexes."

Leading the Canadian contingent was Denison's Washington-based seven-year-old niece Flora MacDonald Lapham, dressed in a coat emblazoned with a prominent Union Jack. Flanked by the delegation from India and the British Isles, all the Canadians wore sashes printed with "Canada." The doctors also wore their mortar-board caps and academic gowns. En route to the event, Denison and others had stopped in Philadelphia to pay tribute to the birth-place of America's liberty.

Toronto Women Who Headed Deputation to Washington

Sympathetic to the suffrage cause, the *Toronto Sunday World* gave front-page coverage to the Toronto contingent that attended the parade in Washington. In the accompanying photograph of 2 March 1913, the women affirm their imperial and national identity, and in the case of the physicians, their educational attainments. From left to right: Flora MacDonald Denison, Augusta Stowe-Gullen, Jessie Campbell MacIver, Dr. Margaret Johnston, Constance Hamilton, Dr. Margaret Gordon, and Harriet Prenter.

Some Canadian press coverage referred to the parade as "suffragette" activity and speculated on the militancy of its Canadian participants. When the women departed from Union Station, a *Globe* writer closely scrutinized their appearance and luggage for signs of belligerency. He described Denison and company as "in appearance and attitude ... much as other women are, all middle-aged or young and dressed in the latest fashions." This apparently surprised him, as he assumed that "such handsome women" would hardly support militancy. He was equally relieved to see no banners in their possession. The same author compared their trip to a pilgrimage, akin to that of "General" Rosalie Jones, an ardent American follower of Pankhurst, who had marched a group of more than two hundred women from New York to Washington in 1912. In contrast, the liberal-leaning *Toronto Star* offered no editorializing: its women's section gave a lengthy description of the parade plans and photos of the costumes.

Toronto World previewed the delegation's trip and later produced a full-page photo collage to celebrate Canada's representation. Stately figures pose before a statue along the parade route, giving seven-year-old Lapham a prominent place. Photos of Canadians are ranged around a glamorous shot of Inez Milholland and a group of young American suffragists, spliced in with images from the inauguration of President Wilson. The photos could just as easily have been taken during an Empire Day celebration, as they give no suggestion that the parade was a radical or unacceptable mobilization for equality. Equally revealingly, the *World* ignored the hostility of hecklers and a male mob that harassed the women and regularly delayed the parade. Under Denison's influence, the *World* stressed the respectability and glamour of the event.

In contrast, the *Globe* targeted the "gross indignities" endured by suffragists due to the failure of the police to protect them. The violence was front-page news for the *Star* too. Though it reassured readers that no Canadian woman had been harmed, it featured a photograph of an ambulance taking suffragists away for medical treatment. Later investigations suggested police involvement in the violence. Over two hundred women required medical attention, and the army was called out to restore order. But the participants were made of stern stuff, and they finished with a tableau that featured women dressed as Justice, Liberty, Peace, Hope, and Charity. Paul and Burns hailed the event as a victory in raising awareness. They would continue with acts of civil disobedience, including vigils and pickets outside the White House, which led to their arrest and subsequent prison hunger strike.

Canadian participation in the Washington march represents the transnational ties among suffragists and the perceived value of international solidarity. But Premier Whitney remained unswayed. Like the 100,000-signature petition of March 1909, the spectacle of eight thousand marchers in Washington did not convince him. After all, only eighteen were from Ontario. Yet the public nature and visual impact of the parade were undeniable. Suffrage activism and support were increasingly impossible to deny or ignore. The choreography and costuming by Paul and Burns helped cast the franchise cause as noble and beautiful, deflecting attention from Pankhurst's less palatable militancy. North American observers were reassured that "their" suffragists sought social and political change through legal, if increasingly public, channels and methods.

A cohort of Ontario participants in the Washington march was sufficiently inspired to ask the TDLC for permission to join the 1913 Labour Day parade. Denison and Stowe-Gullen had already done so in 1909, but the CSA participation in 1913 was more widely celebrated. *Woman's Century* reported that the suffragists' intention was to "impress the immense crowds" with "the reality of the movement for franchise equality." One stumbling block had been the timing of the parade: unlike their working-class counterparts, too many suffragists were out of town on extended summer holidays. However, Denison, Gordon, and MacIver rode in a horse-drawn carriage decorated with yellow bunting, maple leaves, and two signs: one read "Votes for Women" and the other stated "Toronto Women want to be Citizens." They were joined by Ida Edna Fagan Campbell (1863–1919), the wife of a Toronto bookseller, mother of three, and president of the Beaches Progressive Club. *Woman's Century* insisted that the four suffragists attracted much applause and only the occasional "hiss" by "men who did not look like Canadians." It later admitted, however, that the carriage was pelted with acorns, burrs, and celery. MacIver nevertheless said that she took comfort in the warm welcome by the unionists, whom she called "our friends" and good allies because they "have votes behind them."

MacIver gave no hint of the often uncomfortable relations between suffragists and the labour movement. Yet the CSA involvement in the Labour Day parade triggered a public airing of the problem. In a letter to the *Industrial Banner*, Prenter called the CSA arrogant for joining the parade, given that none of the women belonged to a union. She apologized to unionists for the "butting in" and assured them that "suffragists of this town are by no means a unit." Instead, she hoped that labour and suffragists could "bring democracy a little closer" without intruding on each other's territory. Prenter's public shaming of her sister suffragists served as a prelude to the friction that would arise in Toronto and splinter the movement in 1914.

The declaration of war in August 1914 sent the entire suffrage movement into a tailspin, and thus it is difficult to measure how the Ontario campaign was affected by the intensifying anti-suffragist dialogue, the fragile labour-suffrage alliance, and British and American militancy. The urgency of the global conflict both stunted and invigorated the final three years of the provincial crusade. Many suffragists shifted to patriotic war work, whereas a minority campaigned for peace. Others pointed to women's wartime volunteerism and paid labour as proof that they deserved equal citizenship rights. With a new Conservative premier, William Howard Hearst, in office, suffragists and allied Liberal MPPs rallied in delegations and bills during 1915–16. Though these efforts were defeated, suffrage victories in Manitoba and Saskatchewan in 1916, followed by British Columbia in early 1917, forced change in Ontario.

Many women are now filled with the spirit of patriotism, and the primal instinct to conserve and help is meritoriously showing itself in work being done, but let not the glamour of victory, nor the sorrow of defeat blind women to the real important issues. The important issue before, during or after the war is Democratic Freedom, and there is no freedom and no democracy while women are a disenfranchised class.

– FLORA MACDONALD DENISON, *WOMEN AND WAR*, 1914

SIX

VICTORY AMID DISCORD AND WAR

"The Emancipation Easter Hatch," *Brantford Expositor,* 3 April 1917.
The suffrage bill passed by the Ontario legislature
is presented as born of women's war work and sacrifice.

FOR ONTARIO SUFFRAGISTS, 1914 was a miserable year. Three franchise bills met defeat in the Legislative Assembly. The first formal anti-suffragist organization approved its constitution. Controversial leader Flora MacDonald Denison resigned her presidency of the Canadian Suffrage Association (CSA) in an attempt to keep the peace amid an increasingly fragmented movement. The Great War forced many activists to abandon the suffrage movement in order to dedicate more time to war or peace work. Optimistic dreams that soldiering male kin would return home by Christmas disappeared. In this grim reality, a suffrage victory felt very far away, a familiar experience for those who were active in, or at least aware of, the movement's forty-year-long cycle of swelling and waning support, small victories and persistent public hostility, allies made and lost, and the fatigue and personal sacrifice attached to fighting legislative obstruction and social norms. Yet, ultimately, all the obstacles proved no match for decades of momentum and the persistence of hundreds of suffragists. After victories in Western Canada, in the spring of 1917, Ontario finally became a member of the suffrage camp.

It took another year for Ottawa to remove exclusion by sex from the federal franchise, and property qualifications were not eliminated provincially and federally until 1920. Notably, however, property ownership persisted for voting and holding municipal office in most Ontario communities until well into the 1970s. This routinely disenfranchised many tenants who paid lower rents. Equally toxic was the persistence of racial exclusion. The assimilationist goals of the federal Indian Act meant that the

First Nations people who held Indian status were barred from voting provincially in Ontario until 1954. By 1950, most Inuit men and women had voting rights; however, it was not commonplace for ballot boxes to be brought to Arctic communities until 1962. While all other Ontario women saw their political rights expand, Indigenous women endured a colonial system of governance that offered little political autonomy or participation. In fact, the only First Nations woman with Indian status who was able to vote in Ontario between 1917 and the Second World War was Edith Anderson Monture, a Haudenosaunee military nurse. Her identity as a veteran of the Great War trumped the exclusions of the Indian Act.

PRE-WAR FRICTION AMONG SUFFRAGISTS

In the years leading up to the First World War, multiple suffrage organizations operated in Toronto and across the province, often harmoniously. Under Flora MacDonald Denison's leadership, the CSA focused on the provincial vote, whereas its local branch, the Toronto Suffrage Association (TSA), led by Dr. Margaret Gordon, concentrated on adding married women to the municipal electorate. Affiliated branches were active in Ottawa, London, Mount Forrest, Owen Sound, and Port Arthur-Fort William. CSA representation also existed in Montreal, Saint John, Victoria, and Winnipeg. In Toronto, new suffrage bodies emerged within specific interest groups. Focused on the fight for equal pay, the Toronto Teachers' Suffrage Association was a workplace collective, and the Junior Suffrage Club catered to young women and girls. Also active was the Men's League for Equal Franchise led by James Hughes. Most Woman's Christian Temperance Unions (WCTU), Local Councils of Women, and Progressive Clubs had franchise committees, which meant that even if a city or town lacked a club devoted to suffrage, residents could join the cause. Unfortunately, no suffrage association – even the CSA – left records. Newspaper reports and personal papers are the only guides to the scope, ideology, and work.

By 1912, however, good relations had become increasingly uncertain, caused in part by an exodus of members from the CSA.
More broadly, resentment simmered over Denison's leadership.
Augusta Stowe-Gullen and her sister physicians remained with
Denison, but Alice Chown, Sonia Leathes, Constance Boulton, and,
later, Harriet Prenter joined with Constance Hamilton to form the
Equal Franchise League (EFL). Since both groups included conservative feminists (Hamilton and Boulton), as well as socialist-
leaning feminists (Chown and Prenter), no tidy ideological reason
explains the spilt. Those who set up the EFL tended to be newer to
the movement and may have felt estranged from the inner circle,
whom Dr. Emily Stowe or her daughter had recruited. Unlike that
group, Hamilton and most of her followers did not work outside
the home and may have felt alienated from the older generation
of professional women who had long been dominant in the CSA.
Chown dismissed rumours of tension, explaining that the new organization would federate with the CSA. She observed that the
CSA had dozens of new members but that the deadline to qualify
to vote at its upcoming annual meeting had passed; thus, suffragists wishing for more immediate leadership opportunities
started their own group. The EFL decided to prioritize voter education, concentrating on educating women about "social evils to
be remedied after suffrage was attained," rather than on getting
the vote. Denison herself attended the first EFL meeting to welcome it to the movement.

There were early signs of co-operation – members of both the
CSA and the EFL walked side by side in the 1913 Washington suffrage parade. They also collaborated on the 1913–14 municipal
referendum campaign, a major undertaking led by the TSA. On
Gordon's urging, Toronto City Council agreed to hold a referendum on expanding the municipal electorate to include married
female property holders. Partly due to the strong participation
of single and widowed women, the New Year's Day 1914 referendum passed massively: 26,516 to 12,606. In the aftermath of this

achievement, Gordon sent letters to the mayors and reeves of 850 Ontario town and city councils, asking them to hold suffrage referendums. This province-wide initiative, co-ordinated with Local Councils of Women and the WCTU, brought in phenomenal results.

From rural hamlets to industrial centres, another seventy cities and municipalities from every region of the province held suffrage referendums or circulated petitions by the end of 1914. Supporters outside of Toronto included the province's biggest cities – Hamilton, Ottawa, St. Catharines, and Port Arthur-Fort William. Smaller suburban and rural districts were also supportive: Albemarle, Artemesia, Arthur, Ayr, Beeton, Biddulph, Blenheim, Bobcaygeon, Bosanquet, Bruce, Caradoc, Cayuga, Charlotteville, Chesley, Clinton, Collingwood, Dunchurch, East Zorra, Englehart, Etobicoke, Fergus, Galt, Goderich, Gosfield North, Griffith and Matawatchan, Hagerman, Haileybury, Harley, Huntsville, Kenilworth, Keewatin, Kincardine, Lakehurst, Lindsay, Matheson, Meaford, Medonte, Midland, Mitchell, Monck, Morley, Mount Brydges, New Toronto, North Williamsburg, O'Connor, Onondaga, Orono, Paisley, Paris, Parkhill, Penetanguishene, Port Carling, Rawdon, Renfrew, St. Marys, Springbrook, Stafford, Strathroy, Thessalon, Thorold, Tisdale, Vanbrugh, Wainfleet, Watt, Watford, and Welland. Over the next year, more than one hundred additional communities sent Gordon favourable petitions. The overwhelmingly positive response suggests that a sea change had occurred in mainstream opinion. Yet Premier Hearst remained obstinate, stating that because municipal voters were mostly men and single women, the results failed to show what the "great majority of women" actually wanted, especially married women.

Despite co-operation, the EFL withdrew as a CSA affiliate in the spring of 1914. Ontario suffragists were not alone in experiencing such fragmentation. Both the United States and Britain had a long history of rival groups. Emmeline Pankhurst would soon eject her daughter Sylvia from the WSPU because of political

Suffrage supporters in Little Britain, an agricultural village in
the Kawartha Lakes region, gather at the home of Mary Jane Hall
(seated at far left) in about 1910. The wife of a doctor, Hall rallied
members of local women's organizations, including the WCTU,
to create a suffrage club.

differences. Partisan politics and disagreements over strategy
split the Montreal Local Council of Women during the same
period. Lack of evidence makes it difficult to ascertain exactly
why the EFL withdrew from the CSA, though hostility between
Hamilton and Denison appears to be at its root.

From the CSA perspective, the EFL presence at meetings had
produced "a spirit of jealousy" and "absolute lack of harmony,"
which put the cause itself in jeopardy. According to EFL sources,
"rebellion had been brewing" for months between "old regime"
and "progressive" members, the latter disenchanted by the CSA
executive's lack of democracy and transparency. Denison's sympathy with militants and membership in the WSPU also fuelled discord. In particular, a comment she made during Pankhurst's 1913

Toronto visit caused a great stir. Pankhurst had recently declared herself at war against the British government. Under this context, Denison provocatively stated, "I shouldn't condemn Mrs. Pankhurst any more for shooting Premier Asquith," she said, imagining a hypothetical confrontation between the suffragette and the British prime minister, "than I condemn British soldiers for shooting down the Boers in the South African war." To Denison, Pankhurst was a warrior, plain and simple. It was only natural that a warrior fought for her cause with violence. Even though Denison couched her proclamation with the insistence that she believed wars were wrong, the next day's headline read: "Mrs. F. McD. Denison says Murder Is Justifiable to Get Vote." Whether one supported Pankhurst or not, no one could argue such hyperbole was productive to the suffrage cause.

In rebuttal, Denison blamed a power-hungry Hamilton and her "obstructionist" supporters. She denied that the CSA had allied with Pankhurst to the detriment of the Canadian movement: "I personally am a great admirer of the woman, and have repeatedly said so, but in an entirely personal capacity, and not in any way hinting that such methods should be introduced to Canada." Given that Denison was the CSA's most prominent voice during the militancy era, some CSA members and the public could readily misinterpret (or rightly interpret) her enthusiasm for Pankhurst. In terms of strategy, dissociating itself from the British suffragettes probably made EFL activism more palatable. However, the EFL's attitude to the WSPU was far from clear-cut. Only a month after it spilt from the CSA, the EFL hosted British suffragette Dorothy Pethick, who recounted the horror of her fourteen-day prison term, hunger strike, and forced feeding in 1914.

If militancy were an uncertain contributor to disagreement, class was more obvious. As a dressmaker turned entrepreneur, Denison was set apart from women like Hamilton, who had never needed to support themselves. In a letter to Rosaline Kennedy Torrington (1851–1941), president of the National Council of

After residing in England and Winnipeg, Constance
Hamilton jumped into the Toronto suffrage cause during
the early twentieth century, quickly sparring with Flora
MacDonald Denison over the movement's direction and
leadership. One outcome of the 1917 suffrage victory was
Hamilton's election to Toronto City Council in 1920.

Women of Canada (NCWC), Denison alluded to social condescension: "For myself, I understand the smug snobbery existing in
Toronto Church and Social circles and do not look for courtesy
but for my position as President of the Canadian Suffrage Association." Prejudice was echoed in an anonymous letter of 1914: addressed to "Mrs. Flora Denison, Dressmaker," it warned her to cease
her critique of Hamilton, whom it referred to as the "honored

president of the Equal Franchise." "Keep to your own class," it
ordered the veteran suffragist, and leave the fight to "good ladies."
It named Sonia Leathes and Constance Boulton as examples of respectable women. In addition to attacking her class, the term
"good ladies" may have referred to Denison's recent separation
from her husband. In the past, Denison had been protected by
Augusta Stowe-Gullen and the other progressive professionals,
but her open admiration for Pankhurst and her status as a crafts-
woman, not to mention her more eccentric beliefs about religion
and free love, increasingly made her a pariah.

Amid this feud, the CSA took a boldly partisan stance for the
first time. During the 1914 provincial election, it came out in
favour of the Liberals, likely alienating any suffragists – such as
Hamilton – who supported the Conservative Party. In "An Open
Letter to the Electors," penned by Stowe-Gullen, Denison, and
Gordon, the CSA condemned the Whitney Conservatives for
their long-standing "antagonism" and urged voters to opt for
the Ontario Liberals, whose new leader, Newton Wesley Rowell,
had publicly endorsed temperance and women's suffrage. As the
MPP for Oxford North, Rowell, a lawyer and lay preacher, had
sometimes crossed party lines to vote in favour of the municipal
and provincial suffrage bills of Conservative members Thomas
Richard Whitesides and John Wesley Johnson, Labour member
Allan Studholme, and Liberal member John Campbell Elliott – all
of which were defeated between 1912 and 1914.

Rowell's suffrage sympathies owed something to his sister,
Sarah Alice Rowell Wright. Raised in a strict Methodist household
in London, Ontario, both siblings inherited a keen sense of
duty and were high achievers in their respective realms of public
service. A quintessential clubwoman and ardent temperance
crusader, Wright held membership and leadership positions in
multiple local, national, and international temperance and
women's organizations. Most notably, she was elected president of
the WCTU national body in 1905, a post she held until her death

in 1930. A relative latecomer to suffrage, Wright became president of London's new Equal Suffrage Club during the 1910s and later threw her weight behind Hamilton. Like many suffragists, Wright contextualized her interest in women's voting rights as a means through which to create a more moral world. Unfortunately, her brother Rowell turned out to be a relatively powerless ally in the election. Much to the CSA's dismay, the Liberals did badly, winning only twenty seats against the eighty-three taken by the Conservatives. Later, Rowell was better able to fulfill his role as an advocate of women's rights when he returned to the practice of law and argued before the Supreme Court on behalf of the Famous Five's case that women were considered persons and were therefore eligible for senate appointments.

With the CSA loss of membership and influence, Hamilton introduced an ambitious plan to create a nationwide suffrage movement under EFL leadership. Suffragists across the country were invited to the first EFL annual general meeting. Representatives from Montreal, Winnipeg, Ottawa, and London took part, and support came later from a newly formed club in Brantford. The latter couched its recent initiative in decidedly non-militant terms: "Brantford women are never dull nor dead, but as we are somewhat peacefully inclined we trust that you do not demand too much excitement." According to Leathes, the EFL aimed to "gain the confidence of the somewhat timid and conservative country woman." To this end, it invited 740 branches of the Women's Institutes (WI) because it knew that rural women wanted to "hear more." Aware that WI founder Adelaide Hoodless had banned using WI funds for suffrage activity, Leathes offered EFL funding for suffrage speakers. Hamilton also made an effort to engage working-class women. In 1915, she invited an organizer from the Union of Waitresses and Women Cooks, to address EFL members. By this point, many of the affiliated Toronto groups, including the Beaches Progressive Club, the Junior Suffrage Club, and the Teachers' Suffrage Association, had switched allegiance to Hamilton, dropping out of the CSA entirely. The EFL also had the endorsement of Nellie McClung, one of Western Canada's most prominent suffragists. Fragmentation had, however, not ended. By 1915, Harriet Prenter had formed an entirely new club: the Political Equality League, borrowing the name of McClung's Winnipeg suffrage club. Given that Prenter was becoming increasingly sympathetic to socialism and pacifism, her parting with the staunch Conservative Hamilton was foreseeable.

Following the annual general meeting, Hamilton reorganized the EFL into three distinct divisions, aiming at the municipal, provincial, and federal franchises. Hamilton put Boulton in charge of the municipal division. The provincial division came under the leadership of Sarah Ann Armstrong Ormsby, the wife of a prominent Toronto industrialist, who opened her large estate in Mimico to suffrage gatherings. Hamilton herself pursued plans to form a new national association and, to reflect this goal, changed the name of the EFL to the National Union of Woman Suffrage Associations (NUWSA), whose title was similar to those of moderate suffrage bodies in both the United States and Britain. As it turned out, wartime disruptions and entrenched Western and Atlantic provincial movements stymied Hamilton's national vision.

With the CSA struggling for relevance, Denison resigned as president in the fall of 1914 and was replaced by Gordon. Her last act was to preside over a ceremony in which a bust of Dr. Emily Stowe, commissioned by the CSA, was placed in Toronto City Hall. After her resignation, Denison moved to Napanee, working as a dressmaker to support her son's university education as an architect in the United States until his studies were waylaid by the war. Occasionally, she returned to Toronto for CSA meetings and delegations to the Legislative Assembly, and was briefly employed by the New York state suffrage movement. Increasingly, however, Denison shifted her attention to other interests, notably spiritualism, socialism, the Walt Whitman movement, and Bon Echo, her wilderness retreat.

SUFFRAGE DEBATED AT KENT PUBLIC SCHOOL

Children's thoughts on suffrage rarely make it into the historic record. One incident from May 1914 in Toronto demonstrates that young people were well aware of the controversial issue and had indeed chosen sides. Furthermore, the issue of suffrage affected their own decisions about student governance. According to the Toronto Star, *the male students at Kent Public School, many of whom the paper described as coming from families fallen on hard times, were keen to start their own parliament in order to participate in the "onward march of democracy and self government." An election occurred to elect a speaker, president, cabinet ministers, and leader of the opposition. Two parties, the Progressives and the Independents, were created, and both were led by boys who were members of the school's cadet program. Apparently, the question of woman's suffrage dominated the election. The Progressives wanted female students to be allowed to participate in parliament. The Independents thought it better for girls to have their own club. The Independents won with a slight majority, meaning that no representatives from the girls' classes were allowed to participate. Subsequently, the parliament addressed issues involving athletics, cadets, and discipline, described as "matters of real interest to the boys." Participation in such a venture, wagered the* Star, *"would make men out of scholars." Nothing further was said about the girls. This piece of microhistory is a reminder of how the battle for suffrage was waged in many corners and that the training for boys to see themselves as active players in democracy – as voters, elected figures, and soldiers – started young.*

HOMEFRONT BATTLES FOR WAR AND PEACE

Following the assassination of Archduke Franz Ferdinand of Austria, Britain joined its allies, Russia and France, in declaring war on Germany on 4 August 1914. As a British dominion, Canada was automatically at war. Over the next four years, more than 600,000 Canadian men left the country; approximately 10 percent of those in service were killed, and another 172,000 were wounded. Recruitment campaigns, such as Savile Lumley's poster – "Daddy, what did <u>you</u> do in the Great War?" – positioned enlistment as a necessary defence of empire and a validation of male patriotism and masculinity. Similarly, women were expected to support the war in ways that reflected their respectability, patriotism, and feminine self-sacrifice. Wives and mothers were pushed hard to cheerfully release male kin to the conflict and to encourage others. Unmarried women were urged to meet labour shortages by performing industrial and farm work that was usually restricted to men or to serve as volunteer or military nurses. From knitting to victory gardens and war charities, female domestic and organizational skills were directed to the morale and well-being of soldiers and to the assistance of civilian refugees from Europe. Gender alone did not create a universal experience; some men and women defied gendered expectations, and race and ethnicity, political affiliation, and religious identities also drove choices. Vast numbers of women across Ontario nevertheless mobilized to win the war.

After August 1914, the defining question for suffragists was whether to continue their crusade. For some, this was less of a conscious decision than a new rhythm in which peacetime efforts at social reform were displaced by war-related volunteerism. Furthermore, the absence of husbands and fathers meant that women became the temporary heads of households, which could reduce their time for outside pursuits. Most suffrage associations did not disband but simply turned to war-related causes.

The NUWSA and the CSA joined forces to found a Suffragists' War Auxiliary, which raised money for war charities and encouraged recruitment. Further, they aimed to "prepare women to take the place of men released for active service." Under the mantle of the NUWSA, Hamilton co-ordinated support for widows' pensions, which evolved into fundraising for the Patriotic Fund, a national war charity that dispensed relief to military dependants. For their part, the TSA and CSA suffragists fundraised for French war orphans.

In 1915, *Everywoman's World* declared that female enfranchisement was either a "certainty" or "a dead issue," depending on whom was consulted. The NUWSA opted to suspend all suffrage effort for the entirety of the war, a decision that Hamilton characterized as "the only thing any woman with a woman's heart could do." Meanwhile, the CSA intended to engage in war work and continue to lobby for political equality. Denison outlined her argument for doing so in the seven-page booklet *Women and War*, in which she argued that "this war is the most conclusive argument that has ever blazed its electric message across the sky of human consciousness in favor of politically equality." Not only was it a war in which democratic freedom was at stake but, Denison insisted, women needed a vote to be able to properly protect the lives of their sons. Hamilton publicly condemned the CSA's choice, insisting that the war required a united effort and that women who allocated time, money, or resources elsewhere were deplorable. Nevertheless, she agreed with Denison that the war portended a revolution: "We are on the eve of a great social re-creation" in which "great results may come, that barriers will be broken down – barriers of class prejudice, or sex-inequality, of national and racial difference and misunderstanding."

If the conflict were indeed a struggle for democracy, a better deal needed to be pursued at home, as well as on the battlefield. Thanks to the private papers of suffragists Anne J. Barrie and Margaret Cole, we can see how women combined war work with suffrage activism. Barrie, one of Port Arthur's leading suffragists, carried on throughout the war as president of the local Women's Press Club, vice-president of the local WCTU, and executive member of the West Algoma Equal Suffrage Association. Her weekly calendar from January 1915, when the battles of the Eastern Front were centre-stage, mentions "get out voting helpers," probably referring to efforts with the Municipal Franchise Referendum Committee. Tuesday through Friday, she attended meetings of the suffrage association, the WCTU, the Music Club, and the Women's Press Club. Saturday found her at a Ladies' Aid Hospital bake sale and a concert, probably fundraisers for war charities. She also kept a scrapbook, and as it progressed through 1915–16, it focused more and more on the war effort. Articles about the Red Cross joined others that spotlighted suffrage-related war work around the province. Her own CSA-affiliated suffrage group held weekly card games to raise money for the Patriotic Fund. Meanwhile, Cole, a resident of Ottawa, dealt with personal tragedy amid global anxiety. Between 1915 and 1917, her diary catalogued the sorrow of the war, including worries about her son and daughter serving overseas, and hopes for her temperance and suffrage endeavours. Through the YWCA and WCTU, she hosted talks by McClung, Pankhurst, and pacifist suffragist Laura Hughes. She also became president of her branch of the Equal Suffrage Association.

If Constance Hamilton suggested that wartime suffrage commitments were potentially disloyal, peace work was far more traitorous. Until the time of the Great War, many local, national, and international women's organizations rallied around the cause of peace. Preventing war united maternal and egalitarian feminists and mobilized religious and socialist circles. But when the hypothetical became the real, peacemaking lost its respectability; cries for peace were considered subversive and generated suspicion about peace activists, conscientious objectors, and pacifists – male or female. Denison continued to champion peace amid war; sections of *Women and War* encouraged women to oppose militarism.

The Women's Home Guard, the brainchild of concert musician Jessica McNab and suffragist Laura McCully, took up the most unconventional war work. The paramilitary club trained women as a reserve militia, prepared to defend Canada should the home front be invaded. Under the supervision of Lieutenant-Colonel James Galloway, a retired militia officer, female recruits dressed in uniform, marched, learned to shoot and fence, and took first aid courses. While figures vary, up to one thousand women – mainly single, middle class, and of British heritage – were thought to have participated in at least one of the meetings in 1915–16. Nicknamed Toronto's Amazons by the Toronto Star, *the Women's Home Guard was alternately cheered and mocked by the press for their efforts. Forced to defend his involvement, Galloway declared to the* Toronto News, *"Some men have said to me, 'but how can you have anything to do with it? There are suffragettes in it.' I don't care whether there are suffragettes or not. They are organizing for service [and] that's all that matters." Owing to a public falling out between McNab and McCully, not to mention heightened public ridicule, the privately funded venture was short lived. Nevertheless, the Home Guard experiment represents the diverse ways women thought they could contribute to the war effort. Considering the association between manhood, citizenship, and soldiering, excelling at home defence could have given suffragists more evidence to demonstrate that women's value lay not only as participants of democracy, but as its defenders.*

In April 1915, over a thousand delegates from neutral and belliger-
ent nations gathered in The Hague for a meeting of the International
Congress of Women. Canadian delegate Laura Hughes (third from
left) was among those who heartily condemned militarism and
debated solutions for peace. This conference prompted the formation
of the Women's International League for Peace and Freedom, a transnational feminist organization that was committed to bringing
about permanent peace.

Contrasting male aggression with more positive female qualities,
she stated that "had women stood shoulder to shoulder with men
in thinking out world problems this war would never have been."
Gordon shared Denison's anti-war sentiments. Prior to the war,
she had chaired the Toronto Local Council of Women subcommit-
tee dedicated to peace and arbitration, and she continued to work
for peace throughout the war, vocally opposing conscription. She
questioned why women so overwhelmingly supported it: Would
mothers whose sons were in the trenches really be so anxious for
other women's sons to die? Her actions prompted the *Globe* to
condemn her and the committee's efforts as "dangerous ground,"
particularly in opposition to conscription. Such pacifism, even
framed as an expression of maternal feminism, further marginalized CSA members.

Ultimately, only a handful of Ontario suffragists persevered for peace. The most prominent was Laura Hughes (1886–1966), daughter of long-time suffrage allies James and Adaline Hughes. She attended the 1915 Women's Peace Congress in The Hague, where Julia Grace Wales, a Canadian academic who taught at the University of Wisconsin, presented a mediation plan for peace. Inspired, Laura returned to Toronto, hoping that the plan would bring the war to an end. She joined with Alice Chown to form a Canadian branch of the Woman's Peace Party, which had been founded in Washington, DC, under the leadership of Jane Addams. It was affiliated with the newly formed Women's International League for Peace and Freedom (WILPF). Illustrating how choices could tear apart families, Hughes was also the niece of Sam Hughes, minister of militia and defence for Prime Minister Borden, in charge of the Canadian military forces. Reportedly, he offered his niece a gift of land if she would surrender her peace activism.

Hughes was closely aligned with labour politics and firmly linked militarism to capitalism. In 1916, she concluded, "The militarists have more power than ever. And after this war the international armaments trust, which is largely in control of the manufacture of munitions on both sides, will have control of most of the money of the world, and therefore be very powerful; and it won't allow its market to be destroyed if it can help it." On behalf of the Toronto District Labour Council, Hughes went undercover in a munition factory and wrote a scathing report of the conditions in which its female employees worked. She encountered routine harassment, with a pro-war crowd threatening to overturn her car. In 1917, her marriage to an American conscientious objector led her to anti-war work in the United States. Another WILPF activist was Harriet Prenter, who, like Stowe-Gullen, had earlier opposed compulsory cadet training for schoolboys. Such commitments divided them from the editor of *Woman's Century*, Jessie Campbell MacIver, who urged NCWC members to consign anti-war materials from Hughes and Prenter "to the wastebasket." In her opinion, talk of peace should not precede victory on the battlefield.

Emmeline Pankhurst, militant suffragette and critic of the government, surprised many supporters with her passionate ratification of the war effort. In September 1914, while recovering from her tenth hunger strike, she insisted that the vote would have to wait until British democracy was preserved from German barbarism. Suddenly a patriotic spokesperson for the very government she had resisted, Pankhurst advocated conscripting men for military service and women for industrial work. She also used WSPU funds to open a home for illegitimate children who had been fathered by deployed soldiers and abandoned by mothers burdened by social stigma and poverty. In aid of recruitment, Pankhurst toured Canada in 1916, barnstorming eight Ontario towns and cities. In Ottawa, she was feted by the wives of parliamentarians, and she addressed the YWCA and the Equal Suffrage Association. In the past, Pankhurst had urged women to defy tradition and the law, but now she asked them to defend the government and dedicate their energies to the war effort. Having arrived in Canada just as the federal government forged its controversial plans for conscription, which roused massive opposition in Quebec and in many progressive communities, Pankhurst warned Canadians that victory required unity. Despite her patriotic rhetoric, familiar suffrage themes surfaced in her speeches. She pointed to the war as doing "more than generations of speaking and lecturing to vindicate the claims so often made" by suffragists that women could do great things for their country. She added, "We begged, argued and even threatened for it, but it needed a war to give us full opportunity to serve."

Many Ontario suffragists agreed. One of these was Agnes Maule Machar (1837–1927), a Kingston author who identified as a Christian socialist, feminist, and novelist. Active in the suffrage movement since the 1870s, when she was a corresponding member of the Toronto Women's Literary Club, Machar had long been a defender of women's rights, particularly in regard to women's access to education. In "The Citizenship of Women," which she wrote for *Woman's Century,* she argued that "the present colossal war has, by its very magnitude and urgency, shown clearly that in war time the State must depend on its women, as well as on its men." Women defended the Empire by replacing men in ammunition factories and performing medical work in hospitals and with the Red Cross. Machar labelled women's maternalism "heroic" because mothers sacrificed "their hearts' treasures." More than ever, the vote was "a charter of freedom and civic responsibility for men, and no less for women. Anything else makes her an incomplete partner in the commonwealth." Addressing the Dane County Equal Suffrage League in Timmins, one male supporter echoed Machar, calling Red Cross nurses "almost as indispensable as the soldier" and emphasizing that "women in war do their share of the work and more than bear their share of the suffering." Such widespread praise for women's war work rapidly became a refrain among politicians, as they strove to account for their change of heart on female suffrage.

Long-standing xenophobia sometimes contaminated this perspective. Anne Barrie's friend, a Mrs. Fife of Port Arthur, pointed out that because so many Canadian-born men had died in Belgium and France, the voting power of "naturalized aliens may in many localities be in the majority." As a result, female enfranchisement was now all the more urgent if "the integrity of the British Institutions" were to be preserved. Given the heightened anxiety of Anglo-Celtic Canadians about the loyalties of French Canadians and eastern and central European immigrants, Fife's nativist rationale found listeners. Whereas anti-feminists had previously damned the vote as a threat to tradition, the war gave it the potential to bring order to chaos.

VOTES FOR (SOME) WOMEN

Western Canada's enfranchisement victory worked with war-time inspiration to strengthen Ontario suffragists. In Manitoba, the Conservative governments of Rodmond Roblin and his predecessors had long waylaid suffrage delegations. In one famous 1914 exchange with Nellie McClung, Roblin insisted that good women simply did not want the franchise. In 1915, his government was swept out of office by the Liberals. They passed a woman's suffrage act in January 1916, making Manitoba the first province to enfranchise women and grant them the right to stand for election. In the spring of 1916, Saskatchewan and Alberta followed with identical legislation. Ontario suffragists immediately set out to shame their politicians. The West Algoma Equal Suffrage Association addressed Premier Hearst in the spring of 1916:

> In past history, Ontario has been the banner province, leading in educational matters, now she is taking a backward step, allowing the bright young western provinces to be foremost in the enfranchisement of their women. It would seem as if the women of Ontario were not so intelligent as western women, but in any case, the western men have proved more abundant chivalry and justice.

Women's wartime labour and sacrifice of husbands, brothers, and sons for the Empire demonstrated their well-earned right of citizenship. Whereas past arguments insisted that they deserved the vote simply by virtue of being human or mothers, the war emphasized their value as citizens.

In March 1916, Liberal MPP William MacDonald (North Bruce) presented a new suffrage bill for Ontario. Still, Premier Hearst resisted, insisting that war-related priorities took precedence. He had previously cited Pankhurst's militancy as proof that women were unfit for the franchise, but now he used her apostasy to justify his opposition: "Women of the liberal and conservative persuasion are working side by side in splendid patriotic work." Therefore, "it would be a great mistake to introduce any measure that would have the slightest tendency to divide them." He also hoisted old arguments in implying that women were too irrational to be good citizens. The recalcitrant legislature defeated MacDonald's bill. Ottawa proved somewhat more accommodating, when, after a similar debate, Prime Minister Robert Borden promised to consider female suffrage.

By the fall of 1916, NUWSA provincial leader Sarah Ormsby had called all suffragists, even those who had halted the campaign, such as her friend Hamilton, to join a final push. She proposed another petition and drew upon the expertise of Margaret Gordon, who had managed to procure such outstanding results with her municipal referendum project. Gordon had withdrawn to care for her daughter, who died that year, but with Ormsby's call, she now she returned to the fray. The city of Ottawa skipped the petition stage and went straight to a plebiscite in favour of women's suffrage that was narrowly defeated, 4,775 to 4,759. Meanwhile, four high-profile public forums in Toronto rallied suffragist supporters. The first, in October 1916, saw federal Liberal Party leader Wilfrid Laurier backhandedly approve suffrage in a speech to the Women's Canadian Club in London, Ontario. "I do not think that women's suffrage will achieve all the good its exponents claim for it," he said, but added, "And I am sure it will not result in all the bad its opponents expect from it." This tepid conversion allowed provincial leader Newton Rowell to officially add suffrage to the Ontario Liberal platform when the legislature opened in February 1917.

The other three events – a debate, a play, and a conference – affirmed determination to renew the campaign. After Laurier's speech, Prenter debated three anti-suffragists at the Toronto WCTU headquarters, "resolved that in the interests of humanity women should be enfranchised." An equally theatrical event occurred in Hamilton during the annual WCTU meeting. Mrs. W.H. Allen of Newmarket organized a tableau that recollected Alice Paul's White House picket. Dressed in white, wearing yellow suffrage sashes, and holding shields with the slogan "We Want the Vote," suffragists represented enfranchised countries, states, and provinces. In the background stood a bound woman in black, representing Ontario. At the end, a woman in white freed the province and everyone sang "Better Days Are Coming." Finally, in a rare show of co-operation, Ormsby, Hamilton, Prenter, and Gordon addressed an all-day suffrage conference in Toronto that was dedicated to preparing women for the vote. Here, once again, was a showcase for their resolve and talent.

When the Ontario legislature opened in February 1917, Rowell took the initiative. He invited Conservatives and Liberals to join in a non-partisan suffrage bill. As precedent, he cited the unanimous passage of the 1916 Ontario Temperance Act, which had banned the sale of alcohol as an emergency war measure. Rowell's call took the form of a motion attached as an amendment to Hearst's Throne Speech, but Hearst himself declared the motion out of order. After a five-day deliberation, the Speaker agreed. In the meantime, three different suffrage bills came forward, one presented by frequent supporter Liberal William MacDonald and two, one for municipal and one for provincial suffrage, by Conservative John Wesley Johnson (Hastings West). On 27 February, each bill received a second reading. Hearst provided the showstopper when, for the first time publicly, he spoke in favour of enfranchisement. Citing women's war work, the premier concluded, "Having taken our women into partnership with us in our tremendous task I ask, can we justly deny them a share in the government of the country, the right to have a say about the making of the laws they have been so heroically trying to defend? My answer is, I think not." His conversion was undercut by his continued insistence that most women were indifferent to the vote. Not surprisingly, the Liberals saw his transformation as grounded in wily political pragmatism rather than principle. Hearst also spoke about the possibility that women might be the deciders of Ontario's future: with so many men overseas and lost to war, women could be the majority of voters in the following election. Nevertheless, the package of women's suffrage bills unanimously passed, granting the municipal and provincial franchise to single and married women. On 12 April 1917, the bills, repackaged as the Ontario Franchise Act, received Royal Assent. Unlike the Prairies, Ontario did not empower women to hold elected office. Giving tacit approval to the reform was Isabella Jane Duncan Hearst, the premier's wife, who joined several other Conservative spouses on the house floor when the bill passed into law.

A day later, the *Toronto Star* published a domestic comedy cartoon titled *Keeping Up with the Joneses*. The four-panel strip of that day, entitled "Showing How Ethelbert Fell," featured Aloysius, the increasingly exasperated family patriarch, lambasting a younger man, Ethelbert, for reneging on his promise to oppose suffrage. "You're a fine example of man, you are?" he lectures. "You was going to stick with ME on this here suffrage question, huh?" Given that the cartoon was syndicated out of New York, it was not a direct satire on Hearst's about-face. It nevertheless conveyed collective male angst. Whereas Ethelbert blamed a flock of pretty women for his change of heart, political expediency appears to have had the same effect on the premier. British Columbia had enfranchised women just a week before Ontario. With all the Western provinces in line, suffrage may have appeared inevitable. Liberal governments had been women's champions out west, two of them immediately after defeating Conservative majorities. Ontario Conservatives hoped to steal Rowell's thunder (not to mention future voters) and retain power. Meanwhile, Prime Minister Borden, facing a federal election in the fall of 1917, had started discussions about limited enfranchisement. In particular, he focused on the female kin of soldiers, who seemed likely to support conscription. Borden's calculation encouraged Hearst to accept suffrage as part of the Conservative Party's national vision.

Forty-one years after the founding of the Toronto Women's Literary Club, Ontario women finally had the vote. The paternalistic *Toronto Star* reassured its readers: suffragists in the visitors' gallery at the legislature demonstrated "no hysterics over victory," only "wonder, pleasure." A cheerful quote from Gordon downplayed any radicalism: "Just delighted that it's really true. We've worked hard for it and should have had it long ago. It will benefit Ontario in every way." Accompanied by her niece, Stowe-Gullen paid tribute to her mother's efforts as a suffrage pioneer and expressed amazement that their shared dream had become a reality. Perhaps more threatening for erstwhile defenders of male privilege, Hamilton foresaw a future in which "we are going to be taken into partnership. Wherever women have had the franchise they have forwarded legislation along the lines of their interests." Also pointing toward the future, Ida Campbell stressed that the work of suffragists was not over. Their next duty would be to "train the women to use the vote" as well as fight for suffrage elsewhere in Canada and federally. Following this victory, voter lists needed updating to include all female British subjects over twenty-one who had the same property qualifications as men.

AN EXCEPTIONAL VOTE: CHARLOTTE EDITH ANDERSON MONTURE

Almost all Ontario women gained the provincial vote in 1917. Unlike the franchise laws of British Columbia, which specifically excluded people of Asiatic descent from the vote, Ontario's contained no specific racial exclusions. This is not because Ontario was more progressive, only that fewer non-white immigrants had settled within its borders. For their part, First Nations women (and men) were left out due to the restrictions of the federal Indian Act, unless they chose to relinquish their Indian status.

Between 1876 and 1917, few men opted for enfranchisement as they would automatically lose their status. In 1885, John A. Macdonald's revisions to the Franchise Act enabled some First Nations men living east of Lake Superior to vote in the federal elections of 1887 and 1891. As a result, Ontario Liberals and Conservatives courted some Haudenosaunee men on the populous Six Nations of the Grand River Reserve. Such enfranchisement divided the community, with many on the reserve rejecting engagement with colonial politics. In any case, the 1885 extension was short-lived. In 1898, Laurier's Liberals reinstated the Indian Act limitations on Indigenous enfranchisement. These shifts demonstrate the constructed and expedient, not to mention racist, nature of voting rights.

The First World War raised the electoral stakes. In need of reinforcements for the Western Front, Borden was desperate to introduce conscription. Believing that soldiers generally supported it, he passed the Military Voters Act. This enfranchised Canadians serving in the Allied armed forces who were normally denied the federal franchise due to residency requirements, property qualifications, age, race, or sex. Thus, approximately four thousand Indigenous soldiers, plus hundreds of Canadians of Asian descent and three thousand female military nurses in the Canadian Army Medical Corps, gained the federal franchise. In December 1917, these new voters helped sweep Borden's Union coalition into power.

Among the newly enfranchised nurses was Charlotte Edith Anderson Monture (1890–1996), the only First Nations woman known to have served in the Allied armed forces during the First World War. A Mohawk from a prominent family, Monture grew up on the Six Nations of the Grand River Reserve. Racial barriers excluded her from all Canadian nursing schools. Approximately fifty years after Emily Stowe left Canada for New York City, Monture set off to study nursing in New York, staying on after graduation to work as a public health school nurse. When the

United States entered the war in 1917, Monture, now twenty-seven, volunteered as a nurse for the American forces. Back home, some three hundred men from her reserve also volunteered, and some women joined the Six Nations Women's Patriotic League.

Stationed in France, Monture assisted in surgeries, treated the victims of mustard gas, cared for amputees, and offered moral support, often writing letters on behalf of her patients. Her June 1918 diary entry reported, "My pet patient Earl King ... had a hemorrhage at 3:15 A.M. The poor boy lost consciousness immediately. My heart was broken. Cried most of the day and could not sleep." As a member of the Allied forces, Monture was qualified to vote in the December 1917 Canadian federal election, but she was nowhere near a ballot box. She did not exercise her new voting privileges until after the war.

With the war's end, the franchise rights of First Nations veterans remained on record, but policies were often at the arbitrary whim of local Indian agents. Between 1918 and 1924, the Department of Veterans Affairs and the Department of Indian Affairs could be at odds about whether veterans living on reserves were entitled to military pensions and voting privileges. According to Monture's daughter, Helen Monture Moses, her mother enthusiastically voted after she returned to the reserve: "She felt it an obligation, as a Canadian citizen, to exercise this right." Monture married, had five children, and lived on a farm at the edge of the reserve. "We weren't really a political family. We just did our citizen's duty," Moses recalled. "I know my parents were always up on what was going on."

Until the Second World War, when more Indigenous women entered the armed forces, Monture was probably the only enfranchised woman in Ontario who held Indian status. For three decades, as no polling stations existed on her reserve, she had to travel to Onondaga to cast her vote. In 1954, Ontario status Indians, including women, were enfranchised in provincial elections. Monture and her husband then opened their Grand River home as a polling station and acted as scrutineers. Her daughter recalls driving her and a sealed ballot box to the elections office. Although some members of Monture's reserve often opposed involvement in settler politics, her actions suggest that voting was important to her as a Haudenosaunee person, a woman, and a veteran.

Nurses were not the only women who were allowed to vote in the 1917 federal election. Under a different law, the provocative Wartime Elections Act, Borden temporarily granted the federal franchise to women with brothers, fathers, husbands, or sons – living or dead – in the armed forces. The act was meant to reward these particular women for sacrificing their male kin. Unlike the Military Voters Act, it specifically excluded First Nations women with Indian status, an exemption that ignored their equivalent maternal sacrifice. It also implied that these Indigenous women were untrustworthy and potentially disloyal since they were grouped alongside conscientious objectors and enemy aliens, who were disenfranchised by the same act. Overall, the restrictions of the Wartime Elections Act created a voting cohort that was assumed to be personally invested in reinforcing the front and whose loyalty to Canada and Britain was considered absolute.

The act pleased suffragists who felt that women who had made the greatest sacrifices should be enfranchised first. Constance Hamilton and Rosaline Torrington were among its early promoters, joining a telegram campaign to urge leading women's organizations across the country to support the initial wave of limited enfranchisement. Other suffragists were equally fierce in their denunciation. For them, the emphasis was not on principle but on expediency and gerrymandering. As Margaret Gordon pointed out, "It would be more direct and honest if the bill simply stated that all who did not pledge themselves to vote Conservative would be disenfranchised." Augusta Stowe-Gullen similarly objected, dismissing the act as unappealing to most suffragists and decrying a situation in which even an anti-suffragist would be

In this 1919 photo, Monture displays the ribbon bar awarded with
her Allied Victory and US Victory medals. Each chevron on her
sleeve stands for six months of service. The shoulder patch
represents her assignment to the US Army Services of Supply, and
the "AS" indicates that she was in the Advanced Section, providing
care to troops immediately behind the front lines.

permitted to vote, as long as she had the right male kin, whereas
a woman who had campaigned for the franchise but who lacked
the appropriate male relatives remained barred. J.H. Fisher, the
Conservative MP for Brant (home of the Six Nations), also made a
highly unusual intervention on behalf of First Nations women:

I would be remiss in my duty if I did not say a word in regards to the splendid work that has been done along patriotic lines by the Indian women on the reserve. I would simply say, in a word, that the work they have done has not been surpassed in any part of this Dominion, and I trust that when woman suffrage comes, as I have no doubt it will come, the Indian women on the Reserve will be accorded equal rights with their white sisters. They are well deserving of it, and I believe they will exercise the franchise just as well as the white women could or will.

His break with prejudice went largely unheard until after the Second World War. Nevertheless, in May 1918, the long reluctant Union coalition government of Conservatives and Liberals followed through on its promise to enfranchise all, or in fact almost all, female British subjects. Women who were subject to the racial barriers imposed by British Columbia and the Indian Act were still excluded, and additional requirements were placed on certain foreign-born wives. Inmates of prisons, asylums, and charitable institutions were also barred at both the provincial and federal levels. In other words, property and respectability continued to matter. The 1920s would test the consequences of women's voting power in terms of legislative progress and their acceptance as candidates.

EPILOGUE

"MADAM VOTER, INDEED was up bright and early this morning," heralded the *Toronto Star* during the first provincial election following women's enfranchisement. "If there was any doubt concerning her ability to understand the ballots," it patronizingly observed, "that inability did not manifest itself either in her words or actions. She simply came forward, took her ballot, marked it, and walked out with the same air of confidence as the men show." Though more research is needed on voter turnout, fears that Ontario women would be uninterested proved unfounded. As women flexed their voting muscles, Ontario underwent an astonishing, if temporary, political revolution that saw the defeat of William Hearst's Conservative government, and a brand new party, the United Farmers of Ontario (UFO), come to power. This upheaval cannot be attributed entirely to women, but it signalled considerable openness to change and the utility of the ballot. Furthermore, the 1921 federal election victory of Agnes Macphail, an Ontario teacher, appeared to reward suffrage efforts and display public confidence in female politicians. Nevertheless, Macphail's solitary status as the only female MP in the House of Commons until 1935, and the absence of female MPPs in Queen's Park until she won a seat there in 1943, demonstrates the resistance to women as politicians. Unquestionably, the suffrage victory did not erase gendered barriers to their full participation in politics. That work was still ahead, and remains today. Nor did enfranchisement eliminate the need for grassroots activism as a critical tool for women's political engagement.

VOTER EDUCATION

Immediately following the 1917 Ontario Franchise Act, observers debated whether women would vote in a bloc based on gendered

Is Women's Suffrage a Fizzle?

THE VACANT THRONE.
The politicians still are able to say "It was a dangerous experiment to extend the vote to women, but no great harm has been done, for, owing to our prompt efforts they have been taken into the party folds and safely divided."

THE WAY

HUBBY VOTES

VICTOR CHILD

Cartoons by
VICTOR CHILD

Has the woman voter sacrificed the interests of her sex to mere party allegiance?

By ANNE ANDERSON PERRY

Illustration by Victor Child from a 1928 *Maclean's* article by Anne Anderson Perry, scrutinizing whether female enfranchisement changed the landscape of Canadian politics. Titled the "The Vacant Throne," it asserts that women had a negligible impact because they voted just like their husbands. Still more cynically, it suggests that politicians had quickly regrouped to preserve the status quo: "It was a dangerous experiment to extend the vote to women, but no great harm has been done, for, owing to our prompt efforts they have been taken into the party folds and safely divided."

interests or succumb to conventional party politics. "Women must not be attached to any political party," insisted Dr. Elizabeth Smith-Shortt in a speech to the Ottawa Equal Suffrage Association. Elaborating, Smith contended, "The three bogies which women and all other conscientious voters must meet to effect the purification of politics are secret party funds, the patronage evil, and machine nomination." Other pundits debated whether women would overrun one of the long-standing parties. Some suspected that they would flood into the Conservative Party as a thank you to Premier Hearst for their enfranchisement, as well as his enactment of wartime prohibition. Interviewed in March 1917, one Conservative Party organizer in Toronto reported the recent admission of female members and predicted that more would come. After all, "women are just as human as men. I don't think politics will be so very much changed after they get the vote." Dr. Caroline Brown agreed, noting that identification as a Conservative had helped her win election as a school trustee. Others argued that "women voters are not fools," that they would remember the tardiness of the Tory endorsement and would side instead with the Liberals.

Indeed, the Liberal Party saw an upsurge of female members after enfranchisement. For example, when Liberals gathered in Dunnville near Lake Erie to choose their candidate for the Haldimand riding, a third of those who attended were female. In reassuring readers that such participants were thoughtful, respectable voters, the *Toronto Star* stated, "none of them [in Dunnville] looked like frivolous creatures catching up to the latest craze. All of them seemed of the stay-at-home, work-all-the time, mind-your-own-business type who knew how to run a farm or a home, and were interested in children, chores and the high cost of living." The article highlighted the role of a Mrs. Lindsey, granddaughter-in-law of Reform Party hero William Lyon Mackenzie, who spoke in favour of Dunnville's only candidate and castigated Hearst for piggybacking on the Liberals' longer support of suffrage. "Woman would have had the vote long since, but for a prejudice antedating the Old Testament," Lindsey declared. After insisting that she herself would be unchanged by voting, she returned to her knitting, an action that the *Star* implied attested to her womanly credentials. In reality, no single party won the hearts and minds of newly enfranchised women; nor was the party machine challenged en masse by female voters.

In the immediate aftermath of suffrage, almost all women's groups took up voter education, which generally entailed devising strategies to maximize women's votes. Across the province, branches of the social reform bodies and Local Councils of Women hosted candidate talks and organized canvassers. They also helped women run for school boards and city council. The long-established Women's Institutes (WI) and newly formed United Farm Women of Ontario (UFWO) provided spaces, and at times competed, for the political allegiance of their rural constituents. Politicization was a change of pace for the WI, with its traditional anti-suffragist stance, fuelled by the prejudices of Adelaide Hoodless, and its fear of jeopardizing government funding. After 1917, its male superintendent agreed that it could encourage women's interest in political matters that affected rural regions. He nevertheless urged members to remain non-partisan and to leave controversies for special interest organizations. In contrast, the UFWO was openly partisan in its efforts to mobilize farm wives and daughters. It circulated recommended reading lists on politically provocative issues, such as protective tariffs for agricultural goods, rural depopulation, and expanding hydroelectricity.

Voter education also emphasized the practical. In Toronto, a new non-partisan group, the Information Bureau for Women Voters, prepared local women for the 1919 provincial election, which included a referendum on extending prohibition, and for the 1920 municipal election. It set up tables in the city's St. Lawrence market and other civic centres to assist registration, identify voters' correct wards, and explain the timing and conduct of elections. Some problems were beyond its control. As Dr. Augusta Stowe-Gullen pointed out, voter registration was hampered by the chaos of the 1918–19 flu epidemic, with its government-enforced quarantine. The bureau also canvassed women on issues for candidates, which included affordable housing for veterans, public transit, playgrounds, female police officers and

Members of the Mount Pleasant Women's Institute stand before a plague erected in 1962 by the Ontario Archaeological and Historic Sites Board to honour Augusta Stowe-Gullen's birthplace. WI members were originally prohibited from advocating for enfranchisement, but times change, as the photo demonstrates. In 1962, in the long shadow of the suffrage victory, the WI openly took pride in the accomplishments of Stowe-Gullen and her mother, attesting to their work as "ardent feminists" who "organized the Canadian movement for suffrage" and "devoted themselves to the advancement of women in education and public life."

magistrates, and "clean" movies and plays. Since Toronto elections traditionally occurred between Christmas and New Year's Day, the bureau lobbied city council to shift the date to a time when women were burdened with fewer domestic responsibilities. The city did not change the dates until 1950.

Once suffrage had been gained at both the provincial and federal levels, the Canadian Suffrage Association dissolved, leaving

Stowe-Gullen and Dr. Margaret Gordon to lobby for social and political change through the National Council of Women of Canada (NCWC). As chair of the NCWC Citizenship Committee in the 1920s, Stowe-Gullen canvassed Local Councils of Women and identified equal pay, an eight-hour workday, child labour laws, healthy working conditions, mothers' custodial rights, age of consent for marriage, revision of property acts, and more equitable divorce laws as key issues to resolve. Meanwhile, the National Union of Woman Suffrage Associations evolved into the Ontario Women's Citizens' Association, led by Sarah Ormsby, and the United Women Voters, chaired by Constance Hamilton. These two organizations co-hosted public lectures at Massey Hall in Toronto, where Nellie McClung and Emmeline Pankhurst promoted women's role in post-war reconstruction. Hamilton also pushed Prime Minister Borden and future Conservative prime minister Arthur Meighen concerning her club's recommendations that women have a role in the reintegration of veterans and that at least one Canadian woman be included at the Paris peace talks. Initially, Hamilton intended to establish a Woman's Party. Imagined as a unifying force that would put forth female candidates and take up women's issues, this short-lived party was immediately hobbled by its commitment to imperialism and resistance to radicalism. It never gained traction outside of Hamilton's Toronto-based clique. By 1919, the organization, if perhaps not the idea, had disappeared.

Undeterred, Hamilton declared herself a candidate for Toronto City Council and competed with eight men for one of the three seats in Ward 3. Her platform was multifaceted. Among her maternal-feminist-aligned goals was the expansion of playgrounds. Otherwise, she endorsed a stronger police force and public ownership of streetcars and hydro, likewise progressive demands. In a spirit of feminist support, she mended her damaged relationship with Stowe-Gullen sufficiently enough that the latter introduced her at campaign events. Victorious in 1920 and again in 1921, Hamilton became the second woman in Canada to hold municipal office, right behind Calgary's Annie Gale. She joined a council that the *Toronto Star* nevertheless characterized as the "old Boy's club" due to its lack of diversity. Among its twenty-nine members, twenty-six were white, male, Anglo-Saxon Protestants. Once in office, Hamilton supported an eclectic array of causes, including appointing more women judges, establishing a minimum wage, and boosting public funding to combat venereal disease. Joining Hamilton in 1921 was Ethel Small, chair of the Voters' Bureau and an active member of the Woman's Christian Temperance Union (WCTU) and the Big Sisters. After being elected twice more, Hamilton did not again seek office but returned to non-governmental organizations and ran a hostel for indigent female artists and workers.

After the war, long-time activists Constance Boulton, Edith Sarah Lelean Groves, and Ada Mary Courtice were elected or re-elected to the Toronto Public School Board. Female representation on the board remained minor: between 1893 and 1930, only nine women were elected to the office, and only sixteen female candidates ran for some twenty-four positions that came available every two years. In Hamilton, journalist Nora Henderson was eager to see more women represented in city government beyond school boards and city councils. For example, she pushed for female appointees to the hospital board, a change that occurred in 1919. In 1931, Henderson herself was the first woman elected to Hamilton City Council. In 1934, she became the first woman in Canada to be elected to a municipal board of control.

Progress was slower outside the largest cities. Scholars attribute this shortfall to multiple factors, including the lack of economic autonomy and the domestic workload that characterized the lives of most women, a combination that was irreconcilable with the financial needs, schedule, and demands of politics.

Candidates who were wives and mothers were frequently slandered for neglect, and all were regarded as inferior leaders. Furthermore, mainstream parties and the public largely viewed female candidates as risky. Conservatives refused to field any female nominees, whereas the Liberals were at best tentative during the interwar years. "The men won't support them; they don't want them," Caroline Brown admitted as she reflected on the roadblocks she had witnessed, including her own failure to secure the Conservative nomination for her Toronto riding in 1924 and 1925. Her contributions as a long-time Conservative supporter and frequently elected school trustee meant nothing; experience was no match for gender bias. Following the landmark Persons case of 1929 – the constitutional ruling that confirmed women counted as persons, and therefore could sit on the senate – the political establishment grudgingly selected two Ontario women as senators: Liberal appointee Cairine Wilson (1885–1962) in 1930 and Conservative appointee Iva Campbell Fallis (1883–1956) in 1935. Although their leadership in the women's auxiliaries of political parties proved to be the winning ticket in securing their senate seats, auxiliaries more typically kept women on the margins of their own parties. The exception was the slightly better record of leftist parties in nominating and occasionally electing female candidates – but then, they were accustomed to backing underdogs.

AGNES MACPHAIL AND THE LIMITS OF PROGRESSIVE POLITICS

The rise of the UFO offered a platform for political newcomers, including women. It was not coincidental that Canada's first female parliamentarian emerged from its ranks. Demands for progressive alternatives had been brewing since 1914, when co-operative movements and farmer associations merged to form the UFO. In particular, many farmers felt betrayed by the war

In the House of Commons, schoolteacher-turned-politician
Agnes Macphail famously stated in 1925, "I do not want to be
the angel of any home: I want for myself what I want for other
women, absolute equality. After that is secured, then men
and women can take turns being angels."

measures of Borden's Union government, which included the
conscription of farmers' sons. Working in conjunction with
its women and youth auxiliaries, the UFO built momentum
throughout the war by linking a social and political critique of
the establishment with pathways to a more just society and an
agrarian-centred economic policy. In the lead-up to the 1919

provincial election, the party numbered fifty thousand members. On election day, it received enough votes to form a coalition government with the Independent Labour Party.

Many Canadians were startled at the political upheaval. Some blamed new women voters rather than rural populism and discontent. UFO supporter Louise Collins rhetorically asked the editor of the *Farmer's Sun*, "Oh! When will we poor long-suffering women cease to get the blame for every calamity that falls on Man?" In response to complaints that new voters could not distinguish Grits from Tories, she cheerfully agreed: there was no difference! Only the UFO promised a change. Other women happily took credit for the upset. Supporter Anna Elexy Duff of Lanark identified victories in Ontario and later Ottawa as proof that whenever "we women drop the ballot, it will be time to take note." For a moment, hopes soared. By 1923, however, the UFO had collapsed, and the province slid back into Conservative and Liberal domination.

The brief triumph of the UFO spoke to the high hopes of a population scarred by five years of war and economic turmoil. Rural women gained their first platform for causes that were critical to their well-being. Gender-specific issues – from widows' pensions to mothers' allowances, maternity benefits, and free health care for expectant mothers – roused UFO activists. Women's enhanced participation in politics, just as with the war, forced overdue recognition of their economic contribution and heavy workload.

In 1921, the UFO joined forces with United Farmers Parties in Manitoba and Alberta, and with the Canadian Labour Party, to emerge as the Progressive Party of Canada and to win fifty-eight seats in the federal election of that year. Agnes Campbell Macphail (1890–1954) took the Grey Southeast constituency on the Bruce Peninsula. Born in Proton Township to a struggling farming family of Scottish origins, Macphail spent years convincing her parents to allow her to attend high school in Owen

Sound, followed by teacher's college in Stratford. For a decade, she taught in Ontario and Alberta. Though not openly active in the suffragist movement, Macphail reportedly condemned the actions of British suffragettes, though she assigned her students publications written by Nellie McClung. Involved in UFO politics from its inception, Macphail became a columnist for a UFO newspaper, joined the UFWO, and helped organize UFO branches. Noted for her intelligence and oratory, Macphail overcame significant resistance to win the Progressive Party federal nomination, defeating eleven male would-be candidates. She won her seat in the House of Commons by a margin of 210 votes over her Conservative and Liberal male rivals. Her base was particularly strong among farmers in the county and township polling stations. Four other Ontario women ran unsuccessfully, including suffragist, socialist, and pacifist Harriet Prenter.

Macphail was re-elected to Parliament three times before being defeated in 1940. She entered provincial politics for the Co-operative Commonwealth Federation (CCF) in 1943, running in the Toronto riding of York East. She won two of four elections for York East, in 1943–45 and 1948–51. Given the volatile evolution of progressive parties throughout her career, Macphail's party allegiance fluctuated. In total, she was elected as the representative of four different parties: Progressive, United Farmers of Ontario-Labour, United Reform, and CCF.

During Macphail's campaign and time in office, her sex remained contentious. Scorned both as a woman and for not being womanly enough – she was unmarried – Macphail was the target of bigotry from the press, public, and male parliamentarians. "I couldn't open my mouth to say the simplest thing without it appearing in the papers. I was a curiosity, a freak. And you know the way the world treats freaks," she told *Maclean's* in 1949. Undaunted, she pursued a human rights agenda that advocated for workers, women, immigrants, prisoners, children, seniors, and farmers. Her support for disarmament gained her a seat in the Canadian delegation to the League of Nations. Compared to those of most suffragists, Macphail's causes were broadly progressive. One of her proudest moments was contributing to the passing of Ontario's first (albeit preliminary) equal pay act in 1951. Yet her imagination had limits. Like McClung and most feminist contemporaries, Macphail supported eugenics and the sterilization of those classified as feeble-minded.

Throughout her time in office, Macphail did not shy away from the term "feminist." Declaring famously in 1927, "I am a feminist," she defined this to mean the pursuit of "absolute equality" with men. She expressed her convictions by supporting bills that provided for women's equitable treatment in divorce proceedings, equal pay legislation in government contracts, teachers' pensions, and daycare. During the Great Depression, she highlighted the differing ways in which men and women were affected by unemployment and poverty, asking about the lack of relief programs for single, unemployed women: "If men are not capable of taking care of themselves during periods of stress and unemployment, does Parliament think that women are capable of taking care of themselves?" She also spoke publicly about the personal sacrifices she had made for her career and her regret that she had no time for marriage and children.

For all she accomplished, Macphail remained an anomaly in the House until 1935, when she was joined by Martha Black, an Independent Conservative from the Yukon, who ran to hold her incapacitated husband's seat. The Ontario legislature was even worse, again lagging behind Western Canada, which began to elect women in 1917. Between 1919 and 1937, twenty women ran unsuccessfully in the Loyalist province. With the exception of a few Liberal candidates, most represented new progressive farmer or labour parties, mainly from Toronto. All were soundly defeated. Such disappointment can be explained by the reign of Howard Ferguson's Conservative government between 1923 and 1934. The Conservatives never even nominated a female candidate during that period, and they prioritized the repeal of temperance, a long-time feminist cause. The failure was, however, non-partisan: from 1934 to 1943, no women held seats in Mitchell Hepburn's Liberal government. Not until 1943 did Macphail and Rae Luckock (1893–1972), another Toronto CCF candidate, sit in the Ontario legislature. The fact that, after a lifetime of public service, Macphail ultimately experienced financial penury provided a bitter footnote on women's value.

The efforts of First Nations women are instructive. They were not permitted to vote in band council elections or run as candidates until 1951, when the Indian Act was amended. In 1952, Elsie Marie Knott (1922–95) of the Anishinaabe Curve Lake First Nation, northeast of Peterborough, became Canada's first female chief of an elected council. A mother of three, Knott argued for equal access to education, condemning the long history of local school segregation and the lack of transportation to get children to off-reserve schools. When she was asked to run for chief by community members, at first Knott thought the notion was the "biggest joke ever." She defeated her two male rivals and won the election in a landslide; her political career turned out to be far from a joke. Knott governed over the Curve Lake First Nation for sixteen years, winning eight elections in total. As chief, she prioritized improving life for band members, defending treaty rights, and seeking more autonomy from Ottawa. Serving on the board of the National Indian Brotherhood, Knott advocated opening the federal franchise to Indigenous people because they "felt left out of things as long as they could not vote." In 1960, the Canadian Elections Act was repealed to allow First Nations people to vote without incurring the loss of their Indian status. Knott's resistance to the Canadian state's control of Indigenous peoples continued with her vocal criticism of Prime Minister Pierre Trudeau's White Paper on Indian Policy in 1969. Much like Macphail, Knott often worked in a largely male environment, even as her career and overall commitment demonstrated how Indigenous women continued to find ways to lead their communities, protect the land, and challenge inequities.

Writing in 1946, social conservative feminist Charlotte Whitton (1896–1975) lamented the failed experiment of Canadian women in politics, no more than a "sad memorial to the dreams and aspirations" of suffrage. Placing the blame on women's disillusionment, compliance, and lack of interest, Whitton condemned individual inaction as the root cause. Born in Renfrew, Whitton graduated from Queen's University and pursued a career in social work, becoming the founding director of the Child Welfare Council of Canada. Two decades spent working as an adviser to the federal government and the provinces on matters related to relief and children's well-being fuelled political ambitions that saw her elected to the Ottawa Board of Control in 1950. A year later, she became mayor of Ottawa, the first female mayor of a major Ontario city, a position to which she was re-elected four times. (The small town of Webbwood had the honour of electing Ontario's first female mayor, in 1936.)

Whitton's comments have been rightly interpreted as contemptuous, but she was nevertheless a feminist, once proclaiming, "Women of the world unite; you have nothing to lose but your shackles." As mayor, she championed equal pay but dismissed birth control, sex outside of marriage, and divorce as immoral. She also set herself apart from progressive activists by fiercely opposing Canada's slow transition into a welfare state. Nor did she champion women in politics, unless they were single and childless; married women and mothers might neglect their domestic responsibilities. Whitton publicly celebrated her celibacy, which she proclaimed desirable for men and women who were dedicated to public service. Such conservatism did not shield her from sexist vulgarities. As in the case of Macphail, the fact that Whitton was female informed recurring public dialogue about her mayoral reputation, physical appearance, and personal life. Decades later, Whitton's papers revealed her long-term, passionate relationship

Mrs. Lilian Williams of the Aamjiwnaang First Nation made front-page news when she cast her ballot for chief and council members in June 1952. This historic act followed a 1951 amendment to the Indian Act, which granted First Nations women the right to vote in local band elections. Williams was one of eighty women on her reserve who were newly eligible to vote. The local Indian agent and church minister acted as scrutineers, representing the long arm of colonialism in the continuing management of Indigenous governance.

with a woman and prompted reconsideration of her sexual orientation and private burdens. Like all the women who are featured in this book, Whitton remains a figure whose politics, feminism, and actions are not readily summed up.

Ottawa's worthy mayor should not, however, be left with the last word. The steadfast Macphail rejected Whitton's claim that women had been a "flop" in Canadian politics. Although she acknowledged that they "have fallen far below the standard of citizenship which those who fought for suffrage set," she held that political activists had "done very well." Rather than blaming her sex, Macphail condemned the persistence of politics and business as "very much a man's world." Achieving justice and equality would "take time."

⌘

The overall message of the story told in these pages, and indeed of the other books in the series, is that the struggle continues for a fair deal in politics, as in much else. It took forty years of dedicated suffrage activism to convince Ontario that women could be effective voters, and more years would elapse before they could be elected to public office. In this quagmire, women's organizations continued to channel female activism. Established groups such as the NCWC and the YWCA remained predominant players in attempting to speak for women's reform interests. The 1927 repeal of prohibition signalled the significant decline of the WCTU, though women's church work remained a powerful site of activism. In the interwar years, new groups focused on university, professional, and businesswomen. Working through unions and Socialist and Communist Parties, as well as ad hoc mothers' groups, radical women kept up the demand for improved rights and representation in the labour movement. They organized consumer boycotts, tenant resistance, and price control protests in the face of recessions and the Great Depression.

As in the past, racially and ethnically marginalized women mobilized within their own communities, sidestepping mainstream women's organizations that were at best ignorant of the issues affecting non-white, non-Christian, or non-British women. Founded in Toronto in 1916, Hadassah mobilized Jewish women in health, welfare, and education reform efforts. Black women were a force in the Toronto branch of the United Negro Improvement Association, a Garveyite movement dedicated to generating pride, economic self-sufficiency, and an independent black nation in Africa. The Canadian Negro Women's Club, founded in 1951 by radio personality Kay Livingstone (1919–75), concentrated on fundraising and community initiatives, such as scholarships for black students. Long active on the board of the Toronto Woman's College Hospital and University Settlement House, Chinese Canadian restaurateur Jean Lumb (1919–2002) lobbied in the early 1950s to reunite families separated by the Chinese head tax immigration policy. Though the strong drive of the suffrage campaign had waned, the period between 1917 and the women's liberation movement of the 1960s and 1970s was anything but dormant. Women such as Livingstone and Lumb, born on the eve of suffrage victory, used traditional tactics for political engagement and challenged the status quo in ways they hoped would improve their own lives and their communities.

Ultimately, the suffrage victory provided essential legal recognition of the vision, labour, and leadership demonstrated by women since the earliest days of Ontario. The intrepid activist Flora MacDonald Denison summed up the result: suffrage "demands political rights for women because it recognizes the vote as the only dignified and honourable means of securing recognition of needs and aspiration." Official inclusion in the formal democratic process gave women a say in the making of laws and the spending of public money, validating their identities as citizens. A voice on election day empowered lobbying in nongovernmental organizations and further legitimized claims for equal rights in the home, workplace, and community. Suffrage was a wave, interrupted, uneven, and sometimes broken, but nevertheless a confirmation of women's courage and persistence in the face of insult and injury. It was an essential part of the story of greater equality to be won in education, the economy, the law, and everyday life. Even though gender alone never solely determines women's experiences or perspectives, their inclusion as potentially equal electoral participants generated a new politics of possibility for democracy.

Even as the accomplishment should be stressed, twenty-first-century Canadians confront a land in which the frequent hopes of suffragists for a fair deal ultimately stumbled. As much as the great cause was a progressive idea for its time, it too often focused on inclusion in, rather than transformation of, the status quo. Diversity was rarely welcomed, and inequalities ranging from race to religion and sexuality still reigned. The fact, however, that the suffragist demand for electoral inclusion, so often expressed in legal and respectful language, roused both determined opposition and fears of apocalypse, should remind later generations that gender equality was, and indeed remains, a radical claim. For all their imperfections, suffragists battled a province and nation that were still more flawed. The words of Augusta Stowe-Gullen deserve to be remembered: "If our fight is at moments dispiriting, and apparently hopeless it is well to forget the hours of labour and unceasing toil, with so little practical success, and merely to recollect that ultimately there can be no defeat." As she maintained, "Woman must be free. Civilization demands her freedom."

ACKNOWLEDGMENTS

THIS BOOK IS DEDICATED to Nikki Strong-Boag for her vision and support in seeing that Canada's suffragists got another reckoning. I wish to express my gratitude to Darcy Cullen, Katrina Petrik, and everyone at UBC Press for valuing a series on the history of suffrage and for their patience with my manuscript. I am also much in debt to the other series authors, Denyse Baillargeon, Lara Campbell, Sarah Carter, Lianne Leddy, Heidi MacDonald, and Joan Sangster, for sharing their struggles and wisdom. In particular, I am grateful to Lianne and Nikki for offering thoughtful feedback on earlier drafts. I also wish to thank the anonymous reviewers for their numerous suggestions, which made the manuscript stronger.

A big thank you goes to Heather Steel for passing along her archives of suffrage primary sources and to Alison Norman for sending me in the right direction in regard to Toronto suffrage history. Thank you to Cecilia Morgan and Charlotte Skeet for kindly debating the 1844 election with me and to Jason Ellis, Alison Prentice, R.D. Gidney, and W.P.J. Millar for answering my seemingly endless questions about school boards and trustees. I am very appreciative of Bob Hasler for sharing his database of women voters, drawn from records in the Paris Museum and Historical Society. I am most grateful to John Moses and Helen Monture Moses for their generosity in answering my questions about their family history and for giving me a copy of Edith Anderson Monture's diary. I am also most appreciative of Shirley

Victoria Hodgson, Oliver Penrose, and Jonathan Penrose for opening their home and memories to me so I could learn more about their grandmother Sonia Leathes. I am eternally grateful for the archival research collected and analyzed by my amazing research assistants: Funke Aladejebi, Shannon Brown, Jenna Carew, and Cody Groat. Archivists and librarians were incredible vessels of knowledge. In particular, I would like to single out Margaret Deans, Gary Jermy, Cindy Preece, Dana Thorne, and Thorold J. Tronrud, who went out of their way to help me secure images. Thank you to my colleagues, friends, and family for putting up with me on this suffrage detour, especially Dennis and Juliet.

SOURCES AND
FURTHER READING

I AM BEHOLDEN to generations of historians working in women's history, Indigenous history, political history, social history, military history, and the history of Ontario, whose books and articles provided context, inspiration, and rabbit holes to jump down. Below is an account of texts that proved most relevant to each chapter and suggestions for further reading on the subjects. The primary sources consulted are cited in the endnotes.

PREFACE

As discussed, Catherine Cleverdon, *The Woman's Suffrage Movement in Ontario* (Toronto: University of Toronto Press, 1950), and Carole Lee Bacchi, *Liberation Deferred? The Ideas of the English-Canadian Suffragists, 1877–1918* (Toronto: University of Toronto Press, 1983), were valuable sources of chronology, context, and argument. Rose Fine Meyer, "Including Women: The Establishment and Integration of Canadian Women's History into Toronto Ontario Classrooms 1968–1993" (PhD diss., University of Toronto, 2012), examines the ways in which suffrage history was incorporated into the Ontario high school curriculum. I would also like to call attention to the anthology of primary sources curated and edited by Maureen Moynagh and Nancy Forestell, *Documenting First Wave Feminisms*, vol. 1, *Transnational Collaborations and Crosscurrents* (Toronto: University of Toronto Press, 2012), and *Documenting First Wave Feminisms*, vol. 2, *Canada – National and Transnational Contexts* (Toronto: University of Toronto Press, 2013).

Page xi   **Suffragists' dogged determination in the face of apathetic and sexist opposition:** Charlotte Whitton, "Is the Canadian Woman a Flop in Politics?" *Saturday Night,* 26 January 1946.

ONE: WOMEN'S RIGHTS IN INDIGENOUS AND COLONIAL ONTARIO

For the section on Indigenous women, much of the information on women's status and political duties was drawn from Kathryn Labelle, "'They Are the Life of the Nation': Women and War in Traditional Nadouek Society," in *Rethinking Canada: The Promise of Women's History*, ed. Lara Campbell, Tamara Myers, and Adele Perry, 7th ed. (Oxford: Oxford University Press, 2015), 12–22, Rick Monture, *We Share Our Matters: Two Centuries of Writing and Resistance at Six Nations of the Grand River* (Winnipeg: University of Manitoba Press, 2014), and Renée Jacobs, "Iroquois Great Law of Peace and the United States Constitution: How the Founding Fathers Ignored the Clan Mothers," *American Indian Law Review* 16, 2 (1991): 497–531. General information on the region came from Edmund Jefferson Danzinger Jr., *Great Lakes Indian Accommodation and Resistance during the Early Reservation Years, 1850–1900* (Ann Arbor: University of Michigan Press, 2009). Interpretation of the Sky Woman story is from Lina Sunsero, *Being Again of One Mind: Oneida Women and the Struggle for Decolonization* (Vancouver: UBC Press, 2011). Elizabeth Elbourne's work on Molly Brant in "Family Politics and Anglo-Mohawk Diplomacy: The Brant Family in Imperial Context," *Journal of Colonialism and Colonial History* 6, 3 (Winter 2005) was important to my understanding of her role and status. For more on the subject, I recommend Robin Jarvis Brownlie and Valerie J. Korniek, eds., *Finding a Way to the Heart: Feminist Writings on Aboriginal and Women's History in Canada* (Winnipeg: University of Manitoba Press, 2012). The section on Fletcher's observations was drawn from Sally Roesch Wagner, *Sisters in Spirit: Haudenosaunee (Iroquois) Influence on Early American Feminists* (Summertown, TN: Native Voices, 2001).

Numerous texts contributed to the section on women's status in Upper Canada. Notably, these are Elizabeth Jane Errington, *Wives and Mothers, School Mistresses and Scullery Maids: Working Women in Upper Canada, 1790–1840* (Montreal and Kingston: McGill-Queen's University Press, 1995), and Cecilia Morgan, *Public Men and Virtuous Women: The Gendered Languages of Religion and Politics in Upper Canada, 1791–1850* (Toronto: University of Toronto Press, 1996). Beth Light and Alison Prentice, eds., *Pioneer and Gentlewomen of British North America, 1713–1867* (Toronto: New Hogtown Press, 1980), provide an excellent collection of primary source documents on the lives of settler women. Maureen Elgersman Lee, "Slavery in Early Canada: Making Black Women Subject," in *Rethinking Canada: The Promise of Women's History*, ed. Mona Gleason and Adele Perry, 5th ed. (Oxford: Oxford University Press, 2006), 45–60, was critical to my understanding of how race and racism constructed black women's colonial experiences. For Simcoe's thoughts on slavery, see Robin Winks, *The Blacks in Canada: A History*, 2nd ed. (Montreal and Kingston: McGill-Queen's University Press, 2005). Lori Chambers, *Married Women and Property Law in Victorian Ontario* (Toronto: University of Toronto Press, 1997), was essential for understanding the amendments to property laws. So too was Peter Baskerville, *A Silent Revolution? Gender and Wealth in English Canada, 1860–1930* (Montreal and Kingston: McGill-Queen's University Press, 2008). For more information on the immigration experience and Loyalist mindset, I recommend Janice Potter-MacKinnon, *While the Women Only Wept: Loyalist Refugee Women in Eastern Ontario* (Montreal and Kingston: McGill-Queen's University Press, 1993).

The contested 1844 election is acknowledged briefly in John Garner's *The Franchise and Politics in British North America, 1755–1867* (Toronto: University of Toronto Press, 1969). Jeffrey L. McNairn also gives a brief account in *The Capacity to Judge: Public Opinion and Deliberative Democracy in Upper Canada, 1791–1854* (Toronto: University of Toronto Press, 2000). Women's voting rights in Lower Canada are explored in depth in Bettina Bradbury, "Women at the Hustings: Gender, Citizenship, and the Montreal By-Elections of 1832," in Gleason and Perry, *Rethinking Canada,* 73–94. A good general history of voting rights can be found in *A History of the Vote in Canada* (Ottawa: Chief Electoral Officer, 2007). I used census and genealogical documents via ancestry.ca to discover the identities of the West Halton women voters.

Page 5   **"Women were respected":** Quoted in Erin Hanson, "Marginalization of Aboriginal Women," Indigenous Foundations, University of British Columbia, https://indigenousfoundations.arts.ubc.ca/marginalization_of_aboriginal_women/.

Page 8   **"The women of every clan of the Five Nations":** From the 1916 written version of the Great Law compiled by A. Parker, quoted in Renée Jacobs, "Iroquois Great Law of Peace and the United States Constitution: How the Founding Fathers Ignored the Clan Mothers," *American Indian Law Review* 16, 2 (1991): 507.

Page 9   **"Our custom of ignoring women":** Quoted in Sally Roesch Wagner, *Sisters in Spirit: Haudenosaunee (Iroquois) Influence on Early American Feminists* (Summertown, TN: Native Voices, 2001), 91.

Page 10   **"A new land of promise":** Nancy Jean Cameron to Margaret MacPherson, 15 May 1785, quoted in Janice Potter-MacKinnon, *While the Women Only Wept: Loyalist Refugee Women in Eastern Ontario* (Montreal and Kingston: McGill-Queen's University Press, 1993), 134.

Page 10   **Upper Canada as "the bush":** Susanna Moodie, *Roughing It in the Bush* (London: Richard Bentley, 1852).

Page 11   **"Bush and flies":** Quoted in Marlene Epp, *Mennonite Women in Canada* (Winnipeg: University of Manitoba Press, 2008), 28.

Page 11   **"A great deal of ignorance":** Mary A. Shadd, *A Plea for Emigration; or Notes of Canada West* (Detroit: GW Pattison, 1852), 26, 32.

Page 13   **"For each a clean young wife":** A Letter from James Murray to John Watt, 2 November 1763, quoted in Maureen Elgersman Lee, "Slavery in Early Canada: Making Black Women Subject," in *Rethinking Canada: The Promise of Women's History,* ed. Mona Gleason and Adele Perry, 5th ed. (Oxford: Oxford University Press, 2006), 48–49.

Page 13 **"Barbarous" wife:** Benjamin Drew, *The Refugee: Narratives of Fugitive Slaves in Canada* (Cleveland: John P. Jewett, 1855), 194.

Page 14 **"Legal existence of a woman":** Quoted in Lori Chambers, *Married Women and Property Law in Victorian Ontario* (Toronto: University of Toronto Press, 1997), 14.

Page 17 **"For surely no man of sense":** Charles Fothergill, "District of Newcastle Meeting," *Niagara Gleaner,* 10 March 1832, quoted in Jeffrey L. McNairn, *The Capacity to Judge: Public Opinion and Deliberative Democracy in Upper Canada, 1791–1854* (Toronto: University of Toronto Press, 2000), 226.

Page 17 **"Mackenzie has got in again":** Mary O'Brien, *The Journals of Mary O'Brien, 1828–1838,* ed. Audrey Saunders Miller (Toronto: Macmillan, 1968), 138.

Page 17 **"Every advantage":** Ibid., 273.

Page 17 **"Did what little [she] could to serve":** Quoted in John Thurston, *The Work of Words: The Writing of Susanna Strickland Moodie* (Montreal and Kingston: McGill-Queen's University Press, 1996), 73.

Page 17 **"The trampled Despot":** Susanna Moodie, "Canadians Will You Join the Band," *Palladium of British America and Upper Canada Mercantile Advertiser,* 20 December 1837.

Page 17 **"Women entered deeply into this party hostility":** Susanna Moodie, *Life in the Clearings versus the Bush* (London: Richard Bentley, 1853), 35.

Page 18 **"Asking if she was happy here in Canada":** Anna Brownell Jameson, *Winter Studies and Summer Rambles in Canada* (London: Saunders and Otley, 1838), 2:45.

Page 19 **"Public interest, decency":** Quoted in Bettina Bradbury, "Women at the Hustings: Gender, Citizenship, and the Montreal By-Elections of 1832," in Gleason and Perry, *Rethinking Canada,* 89.

Page 20 **"The fate of the petition":** *Upper Canada Herald,* 24 December 1844, 3.

Page 22 **"The Committee could not take for granted":** All quotes are from Alfred Patrick, ed., *Digests of Precedents or Decisions, Upper Canada Contested Elections, 1824 to 1840* (Toronto: Lovell and Gibson, 1851), 57–62.

Page 23 **"That no woman is or shall be entitled to vote":** *Provincial Statutes of Canada* (Montreal: Stewart and Derbishire and George Desbarats, 1849), 189.

Page 23 **"Tumultuous constituency":** *Globe* (Toronto), 22 March 1848 and 1 June 1850, quoted in McNairn, *The Capacity to Judge,* 343.

Page 24   **"Fit and proper persons":** *An Act for the better establishment and maintenance of Common Schools in Upper Canada,* 1850, 13 & 14 Vict., c. 9, s. 23, s. 27.

Page 24   **Contemporary observers interpreted … agitation for:** Elizabeth Cady Stanton, Susan B. Anthony, and Matilda Joslyn Gage, "Female Suffrage in Canada," *History of Woman Suffrage,* vol. 1 (Rochester, NY: Charles Mann, 1889), 870.

Page 24   **"Rather strange and modern reformation":** "From Our Hamilton Correspondent," *Globe* (Toronto), 15 March 1855.

Page 24   **"A friend of mine in Canada West":** Straton, Anthony, and Gage, "Female Suffrage in Canada," 651.

Page 25   **"Unfit for the office":** "The School Elections," *Globe* (Toronto), 13 January 1853.

Page 25   **"Never make headway in Canada":** "Legal Rights of Married Women," *Globe* (Toronto), 26 December 1856.

TWO: ORIGINS OF FEMINIST THOUGHT AND ACTION

For a detailed biography and analysis of Mary Ann Shadd Cary's career, please see Jane Rhodes, *Mary Ann Shadd Cary: The Black Press and Protest in the 19th Century* (Bloomington: Indiana University Press, 1998). Two essays in Peggy Bristow, ed., *"We're Rooted Here and They Can't Pull Us Up": Essays in African Canadian Women's History* (Toronto: University of Toronto Press, 1994), were central to grounding the experience of black women in nineteenth-century Ontario. These were Peggy Bristow, "'Whatever You Raise in the Ground You Can Sell It in Chatham': Black Women in Buxton and Chatham, 1850–65," 69–142, and Afua Cooper, "Black Women and Work in Nineteenth Century Canada West: Black Woman Teacher Mary Bibb," 143–70. The emergence of black and white women's literary societies is covered in Heather Murray, *Come, Bright Improvement! The Literary Societies of Nineteenth-Century Ontario* (Toronto: University of Toronto Press, 2002). Another perspective on black women's organizing appears in Lorene Bridgen, "'Lifting as We Climb': The Emergence of an African-Canadian Civil Society in Southern Ontario, 1840–1901" (PhD diss., University of Waterloo, 2016).

Mary Beacock Fryer's *Emily Stowe: Doctor and Suffragist* (Toronto: Dundurn Press, 1990) is the most comprehensive biography of Stowe. An earlier work, Janet Ray, *Emily Stowe* (Toronto: Fitzhenry and Whiteside, 1978), is also a useful examination of Stowe's life. Works that consider Stowe as a feminist icon include Wayne Roberts, "'Rocking the Cradle for the New World': The New Woman and Maternal Feminism, Toronto 1877–1914," and Veronica Strong-Boag, "Canada's Women Doctors: Feminism Constrained," both in *A Not Unreasonable Claim: Women and Reform in Canada, 1880s–1920s,* ed. Linda Kealey (Toronto: Women's Press, 1979), 15–46 and 109–30.

Alison Prentice and Marjorie R. Theobald, eds., *Women Who Taught: Perspectives on the History of Women and Teaching* (Toronto: University of Toronto Press, 1991), has several chapters on the feminization of teaching in Ontario.

Women's role in social reform and the formation of groups such as the YWCA and the WCTU are portrayed in Diana Pedersen, "'Keeping Our Good Girls Good': The YWCA and the 'Girl Problem,' 1870–1930," *Canadian Women Studies/Cahiers de la femme* 7, 4 (1986): 20–24; Carolyn Strange, *Toronto's Girl Problem: The Perils and Pleasures of the City, 1880–1930* (Toronto: University of Toronto Press, 1995); Sharon Anne Cook, *"Through Sunshine and Shadow": The Woman's Christian Temperance Union, Evangelicalism, and Reform in Ontario, 1874–1930* (Montreal and Kingston: McGill-Queen's University Press, 1995); and Wendy Mitchinson, "The WCTU: 'For God, Home and Native Land': A Study in 19th Century Feminism," in Kealey, *A Not Unreasonable Claim*, 151–68.

For Indigenous women and social reform, see Alison Norman, "Race, Gender and Colonialism: Public Life among the Six Nations of Grand River, 1899–1939" (PhD diss., University of Toronto, 2010). Bonita Lawrence, "Identity, Non-Status Indians, and Federally Unrecognized Peoples," in *Aboriginal History: A Reader*, ed. Kristin Burnett and Geoff Read, 2nd ed. (Oxford: Oxford University Press, 2016), 196–205, outlines the assimilation policies and gendered impact of the Indian Act. For more information on Nahnebahnwequay, see Donald Smith's chapter "Upright Woman: Catharine Sunegoo or Nahnebahnwequay, 'Nahnee' (1824–1865)" in *Mississauga Portraits: Ojibwe Voices from Nineteenth-Century Canada* (Toronto: University of Toronto Press, 2013), 68–97. Nancy Forestell also references Sutton's activism and that of other Indigenous women who resisted colonialism in her chapter for Nancy Janovicek and Carmen Nielson, eds., *Reading Canadian Women's and Gender History* (Toronto: University of Toronto Press, forthcoming).

Page 26   **"I am not the one to set a limit"**: Emily Stowe, "Housewifery, May 1889," untitled newspaper clipping, May 1889, Emily Stowe Scrapbook, file 1.11 microfilm, series 1, Emily Stowe and Augusta Stowe-Gullen (ES-ASG) Collection, Wilfrid Laurier Archives (WLU).

Page 27   **"One of the best Editors our Province ever had"**: *Provincial Freeman*, 22 August 1855.

Page 28   **"Woman, whose nature is to love home"**: Catharine Parr Traill, *The Female Emigrant's Guide, and Hints on Canadian Housekeeping* (Toronto: Maclear, 1854), 27.

Page 28   **"It seems to me it is with woman as man"**: Fannie Belle Irving, "Woman's Place," *Toronto Weekly Graphic*, 29 November 1879, 11.

Page 29   **Neighbours who "belong to a different branch"**: *London Free Press*, 12 August 1964.

Page 30   **"For all irrespective of colour"**: Mary Bibb to Horace Mann, 20 January 1853, quoted in Afua Cooper, "Black Women and Work in Nineteenth Century Canada West: Black Woman Teacher Mary Bibb," in *"We're Rooted Here and They Can't Pull Us Up": Essays in African Canadian Women's History,* ed. Peggy Bristow (Toronto: University of Toronto Press, 1994), 151.

Page 31   **"To recognize equality in the ability of the sexes"**: Quoted in Alison Prentice, "'Friendly Atoms in Chemistry': Women and Men at Normal School in Mid-Nineteenth-Century Toronto," in *Old Ontario: Essays in Honour of J.M.S. Careless,* ed. David Keane and Colin Read (Toronto: Dundurn, 1990), 310.

Page 32   **"Unceasing industry"**: Frederick Douglass, 4 July 1856, quoted in Jane Rhodes, *Mary Ann Shadd Cary: The Black Press and Protest in the 19th Century* (Bloomington: Indiana University Press, 1998), xi.

Page 32   **"New feature in political gatherings"**: *Provincial Freeman,* 5 August 1854.

Page 33   **"Only a busy body in men's matters"**: Horace Hallock to Reverend C.C. Foote, 13 January 1852, quoted in Rhodes, *Mary Ann Shadd Cary,* 67.

Page 33   Directing **"a word"** to black women: "Adieu," *Provincial Freeman,* 30 June 1855.

Page 34   **"The heat and burden of the day"**: "The Late Dr. Emily Stowe," *Canadian Journal of Medicine and Surgery* 13, 6 (June 1903): 436–37.

Page 35   **"As wives, mothers, sisters and dainty housekeepers"**: "Female Medical Students," *Canadian Lancet* 3 (1871): 213.

Page 36   **"My career has been one of much struggle"**: Quoted in Janet Ray, *Emily Stowe* (Toronto: Fitzhenry and Whiteside, 1978), 41.

Page 37   **"How I do wish you were here to advise me"**: George Brown to Anne Nelson Brown, 20 June 1864, quoted in J.M.S. Careless, "George Brown and the Mother of Confederation, 1864," in *Careless at Work: Selected Canadian Historical Studies* (Toronto, Dundurn Press, 1996), 86.

Page 37   **"My Diaries as Miss Bernard did not need"**: Lady Agnes Macdonald, personal journal, 5 July 1867, Family Papers, Baroness Macdonald, Sir John A. Macdonald Fonds, MG 26 A, volume 59A, Library and Archives Canada, http://www.collectionscanada.gc.ca/obj/008001/f2/ladymacdonald-diary-transcript-en.pdf.

Page 40   **"Proposed not only to rock the cradle"**: Lottie McAlister, *Clipped Wings* (Montreal: C.W. Coates, 1899), 25.

Page 40   **"We cannot successfully evade duty"**: Handwritten copy of a sermon given by Mary Ann Shadd on 6 April 1858, quoted in Rhodes, *Mary Ann Shadd Cary,* 127.

Page 42   **"Tales of sorrow":** Letitia Creighton Youmans, *Campaign Echoes: The Autobiography of Mrs. Letitia Youmans, the Pioneer of the White Ribbon Movement in Canada* (Toronto: W. Briggs, 1893), 8.

Page 43   **"It will seem so bold":** Ibid., 106.

Page 43   **"Untold agonies" … only furthered WCTU resolve:** Ibid., 108.

Page 44   **"Enact a prohibitory law":** *One Hundred Years of Temperance: A Memorial Volume of the Centennial Conference Held in Philadelphia* (New York: National Temperance Society and Publication House, 1885), 106–7.

Page 45   **"Male members of the band":** *Indian Act,* S.C., 1876, c. 18, s. 61.

Page 45   **"Wholesale robbery and treachery":** Quoted in Donald Smith, "Nahnebahwequay," *Dictionary of Canadian Biography,* http://www. biographi.ca/en/bio/nahnebahwequay_9E.html.

Page 46   **The irreverent Emily Stowe lectured on**: Emily Stowe, "Woman's sphere," undated, unidentified newspaper clipping, Emily Stowe Scrapbook, file 1.11 microfilm, series 1, ES-ASG Collection, WLU.

Page 46   **"The fiercest dislike":** "Portia's Column," *Toronto Star,* 4 January 1896.

Page 46   **"Widespread intelligence among the women":** Hilda Ridley, "A Synopsis of Woman Suffrage in Canada," undated, 5, SPEC COLL JL 192 R54 SC1145, ES-ASG Collection, WLU.

Page 47   **"General opinion being in favour of the subject":** "Toronto Women's Literary Club," undated, unidentified newspaper clipping, Emily Stowe Scrapbook, file 1.11 microfilm, series 1, ES-ASG, WLU.

THREE: EARLY LEGISLATIVE VICTORIES AND DEFEATS

For more information on Emily Stowe's trial, see Constance Backhouse, *Petticoats and Prejudice: Women and Law in Nineteenth-Century Canada* (Toronto: Women's Press, 1991). Regarding Ontario women's access to higher education, Sara Z. Burke is the expert. Her article "Women of Newfangle: Co-education, Racial Discourse and Women's Rights in Victorian Ontario," *Historical Studies in Education/Review d'histoire de l'éducation* July 2007: 115–33, is a fantastic examination of broader argument for and against coeducation. For specific discussion on the University of Toronto, see her chapter, "Co-education at the University of Toronto, 1884–1895," in *Schooling in Transition: Readings in Canadian History of Education,* ed. Sara Z. Burke and Patrice Milewski (Toronto: University of Toronto Press, 2012), 166–82. Another good discussion on coeducation can be found in Alison Prentice, "'Friendly Atoms in Chemistry': Women and Men at Normal School in Mid-Nineteenth-Century Toronto," in *Old Ontario: Essays in Honour of J.M.S. Careless,* ed. David Keane and Colin

Read (Toronto: Dundurn Press, 1990), 285–317. For an analysis of Sarah Curzon's play, see Céleste Derksen, "Out of the Closet: Dramatic Works by Sarah Anne Curzon Part Two: Re-dressing Gender Inequality: *The Sweet Girl Graduate*," *Theatre Research in Canada* 15, 2 (Fall 1994): 123–35. Gail G. Campbell, "Voters and Non-voters: The Problem of Turnout in the Nineteenth Century: Southwestern Ontario as a Case Study," *Social Science History* 11, 2 (Summer 1987): 187–210, provides a thorough examination of who made use of their voting rights in nineteenth-century Ontario. For background on the gendered labour force of Paris, Ontario, see Joy Parr, *Gender of Breadwinners: Women, Men, and Change in Two Industrial Towns, 1880–1950* (Toronto: University of Toronto Press, 1990). Once again, Lori Chambers, *Married Women and Property Law in Victorian Ontario* (Toronto: University of Toronto Press, 1997), was key to understanding the changes and limits of the new 1885 legislation. I used census and genealogical documents via ancestry.ca to discover the identities of the women whom the Paris voting registry named.

Regarding John A. Macdonald's proposed amendments to the federal franchise, I recommend consulting Veronica Strong-Boag, "The Citizenship Debates: The 1885 Franchise Act," in *Contesting Canadian Citizenship: Historical Readings*, ed. Robert Adamoski, Dorothy E. Chunn, and Robert Menzies (Toronto: Broadview Press, 2002), 69–94, and Colin Grittner, "Macdonald and Women's Enfranchisement," in *Macdonald at 200: New Reflections and Legacies*, ed. Patrice Dutil and Roger Hall (Toronto: Dundurn Press, 2014), 27–57. The rhetoric surrounding women's suffrage in 1885 and beyond is taken up in Michael Dorland and Maurice Charland, *Law, Rhetoric, and Irony in the Formation of Canadian Civil Culture* (Toronto: University of Toronto Press, 2002).

Page 48   **"We ask to have the franchise extended":** Quoted in the "Constitution and Rules of the Canadian Women's Suffrage Association," 9 March 1883 (CWSA Constitution), 15, SPEC COLL JL 192 C359 SC1144, Emily Stowe and Augusta Stowe-Gullen (ES-ASG) Collection, Wilfrid Laurier Archives (WLU).

Page 49   **"In man's legislation":** "Suffragists Are Pleased," unidentified newspaper clipping, c. 1909, Box 8A, Collection of newspaper clippings relating to women's suffrage, 1890–1919, Flora MacDonald Denison Scrapbook, Flora MacDonald Denison Papers, Thomas Fisher Rare Book Library, University of Toronto.

Page 50   **"Let us pray for deliverance from female suffrage":** Francis Parkman, "The Woman Question," *North American Review,* October 1879, 321, 313.

Page 50   **Suffragists fiercely rejected such slurs ... proof that female voters could be trusted:** Julia Ward Howe et al., "The Other Side of the Woman Question," *North American Review,* November 1879.

Page 51 **"Without it the germs of nations":** Goldwin Smith, "Female Suffrage," *Essays on the Questions of the Day: Political and Social,* 2nd ed. (London: Macmillan, 1897), 225.

Page 52 **"So Goody – I mean Goldwin – Please":** "To a Male Scold," *Punch,* 12 January 1889.

Page 52 **Discussion about the relative merits:** "Strong-Minded Women," *Globe* (Toronto), 23 November 1877. See also other letters in November–December 1877.

Page 53 **Dildock run out of the "hen convention":** "O.P. Dildock Visits the Woman's Club: Make Way for Liberty. Great Cackalations," *Toronto Graphic,* c. 1870s, Emily Stowe Scrapbook, file 1.11 microfilm, series 1, ES-ASG Collection, WLU.

Page 54 **Her "woman's rights army":** *Mail* (Toronto), 24 September 1879.

Page 54 **"All questions of a social or moral nature":** *Globe* (Toronto), 13 May 1878.

Page 55 **"I do not feel called upon to commit myself":** Quoted in CWSA Constitution, 15–16, SPEC COLL JL 192 C359 SC1144, ES-ASG Collection, WLU.

Page 55 **When asked the rationale for pursuing female enfranchisement:** *Globe* (Toronto), 7 March 1883.

Page 55 **"To obtain for women the Municipal and Parliamentary":** CWSA Constitution, 15–16, SPEC COLL JL 192 C359 SC1144, ES-ASG Collection, WLU.

Page 57 **"The young men would be demoralized":** Sarah Curzon, *The Sweet Girl Graduate,* in *Laura Secord, the Heroine of 1812: A Drama and Other Poems* (Toronto: C. Blackett Robinson, 1887), 124.

Page 57 **"Now let the New Zealanders boast":** Ibid., 131.

Page 58 **"Unlawful and unjust" exclusion of women:** "University College Petition for the Admission of Female Students," *Globe* (Toronto), 31 January 1883.

Page 59 **"Although she had received her instruction":** "Canada," *The Englishwoman's Review of Social and Industrial Questions,* vol. 14 (London: Trubner and Co., 1883), 384.

Page 59 **"Every unmarried woman and every widow":** *Municipal Amendment Act,* 1844, S.O., 47 Vict., c. 32, s. 15. *Statutes of Ontario,* 1884.

Page 60 **"Great public duty":** "Ontario Legislature," *Globe* (Toronto), 6 March 1884.

Page 60 **Words "unmarried" and "widow" … defeated by ninety-one:** "Ontario Assembly Notes," *Globe* (Toronto), 17 March 1884.

Page 61   **"A dear price to pay for a vote"**: Letitia Creighton Youmans, *Campaign Echoes: The Autobiography of Mrs. Letitia Youmans, the Pioneer of the White Ribbon Movement in Canada* (Toronto: W. Briggs, 1893), 208–10.

Page 61   **"Women were to be seen hustling to the polls"**: "Municipal Elections," *Globe* (Toronto), 4 January 1887.

Page 62   **Howland won a "huge" majority and expressed:** "A Huge Majority!" *Globe* (Toronto), 5 January 1886.

Page 62   **"Men who have only recently learned"**: Emily Stowe to the editor, untitled newspaper clipping, 10 March 1890, Emily Stowe Scrapbook, file 1.11 microfilm, series 1, ES-ASG Collection, WLU.

Page 65   **"Shocked at the idea of women having to think"**: "Political Women," *Toronto World,* 12 February 1884, 2.

Page 66   **"It would create a large vote"**: Canada, *House of Commons Debates,* Hansard, 27 April 1885, 1390.

Page 67   **"Canada would have had the great honour"**: Ibid., 1388.

Page 68   **"You are driven to treat marriage"**: "The Franchise Bill," *Globe* (Toronto), 24 April 1885.

Page 68   **"Old maids"**: Canada, *House of Commons Debates,* 17 April 1885, 1204.

Page 68   **"Deny it to the mothers of this country"**: Ibid., 24 April 1885, 1356.

Page 68   **"No more dangerous element in the voting community"**: "The Franchise Bill," *Globe* (Toronto), 24 April 1885.

Page 68   **"Greatest triumph of his life"**: Letter from John A. Macdonald to Charles Tupper, July 1885, quoted in Gordon Stewart, "John A. Macdonald's Greatest Triumph," *Canadian Historical Review* 63, 1 (1982): 3.

FOUR: WAKING UP TO THE POWER

For an analysis of the Mock Parliament, see Kym Bird, *Redressing the Past: The Politics of Early English-Canadian Women's Theatre:1876–1927* (Montreal and Kingston: McGill-Queen's University Press, 2004). John Markhoof, "Margins, Centers, and Democracy: The Paradigmatic History of Women's Suffrage," *Signs* 29, 1 (Autumn 2003): 85–116, was the source for the discussion about the importance of geographic proximity to the metropole in regard to whether suffrage advanced quickly or slowly. Margaret Evan's *Sir Oliver Mowat* (Toronto: University of Toronto Press, 1992) has a chapter discussing his interactions with suffragists in the 1880s and 1890s. Adaline and James Hughes's long career as educational reformers is explored in Larry Prochner's *A History of Early Childhood Education in Canada, Australia, and New Zealand* (Vancouver: UBC Press, 2010).

For the history of women's socialist action and the roles played by Margaret Haile, Edith Wrigley, and others, see Linda Kealey, *Enlisting Women for the Cause: Women, Labour and the Left in Canada, 1890–1920* (Toronto: University of Toronto Press, 1998), and Janice Newton, *Feminist Challenge to the Left, 1900–1918* (Montreal and Kingston: McGill-Queen's University Press, 1995).

Page 70   **"I am delighted to have met all of you gentlemen here today"**: "A Mock Parliament," unpublished script, adapted by Kym Bird, reconstructing dialogue and stage directions from the 1893 Winnipeg and the 1896 Toronto Mock Parliament Productions.

Page 72   **"On behalf of our downtrodden"**: Ibid.

Page 73   **"Heaps of fun"**: "Portia's Column," *Toronto Star*, 18 February 1896.

Page 73   **"A deep-laid scheme for the new women"**: Undated, unidentified newspaper clipping, Emily Stowe Scrapbook, file 1.11 microfilm, series 1, Emily Stowe and Augusta Stowe-Gullen (ES-ASG) Collection, Wilfrid Laurier Archives (WLU).

Page 74   **"The old idea of female dependence"**: Undated, unidentified newspaper clipping in ibid.

Page 75   **"Woman is man's equal intellectually, morally"**: "Inaugural Address of Principal Garvin," *Woodstock Sentinel-Review*, 9 June 1890.

Page 76   **"Drawn from the ranks of the well-to-do"**: "Shall They Vote?" *Globe* (Toronto), 13 June 1890.

Page 76   **"The best type of public man"**: "John Waters of North Middlesex," *Globe* (Toronto), 10 December 1910.

Page 77   **"Someone must mind the baby"**: "The Woman Suffrage Bill Discussed All Day," *Globe* (Toronto), 28 February 1889.

Page 77   **"Cowboy territory"**: Ibid.

Page 77   **Women did not want "to be dragged into party politics"**: John Dryden, "Speech of Women's Suffrage," Ontario Legislative Assembly, 10 May 1893.

Page 78   **"Evils arising from the traffic"**: "The Methodist Church of Canada on Women's Suffrage," 1883, Emily Stowe Scrapbook, file 1.11 microfilm, series 1, ES-ASG Collection, WLU.

Page 78   **"We can fight Christ's battles"**: Quoted in Sharon Anne Cook, *"Through Sunshine and Shadow": The Woman's Christian Temperance Union, Evangelicalism, and Reform in Ontario, 1874–1930* (Montreal and Kingston: McGill-Queen's University Press, 1995), 101.

Page 79   **"The whites had no compassion on the Black man":** Quoted in Lorene Bridgen, "'Lifting as We Climb': The Emergence of an African-Canadian Civil Society in Southern Ontario, 1840–1901" (PhD diss., University of Waterloo, 2016), 136.

Page 81   **"I believe homemaking, of all occupations":** Emily Stowe, "Housewifery, May 1889," untitled newspaper clipping, May 1889, Emily Stowe Scrapbook, file 1.11 microfilm, series 1, ES-ASG Collection, WLU.

Page 81   **Stowe began by characterizing women as "educated citizens":** "Ladies Make a Raid on the Old Building," *Globe* (Toronto), 9 February 1889.

Page 82   **"Equal suffrage is a fixed element":** James Hughes, *Equal Suffrage* (Toronto: William Briggs, 1895), preface.

Page 83   **"We often hear it is asserted":** Mary McDonnell, "A Century of Progress for Women in Canada," *The World's Congress of Representative Women, 1893* (Chicago: Rand, McNally, 1894), 686.

Page 84   **"The government granting such legislation deserved":** "Ladies who Want Female Suffrage also Make Onslaught on the Knight: May Have Franchise Some Day," *Toronto Star,* 3 March 1894.

Page 84   **"I do not say you will get what you want":** Ibid.

Page 85   **"How many men would be out":** Unidentified, undated newspaper clipping, Box 8A, Collection of newspaper clippings relating to women's suffrage, 1890–1919, Flora MacDonald Denison Scrapbook, Flora MacDonald Denison Papers, Thomas Fisher Rare Book Library, University of Toronto.

Page 85   **Table, sample of voter turnout across Ontario:** "Plebiscite Returns," Ontario Legislative Assembly, Sessional Papers, v. 70, 1894, 1–41.

Page 85   **Anyone who paid property taxes could stand:** *An Act for the better establishment and maintenance of Common Schools in Upper Canada,* 1850, 13 & 14 Vict., c. 9, s. 23, s. 27.

Page 86   **"With all our boasted liberality":** "The Education of Women," *Globe* (Toronto), 30 July 1877.

Page 86   **"If women are forbidden by law to be trustees":** "Women as School Trustees," *Globe* (Toronto), 24 January 1885.

Page 86   **By the 1880s, revisions to Statutes of the Province of Ontario:** Ontario, "Public Schools," *Statutes of the Province of Ontario* (Toronto: Queen's Printer, 1885), 198.

Page 86   **"Been slow to avail themselves of this privilege":** Elizabeth Cady Stanton and Susan B. Anthony, *History of Woman Suffrage,* vol. 3 (Rochester, NY: Charles Mann, 1887), 831–32.

Page 87 **McDonnell petitioned city council to appoint:** "Central WCTU Union,"
Globe (Toronto), 31 January 1888.

Page 87 **Toronto City Council appointed two women:** "Women as School
Trustees," *Globe* (Toronto), 24 April 1888.

Page 88 **"Women's gentle influence":** *Toronto Grip,* 12 December 1891, 373.

Page 88 **"A favorable impression":** "Four of Them in the Field," *Globe* (Toronto),
29 December 1891.

Page 88 **Stowe-Gullen spoke of the need:** Ibid.

Page 89 **An 1892 letter writer who called herself:** "For Woman's Suffrage," *Globe*
(Toronto), 2 January 1892.

Page 90 **"It lowered the queenly name of woman":** "They May Teach," *Globe*
(Toronto), 7 December 1894.

Page 90 **"Engage the best talent":** Ibid.

Page 90 **"No complaints were recorded against the married women":** Ibid.

Page 90 **The board ignored her recommendations, and the illegal:** "School
Board," *Toronto Grip,* 8 July 1893, 420.

Page 90 **"Five or six well-disposed men":** "Lady Trustee Experience," undated,
unidentified newspaper clipping, Scrapbook, 19, box 1, file 1 1881–1926,
Augusta Stowe-Gullen Fonds, EJ Pratt Library, Victoria College.

Page 92 **Mrs. J.H. Brown organized a letter-writing campaign:** "Appeal for
Assistance," *Ottawa Journal,* 3 December 1909.

Page 95 **"The struggle between the classes":** Quoted in Janice Newton, *Feminist
Challenge to the Left, 1900–1918* (Montreal and Kingston: McGill-Queen's
University Press, 1995), 143.

Page 96 **Discuss "things and explain them in our own way":** Margaret Haile,
Justice, 1 June 1895.

Page 96 **"I understand that she has *lost*":** Michael E. Stevens, ed., *The Family
Letters of Victor and Meta Berger, 1894–1929* (Madison: Wisconsin
Historical Society Press, 2016), 55 (emphasis in original).

Page 98 **"Doubt has been expressed":** "Ottawa Liberals," *Globe* (Toronto),
25 April 1902.

Page 99 **"Another red spot on the socialist map":** G. Weston Wrigley, "Another
Red Spot on the Socialist Map," *International Socialist Review* 4 (December
1903).

Page 99   **"A pioneer in every sense of the word":** Letter from Susan B. Anthony
to Augusta Stowe-Gullen, 25 May 1903, S729, file 1.2.1, ES-ASG
Collection, WLU.

FIVE: RESISTING A REVOLUTION

For biographical information on a new generation of suffragists, consult Kathleen
Smith, "Dr. Augusta Stowe-Gullen: A Pioneer of Social Conscience," *Canadian
Medical Association Journal* 126, 12 (1982): 1465–67. The most in-depth biography
of Stowe-Gullen's fellow CSA president, Flora MacDonald Denison, can be found
in Deborah Gorham's excellent chapter "Flora MacDonald Denison: Canadian
Feminist," in *A Not Unreasonable Claim: Women and Reform in Canada, 1880s–1920s,*
ed. Linda Kealey (Toronto: Women's Press, 1979), 47–70. Adam Baldwin, "Wilderness
and Tolerance in Flora MacDonald Denison: Towards a Biopolitics of Whiteness,"
Social and Cultural Geography 11, 8 (December 2010): 883–901, is another thoughtful analysis of her writing and ideas. Sophia Sperdakos, "'For the Joy of the Working':
Laura Elizabeth McCully, First-Wave Feminist," *Ontario History* 84, 4 (1992): 283–
314, provides an account of the poet and student's suffrage activism. For a history
of suffrage in Fort William and Port Arthur suffrage, see Thorold J. Tronrud,
"Thunder Bay Suffragists," *Thunder Bay Historical Museum Society Paper and Records*
19 (1991): 21–34. Information on Mary J.L. Black is in Frederick Brent Scollie, "Black,
Mary Johanna Louisa," *Dictionary of Canadian Biography,* http://www.biographi.ca/
en/bio/black_mary_johanna_louisa_16E.html. For more details on the vibrant
Finnish activist community in Thunder Bay, consult Varpu Lindström's many
works, including *Defiant Sisters: A Social History of Finnish Immigrant Women, 1890–
1930* (Toronto: Multicultural History Society of Ontario, 1998).

For a history of the National Council of Women of Canada, see Naomi E.S. Griffiths,
*The Splendid Vision: Centennial History of the National Council of Women of Canada,
1893–1993* (Montreal and Kingston: McGill-Queen's University Press, 1993). Anne-
Marie Kinahan, "Transcendent Citizenship: Suffrage, the National Council of
Women of Canada, and the Politics of Organized Womanhood," *Journal of Canadian
Studies* 42, 3 (Fall 2008): 5–27, provides a thorough account of how the NCWC
wrestled with the idea of suffrage.

Cheryl MacDonald, *Adelaide Hoodless: Domestic Crusader* (Toronto: Dundurn Press,
1986), provides a thoughtful biography of Hoodless. For the ways in which individual branches of the Women's Institutes approached the question of suffrage, see
Linda M. Ambrose, "The Women's Institutes in Northern Ontario," in *Changing
Lives: Women in Northern Ontario,* ed. Margaret Kechnie and Marge Reitsma-Street
(Toronto: Dundurn Press, 1996), 263–75. The most provocative look at the anti-
suffrage movement is Sheila Eileen Powell, "The Opposition to Woman Suffrage
in Ontario 1872–1917" (master's thesis, Carleton University, 1987).

For suffrage intersections with the Toronto labour movement, refer to Andrea Knight, "Educating Working Women for the Vote: The Response of the Toronto Labour Movement to Women Suffrage" (master's thesis, University of Toronto, 1982), and Ruth Frager, *Sweatshop Strife: Class, Ethnicity, and Gender in the Jewish Labour Movement of Toronto, 1900–1939* (Toronto: University of Toronto Press, 1992). Both texts offer context to key strikes and the relationships formed between suffragists and labour leaders. Karen Dubinsky and Franca Iacovetta, "Murder, Womanly Virtue, and Motherhood: The Case of Angelina Napolitano, 1911–1922," *Canadian Historical Review* 72 (1991): 505–31, give background information on this murder case.

On the topic of militancy in Britain and the United States, I recommend Ian Christopher Fletcher, "'Women of the Nations, Unite!' Transnational Suffragism in the United Kingdom 1912–1914," in *Women's Suffrage in the British Empire: Citizenship, Nation and Race*, ed. Ian Christopher Fletcher, Philippa Levine, and Laura E. Nym Mayhall (London: Routledge, 2012), 103–20. Deborah Gorham considers the specific impact in Canada in her seminal article "The English Militants and the Canadian Suffrage Movement," *Atlantis* 1, 1 (Fall 1975): 83–112. For biographies of Emmeline Pankhurst and Alice Paul, the following texts were helpful: Paula Bartley, *Emmeline Pankhurst* (London: Routledge, 2002), and D. Zahniser and Amelia R. Fry, *Alice Paul: Claiming Power* (Oxford: Oxford University Press, 2014). In regards to anti-suffragette cartoons, see Jaqueline Mcleod Rogers, "Geopolitics in the Anti-Suffrage Cartoons of American John Tinney McCutcheon and Canadian Newton McConnell: Stopping Trans-Atlantic Flow," *Peitho Journal* 17, 1 (2014): 31–45.

Page 100 **"Our whole social structure"**: Flora MacDonald Denison, "The Mental Atmosphere: The Unemployed and Zero Weather," box 2, file: Printed Programs, Flora MacDonald Denison (FMD) Papers, Thomas Fisher Rare Book Library (TFRBL), University of Toronto (UT).

Page 101 **"It is impossible to separate the work"**: Flora MacDonald Denison, "Under the Pines," *Toronto World*, 9 May 1910.

Page 102 **Sunflower badges "symbolizing light and wisdom"**: "Big Notebook, 1911," box 2, Suffrage, FMD Papers, TFRBL, UT.

Page 103 **"All girls should be taught one vocation"**: Augusta Stowe-Gullen, "Woman a Physician," in *Woman; Her Character, Culture and Calling* (Brantford: Book and Bible House, 1890), 122.

Page 104 **"Creature with horns"**: "Half the Ladies Opposed to It," *Ottawa Journal*, 19 May 1898.

Page 105 **"Nature did not divide men and women"**: Quoted in Gloria Geller, "The Wartime Elections Act of 1917 and the Canadian Women's Movement," *Atlantis* 2, 1 (Fall 1976): 95.

Page 105 **One early column reached out ... "indifferent to":** Flora MacDonald Denison, "Under the Pines," *Toronto World*, 9 January 1910.

Page 106 **Quickest route to suffrage would be a walkout:** "Women Should Leave Husbands Till They Vote," 3 January 1912, box 8B, articles and writings, 1907–1918, FMD Papers, TFRBL, UT.

Page 106 **"I have no particular desire to see my husband dead":** "Fair Sex Capture City Council," *Globe* (Toronto), 25 March 1909.

Page 107 **"For the taxes we pay":** Ottawa Equal Suffrage Association Letter, 30 November 1909, box 2, Printed matter, FMD Papers, TFRBL, UT.

Page 107 **"Criticism of an unjust kind":** "Suffragists Hold Meeting," *Ottawa Journal*, 11 June 1909.

Page 109 **Todson predicted that marriage rates would soar:** "An Address Delivered before the West Algoma Equal Suffrage Association," March 1914, Scrapbook, Anne J. Barrie Papers, Thunder Bay Museum.

Page 111 **"I wish you all had votes":** "The Appeal of Women for the Privilege of Voting," *Toronto Star*, 21 November 1906.

Page 112 **Favourable statements by fourteen Toronto ministers:** Toronto Suffrage Association, "Opinions of Toronto Clergymen on Woman's Suffrage," undated, Stowe-Gullen Scrapbook, S729 file 2.2, Emily Stowe and Augusta Stowe-Gullen (ES-ASG) Collection, Wilfrid Laurier Archives (WLU).

Page 113 **"A few faddist women":** "Women Ask for Votes," *Globe* (Toronto), 25 March 1909.

Page 113 **"Would they stand for this injustice for themselves?":** "Open Letter to Whitney and Rowell from Stowe-Gullen," *Mail and Empire*, 9 November 1911, box 1, file 5 clippings, Augusta Stowe-Gullen Fonds, EJ Pratt Library, Victoria College.

Page 114 **"Deny the depth of woman's influence":** "Women Ask for Votes," *Globe* (Toronto), 25 March 1909.

Page 114 **"Call again, and we will try":** Quoted in Hilda Ridley, "A Synopsis of Woman Suffrage in Canada," undated, 12, SPEC COLL JL 192 R54 SC1145, ES-ASG Collection, WLU.

Page 114 **"Greater unity of thought, sympathy and purpose":** From the NCWC constitution preamble, 1893, quoted in Naomi E.S. Griffiths, *The Splendid Vision: Centennial History of the National Council of Women of Canada, 1893–1993* (Montreal and Kingston: McGill-Queen's University Press, 1993), 441.

Page 115 **"After it is quite sure it is the popular thing":** Quoted in Deborah Gorham, "Flora MacDonald Denison: Canadian Feminist," in *A Not*

Unreasonable Claim: Women and Reform in Canada, 1880s-1920s, ed. Linda Kealey (Toronto: Women's Press, 1979), 60.

Page 116 **"Who has been brought face to face":** "New Methods in Education," quoted in Terry Crowley, "Hunter, Adelaide Sophia (Hoodless)," *Dictionary of Canadian Biography,* http://www.biographi.ca/en/bio/hunter_adelaide _sophia_13E.html.

Page 116 **"A woman who has not succeeded":** Quoted in Cheryl MacDonald, *Adelaide Hoodless: Domestic Crusader* (Toronto: Dundurn Press, 1986), 47.

Page 116 **"Good men have never denied":** Ibid.

Page 117 **"Baby hands stretch[ed] out":** Quoted in Sheila Eileen Powell, "The Opposition to Woman Suffrage in Ontario 1872–1917" (master's thesis, Carleton University, 1987), 112.

Page 117 **"So let us continue to hope":** "Anti-suffrage Notes," *Hamilton Herald,* 15 November 1909.

Page 118 **"Women ought to possess the vote":** Quoted in Griffiths, *The Splendid Vision,* 105.

Page 118 **"We have got the suffrage microbe in our District":** Quoted in Linda M. Ambrose, "The Women's Institutes in Northern Ontario," in *Changing Lives: Women in Northern Ontario,* ed. Margaret Kechnie and Marge Reitsma-Street (Toronto: Dundurn Press, 1996), 272.

Page 119 **"Against the best interests of the State":** Quoted in Powell, "The Opposition to Woman Suffrage," 149.

Page 120 **"Difficult to keep the domestic machinery moving":** Elizabeth Becker, "Is the Strain of Business Life Dulling the Home Making Instinct? The Home Life of Professional Women," *Everywoman's World,* December 1915, 13.

Page 120 **"Those that have brain enough":** Ibid., 32.

Page 121 **No need for the "advocacy of equal rights":** Quoted in Ruth Frager, *Sweatshop Strife: Class, Ethnicity, and Gender in the Jewish Labour Movement of Toronto, 1900–1939* (Toronto: University of Toronto Press, 1992), 111.

Page 123 **"Pale blue lips – a ghastly sight":** Quoted in Gorham, "Flora MacDonald Denison," 53.

Page 125 **"The common, everyday longings":** Alice Amelia Chown, *The Stairway* (Toronto: University of Toronto Press, 1988), 120–21.

Page 125 **"Ignorant, illiterate and often the scum":** Quoted in Geller, "The Wartime Elections Act," 95.

Page 126 **Assimilation remained incomplete:** "Women Should Leave Husbands Till They Vote," 3 January 1912, box 8A, Collection of newspaper clippings relating to women's suffrage, 1890–1919, FMD Papers, TFRBL, UT.

Page 126 **"Many people think that women want to become":** Ottawa newspaper clipping, 3 January 1912, Denison Scrapbook, FMD Papers, TFRBL, UT.

Page 127 **"Most likely the effect of temporary insanity":** Sonia Leathes, "The Case of Angelina Napolitano," *Globe* (Toronto), 16 and 21 May 1911.

Page 127 **"Any political solidarity as a sex":** Sonia Leathes, "The Women in Russia," *Woman's Journal,* 16 November 1912.

Page 128 **"Controlled by privilege and reaction":** Quoted in Andrea Knight, "Educating Working Women for the Vote: The Response of the Toronto Labour Movement to Women Suffrage" (master's thesis, University of Toronto, 1982), 54.

Page 129 **"Imperial in its scope":** Quoted in Ian Christopher Fletcher, "'Women of the Nations, Unite!' Transnational Suffragism in the United Kingdom 1912–1914," in *Women's Suffrage in the British Empire: Citizenship, Nation and Race,* ed. Ian Christopher Fletcher, Philippa Levine, and Laura E. Nym Mayhall (London: Routledge, 2012), 106.

Page 130 **Media proclaimed the rabble rouser to be:** Paula Bartley, *Emmeline Pankhurst* (London: Routledge, 2002), 164–65.

Page 130 **"Physical violence was [not] the best method":** "Same Terms as Men," *Globe* (Toronto), 7 December 1909.

Page 132 **"She is neither insane or a fanatic":** "The Appeal of Women for the Privilege of Voting," *Toronto Star,* 21 November 1906.

Page 132 **"Torment members of parliament":** Quoted in Joan Sangster, *One Hundred Years of Struggle: The History of Women and the Vote in Canada* (Vancouver: UBC Press, 2018), 150.

Page 133 **"And thou, who bravedst the whole world's scorn":** Laura E. McCully, "Emily Wilding Davidson," in *Mary Magdalene and Other Poems* (Toronto: Macmillan, 1914), 51.

Page 133 **Olivia Smith rose from the gallery ... "throw a bucket":** "Real Suffragette Heard from at Close of Legislature," *Lindsay Post,* 25 March 1910.

Page 134 **"The movement here is dead":** "Franchise for Women," *Globe* (Toronto), 1 April 1910.

Page 134 **"Policy is to gain supporters for our cause":** "Little Comfort for the Suffragettes," *Globe* (Toronto), 29 August 1912.

Page 135   **"Respectable, law-abiding English women":** A.H.F. Lefroy, *Should Canadian Women Have the Parliamentary Vote?* (Toronto: Equal Franchise League, 1913), 3.

Page 135   **"Beyond any woman in the world":** Quoted in Bartley, *Emmeline Pankhurst*, 170.

Page 135   **"Mrs. Pankhurst will go down in history":** "Miss Lulu Abbot Replies," *Ottawa Journal*, 1 March 1913.

Page 136   **"Ardent suffragist" who "longed to be like":** Adolf Hungrywolf, "Dawn Mist," in *Blackfoot Papers*, vol. 4, *Pikunni Biographies* (N.p.: Good Medicine Foundation, 2006), 1054.

Page 137   **"Might not care to have a coloured person":** "Party Led by Woman of 85 Saw Suffragettes Off," *Globe* (Toronto), 3 March 1913.

Page 137   **"I had no illusions about the women":** Quoted in Allana Lindgren, "In the Family Way: The Politicization of Motherhood in Merrill Denison's *Marsh Hay* (1923)," *Theatre Research in Canada* 27, 1 (2006): 12.

Page 138   **"in appearance and attitude ... much as other women are":** Ibid.

Page 139   ***Toronto World* ... produced a full-page photo collage:** "Canadian Suffragettes at the Inauguration of a New U.S. President," *Toronto World*, 15 March 1913.

Page 139   **"Gross indignities" endured by suffragists:** "Cavalry Charges Washington Mob," *Globe* (Toronto), 4 March 1913.

Page 139   **Featured a photograph of an ambulance taking suffragists away:** "First Pictures of the Suffragette Parade in Washington," *Toronto Star*, 6 March 1913.

Page 140   **"Impress the immense crowds" ... "have votes behind them":** "Parade," *Woman's Century*, October 1913.

Page 141   **Called the CSA arrogant ... "bring democracy a little closer":** *Industrial Banner*, September 1914.

SIX: VICTORY AMID DISCORD AND WAR

An important book on womanhood and the war work of white and Indigenous women is Sarah Glassford and Amy Shaw, eds., *A Sisterhood of Suffering and Service: Women and Girls of Canada and Newfoundland during the First World War* (Vancouver: UBC Press, 2012). Barbara Roberts has published numerous works on women's peace campaigns in the Great War, including *Reconstructed World: A Feminist Biography of Gertrude Richardson* (Montreal and Kingston: McGill-Queen's University Press,

1996). For Margaret Cole's wartime work and family sacrifice, see Stuart Ivison, "The Activities of Margaret Edwards Cole," *Canadian Society of Church History Papers* (1984): 140–56. Kori Street, "'Toronto's Amazons': Militarised Femininity and Gender Construction in the Great War" (master's thesis, University of Toronto, 1991), examines the rise and fall of the Home Guard experiment in female civil defence. Details about the Rowell siblings were taken from Sharon Anne Cook, "Sarah Alice Rowell (Wright)," *Dictionary of Canadian Biography*, http://www. biographi.ca/en/bio/rowell_sarah_alice_15E.html, and Margaret E. Prang, "Newton Wesley Rowell," *Dictionary of Canadian Biography*, http://www.biographi.ca/en/ bio/rowell_newton_wesley_17E.html.

Changes to the federal franchise are the subject of Gloria Geller, "The Wartime Elections Act of 1917 and the Canadian Women's Movement," *Atlantis* 2, 1 (Fall 1976): 88–106, and Julie Evans et al., *Equal Subjects, Unequal Rights: Indigenous People in British Settler Colonies, 1830–1910* (Manchester: Manchester University Press, 2003). Eric Story, "A Dual Identity: The Experiences of Indigenous Casualties of the Great War, 1918–1939" (master's thesis, Wilfrid Laurier University, 2016), provides a good overview of the difficulties that Indigenous men faced when accessing their rights as veterans.

Page 142 **"Many women are now filled with the spirit":** Flora MacDonald Denison, *Women and War* (Toronto: Canadian Suffrage Association, 1914), 7.

Page 146 **"Social evils to be remedied after suffrage":** Unidentified newspaper clipping, 3 January 1912, box 8A, Collection of newspaper clippings relating to women's suffrage, 1890–1919, Flora MacDonald Denison (FMD) Papers, Thomas Fisher Rare Book Library (TFRBL), University of Toronto (UT).

Page 147 **Results failed to show what the "great majority":** "No Franchise for Women," unidentified newspaper clipping, 1916, Barrie scrapbook, Anne J. Barrie Papers, Thunder Bay Museum (TBM).

Page 148 **"A spirit of jealousy":** "Now Two Canadian Suffrage Societies," *Toronto Daily Star*, 25 March 1914.

Page 149 **"I shouldn't condemn Mrs. Pankhurst any more:"** "Human Blood Is to Be Shed by Suffragette," undated, unidentified newspaper clipping, 1913, box A, Clippings, FMD Papers, TFRBL, UT.

Page 149 **"I personally am a great admirer of the woman":** "The Suffrage Breach Widens," *Globe* (Toronto), 28 April 1914.

Page 150 **"For myself, I understand the smug snobbery":** Flora MacDonald Denison to Rosaline Kennedy Torrington, 17 January 1913, FMD Papers, TFRBL, UT.

Page 151 **The CSA condemned the Whitney Conservatives:** "An Open Letter to the Electors," *Globe* (Toronto), 19 June 1914.

Page 152 **"Brantford women are never dull nor dead":** "Letter from Brantford Suffragettes," *Globe* (Toronto), 16 April 1912.

Page 152 **Leathes offered EFL funding for suffrage speakers:** Sonia Leathes, "Suffrage Situation in Canada," *Jus Suffragii,* 1 November 1913.

Page 154 **"Onward march of democracy and self government":** "Boys are Rulers of Own Affairs at Kent School," *Toronto Star,* 14 May 1914.

Page 156 **"Prepare women to take the place of men":** "Suffrage War Auxiliary," brief, box 3, file 8, Augusta Stowe-Gullen Fonds, EJ Pratt Library, Victoria College.

Page 156 **Enfranchisement either a "certainty" or "a dead issue":** "What Twelve Canadian Women Hope to See as the Outcome of the War," *Everywoman's World,* 6 April 1915, 6–7.

Page 156 **"The only thing any woman with a woman's heart could do":** "Suffrage Gives Way to Work for the War," *Globe* (Toronto), 16 June 1915.

Page 156 **"This war is the most conclusive argument":** Denison, *Women and War,* 7.

Page 156 **"On the eve of a great social re-creation":** "What Twelve Canadian Women Hope to See," 6.

Page 158 **"Some men have said to me":** Quoted in David Wencer, "Historicist: The Women's Home Guard," *Torontoist,* 10 November 2012, https://torontoist. com/2017/03/historicist-womens-home-guard/.

Page 159 **"Had women stood shoulder to shoulder":** Denison, *Women and War,* 7.

Page 159 **Condemn her and the committee's efforts:** "Local Council Votes in Favor of Conscription," *Globe* (Toronto), 22 November 1916.

Page 160 **"The militarists have more power than ever":** Quoted in Barbara Roberts, *Reconstructed World: A Feminist Biography of Gertrude Richardson* (Montreal and Kingston: McGill-Queen's University Press, 1996), 247.

Page 161 **"To the wastebasket":** Ibid., 189.

Page 161 **"More than generations of speaking and lecturing":** *Toronto Mail and Empire,* 13 March 1916.

Page 162 **"The present colossal war" ... "an incomplete partner":** Agnes Maule Machar, "The Citizenship of Women," *Woman's Century,* March 1916.

Page 162 **"Almost as indispensable as the soldier"**: "Give Women a Chance to Vote," *Porcupine Advance,* 1 November 1916.

Page 162 **"Naturalized aliens may in many localities"**: "Campaign for Woman Suffrage in This Province," unidentified newspaper clipping, January 1916, Scrapbook, Anne J. Barrie Papers, TBM.

Page 163 **"In past history, Ontario has been the banner"**: Letter to Premier Hearst from the West Algoma Equal Suffrage Association, undated, unidentified newspaper, scrapbook, Anne J. Barrie Papers, TBM.

Page 164 **"Women of the liberal and conservative persuasion"**: Ibid.

Page 164 **Ormsby had called all suffragists**: "Women Are Out to Get the Vote," *Globe* (Toronto), 2 October 1916.

Page 164 **Ottawa ... went straight to a plebiscite**: "People Vote for City Manager by Great Majority; the Plebiscites," *Ottawa Journal,* 4 January 1916.

Page 164 **"I do not think that women's suffrage will achieve"**: "Sir Wilfrid Laurier Declares in Favor of Woman Suffrage," *Globe* (Toronto), 13 October 1916.

Page 164 **"Resolved that in the interests of humanity"**: "Anti-suffragists Score Win in Debate," *Globe* (Toronto), 18 October 1916.

Page 165 **Mrs. W.H. Allen organized a tableau**: "Temperance Workers Not to Rest on Oars," *Globe* (Toronto), 2 November 1916.

Page 165 **"Having taken our women into partnership with us"**: "Ontario Gives Votes to Women," *Globe* (Toronto), 28 February 1917.

Page 167 **"No hysterics over victory" ... "legislation along the lines"**: "Women of Ontario at Last to Get Right to Vote," *Toronto Star,* 28 February 1917.

Page 167 **"Train the women to use the vote"**: Ibid.

Page 169 **"My pet patient Earl King"**: C. Edith Anderson, "Diary of a War Nurse," June 1918, family document, care of John Moses.

Page 169 **"She felt it an obligation"**: Oral History, author interview with Helen Monture Moses, 18 October 2016, telephone interview, recording and transcript in author's possession.

Page 170 **"It would be more direct and honest"**: Quoted in Gloria Geller, "The Wartime Elections Act of 1917 and the Canadian Women's Movement," *Atlantis* 2, 1 (Fall 1976): 104.

Page 172 **"I would be remiss in my duty"**: Canada, *House of Commons Debates,* 14 May 1917, 1387.

EPILOGUE

Frederick Brent Scollie, "The Woman Candidate for the Ontario Legislature," *Ontario History*, 104 (Autumn 2012): 1–27, gives a succinct survey of women's progress in municipal and provincial politics. For a look at women's involvement in the United Farmers of Ontario, see Margaret Kechnie, "The United Farm Women of Ontario: Developing a Political Consciousness," *Ontario History* 77 (December 1985): 268–80, and Kerry Badgley, *Ringing in the Common Love of Good: The United Farmers of Ontario, 1914–1926* (Montreal and Kingston: McGill-Queen's University Press, 2000). The careers and personal lives of Agnes Macphail and Charlotte Whitton are covered in Terry Crowley, *Agnes Macphail and the Politics of Equality* (Toronto: Lorimer, 1990), and P.T. Rooke and R.L. Schnell, *No Bleeding Heart: Charlotte Whitton, a Feminist on the Right* (Vancouver: UBC Press, 1987). Details on Elsie Knott's career and life and those of other Indigenous female leaders are from Cora Voyageur, *Firekeepers: First Nations Women Chiefs* (Montreal and Kingston: McGill-Queen's University Press, 2008).

Page 173 **"Madam Voter, indeed was up bright and early":** "Riverdale Vote Strong, Ladies' Interest Keen," *Toronto Star,* 20 October 1919.

Page 174 **"Women must not be attached to any political party":** "Could Not Agree on Course for Future," *Ottawa Journal,* 24 April 1917.

Page 175 **"Women are just as human as men":** "Women Human, Too. They Talk Patronage," *Toronto Star,* 5 March 1917.

Page 175 **"Women voters are not fools":** "Lining Up the Women," *Globe* (Toronto), 18 January 1918.

Page 175 **"None of them looked like frivolous creatures":** "Liberal Women Help Nominate Candidate," *Toronto Star,* 26 March 1917.

Page 179 **"Old Boy's club":** Mark Maloney, "Toronto Pioneer Mostly Forgotten," *Toronto Star,* 10 March 2005.

Page 180 **"The men won't support them":** Quoted in Frederick Brent Scollie, "The Woman Candidate for the Ontario Legislature," *Ontario History* 104, 2 (2012): 20.

Page 181 **"I do not want to be the angel of any home":** Quoted in Terry Crowley, *Agnes Macphail and the Politics of Equality* (Toronto: James Lorimer, 1990), 94.

Page 182 **"Oh! When will we poor long-suffering women":** Quoted in Kerry Badgley, *Ringing in the Common Love of Good: The United Farmers of Ontario, 1914–1926* (Montreal and Kingston: McGill-Queen's University Press, 2000), 129.

Page 182   **"We women drop the ballot":** Ibid., 128.

Page 183   **Base was particularly strong among farmers:** "Agnes Macphail Re-elected for S.-E. Grey," *Flesherton Advance,* 30 October 1925.

Page 183   **"I couldn't open my mouth to say the simplest thing":** Agnes Macphail, "Men Want to Hog Everything," *Maclean's,* 15 September 1949, 72.

Page 184   **Defined this to mean the pursuit of "absolute equality":** Quoted in Terry Crowley, "Agnes Macphail and Canadian Working Women," *Labour/Le Travail* 28 (Fall 1991): 129.

Page 184   **"If men are not capable of taking care of themselves":** Ibid., 140.

Page 184   **Spoke publicly about the personal sacrifices:** Ibid., 141.

Page 185   **"Biggest joke ever":** Quoted in Cora Voyageur, *Firekeepers of the Twenty-First Century: First Nations Woman Chiefs* (Montreal and Kingston: McGill-Queen's University Press, 2008), 31.

Page 185   **They "felt left out of things":** Quoted in Cora Voyageur, "Making History: Elsie Marie Knott – Canada's First Female Indian Elected Chief," in *Aboriginal History: A Reader,* ed. Kristin Burnett and Geoff Read, 2nd ed. (Oxford: Oxford University Press, 2016), 369.

Page 186   **"Sad memorial to the dreams and aspirations":** Charlotte Whitton, "Is the Canadian Woman a Flop in Politics?" *Saturday Night,* 26 January 1946.

Page 186   **"Women of the world unite":** Quoted in P.T. Rooke and R.L. Schnell, *No Bleeding Heart: Charlotte Whitton, a Feminist on the Right* (Vancouver: UBC Press, 1987), 189.

Page 187   **They "have fallen far below the standard":** Agnes Macphail to Catherine Cleverdon, 22 March 1946, Catherine Lyle Cleverdon Fonds, MG 30 D160, box 1, Library and Archives Canada.

Page 189   **"Only dignified and honourable means of securing":** Canadian Suffrage Association, *Report of Interview with the Right Honourable R.L. Borden, Prime Minister of Canada* (Toronto: Canadian Suffrage Association, 1912).

Page 190   **"If our fight is at moments dispiriting":** Augusta Stowe-Gullen, "Report on Citizenship Committee," in *The Year Book Containing the Report of the Twentieth Annual Meeting of the National Council of Women of Canada* (Montreal: National Council of Women of Canada, 1913), 64.

PHOTO CREDITS

Records of the National Woman's Party, Manuscript Division, Library of Congress.

Page 111: Finnish Canadian Historical Society, 991.1223, Thunder Bay Museum.

Page 130: Newton McConnell, "Wonder Who Told Them We Didn't Encourage the Suffragette Movement in Toronto?" c. 1910. Archives of Ontario, C 301–0–0–0–996.

Page 131: Newton McConnell, "James L. Hughes, One of Toronto's Leading Suffragettes Rehearsing for the Coming of Mrs. Pankhurst," c. 1905–14. Archives of Ontario, C 301–0–0–0–615.

Page 138: "Toronto Women Who Headed Deputation to Washington," *Toronto Sunday World*, 13 March 1913.

Page 143: "The Emancipation Easter Hatch," *Brantford Expositor*, 3 April 1917. Public domain.

Page 148: Donated by Marylou Hall, Kawartha Lakes Public Library.

Page 150: Studio portrait, c. 1901. J.S. Matthews Collection, City of Vancouver Archives.

Page 159: Woman's Library Collection, London School of Economics.

Page 171: Personal collection, courtesy of John Moses.

Page 174: Victor Child, "The Vacant Throne," *Maclean's*, 1 February 1928.

Page 177: Donated by Linda Guest, Mount Pleasant Collection, County of Brant Public Library.

Page 181: Agnes Macphail, c. 1920. Grey Roots Archival Collection, PF22S1F1, Grey Roots Museum and Archives.

Page 187: "Indian Women Vote," *Canadian Observer*, 20 June 1952. Sarnia Observer Negative Collection, 04986-01, Lambton County Archives.

INDEX

Note: "(f)" after a page number indicates an illustration.

from class interests, 94–95; universal suffrage, 121; working-class demands, 93

societies, literary. *See* literary clubs

SPC (Socialist Party of Canada), 93

Spence, F.S., 84

Spencer, Emily, 76

Spencer, Herbert, 55

spheres, public and private. *See* separate spheres

St. Catharines, 29, 75, 146–47

The Stairway (Chown), 125

Stanton, Elizabeth Cady, 51, 74

sterilization, 184

Stevenston, R.J., 122–23

Stone, Lucy, 24, 51

Stormont, 84–85

Stowe, Emily: about, 34–39, 36(f), 46–47, 73, 99; abortion trial, 54, 120; barriers to professions, 35, 38; CWSA leadership, 54–55; death and memorials, 99, 153; DWEA leadership, 75–76, 78; DWEA-WCTU delegations to Mowat, 81–85; education of women, 46–47; egalitarian feminism, 80–81; "Housewifery" (essay), 81; ICW member, 74; lecture tours, 46, 78; life in the United States, 35, 38, 46, 74; marriage and motherhood, 35–36; maternal feminism, 80–81; media coverage, 54; Mock Parliaments, 70, 71(f), 72–74; on municipal franchise, 62–63; physician, 35–36, 38, 54; Quaker, 34, 39, 46, 105; Reform Party, 34; suffragist, 39, 51; teacher, 31, 35; TWLC leadership, xii, 46–47, 53, 54; on women's careers (1889), 26

Stowe, John, 35–36

Stowe-Gullen, Augusta: about, 49(f), 102–4, 177(f); celebration of achieving suffrage, 167; CSA leadership,

102–3, 106, 111–14, 146; on domestic help, 120; DWEA leadership, 102–3; education of women, 103–4; on human rights, 49; Labour Day parades, 140; Liberal Party support, 151; life in the United States, 59; memorial, 177(f); Mock Parliament, 72–74; NCWC member, 177–78; petitions to MPPs, 122; physician, 49(f), 58–59, 106–7; school trustee, 88–91; support for socialist MPP candidate, 97–98; on Wartime Elections Act (1917), 170–71; Washington parade (1913), 137–38, 138(f); on women's freedom, 190; WSPU sympathy, 132

strikes. *See* labour movement

Stuart-Jones, Cornelia Capron, 63

Studholme, Allan, 134, 151

Styres, Mary Smith, 44

suffrage movement: about, vii–viii, 40; all-women vs mixed membership, 55–56, 74; citizenship symbol, xiv; diversity in, x, 127–28, 188–90; fragmentation before First World War, 144, 145–53; histories of, ix–x, xi–xii; lack of militancy, viii, 133; meeting space, 107; Mock Parliaments, 70, 71(f), 72–74, 83; New Woman, 34–35, 103; personal qualities, x; petitions, 110, 111–14, 122; regional vs national, 76; response to other, xi, 46, 103, 120–22; role of class, ethnicity, race, and religion, xi–xii, xiv; school franchise as early victory, 23–25; significance of, xiv–xv; social conservatism, viii, 91, 122; strategies, vii–viii; suffrage, as term, ix; suffragists and suffragettes, as terms, 129; teachers, 31; Washington parade (1913), 135–41, 138(f); white, middle class women, ix–xi, 103–4; First World War's impact on, 155

voter turnout, 61, 63, 84–85, 173
voting rights. *See* federal franchise
(before 1918); federal franchise (1918
and later); Indigenous peoples, franchise; Ontario, provincial franchise
(April 1917)
voting stations. *See* polling stations

Wales, Julia Grace, 160
War, First World. *See* First World War
Warren, Sarah, 119
Wartime Elections Act (1917), 170–71
Waters, John, 60, 76–77
WCTU (Women's Christian Temperance
Union): about, 28, 41–44, 188; African
Canadian communities, 43–44, 78–
80; alliances with socialists, 94–97;
alliances with suffragists, 77–78,
80, 95–96, 102, 148(f), 151–52, 164;
branches, 42–43; decline of, 188;
DWEA-WCTU alliances, 77–78, 81–
85; Indigenous communities, 43–44;
maternal feminism, 80–81; media
coverage, 52; Mock Parliaments, 73;
referendum on municipal franchise
(1913–14), 147; social class, 80; suf-
fragists, 43, 145. *See also* temperance
and prohibition
Webster, James, 4
Welland, 84–85
Wells-Barnett, Ida B., 136
Wendat, 5–6. *See also* Indigenous peoples
West Algoma Equal Suffrage Association, 108, 110, 163
West Halton County, Canada West:
women voters (1844), xiii, 4–5, 18–23
Western Canada: suffrage movements,
76, 91–92
Western Clarion (newspaper), 94–95
Whitesides, Thomas Richard, 151
Whitney, James, 102, 110, 111–14, 133–
34, 140, 151
Whitton, Charlotte, xi, 186–87

widows: colonial era, 12, 14, 15, 20–21,
24; municipal franchise, 59–61,
63–64, 84–85, 106; war widows'
pensions, 156, 182
Willard, Frances, 43, 94
Williams, Hannah, xiii, 20–23
Williams, Lilian, 185(f)
WILPF (Women's International League
for Peace and Freedom), 159(f), 160
Wilson, Cairine, 180
Wilson, Daniel, 58
Wilson, Woodrow, 136, 139
Windsor, 29–30
Winnipeg, 145, 152
*The Woman Suffrage Movement in
Canada* (Cleverdon), xi
"Woman with the Needle" (poem,
Denison), 123
Woman's Century (NCWC magazine), 137,
140, 160–61
Woman's Journal (US suffrage periodical),
127
Woman's Party, 178
Woman's Peace Party, 160
women. *See* feminism; gender; suffrage
movement
Women and War (Denison), 142, 156, 157
Women's Canadian Club, 164
Women's Christian Temperance Union.
See WCTU (Women's Christian
Temperance Union)
Women's Home Guard, 158
Women's Institutes (WIS): anti-
suffragists, 115, 118, 152, 176; EFL
alliance, 152; government funding,
118, 152, 176; homemaking skills,
115–16; Stowe-Gullen's memorial,
177(f); voter education, 176
Women's International League for
Peace and Freedom (WILPF), 159(f),
160
Women's Parliaments. *See* Mock
Parliaments